HUNDRED OF

The Ruins of Fordly Castle
Fordly
heath
Common
OF
eding
Buddington
Upper street
Hollis
LIBERTY OF LODSWORTH
Upperton Com.
River Upperton street
Cowdry Park
Easebourne
Lodsworth
Dance
Netherland
Lurgashale
Gentles
Hills Green
Barkf
Limbo
dehurst
E BRIDGE
dehurst
Palingham
Wharfe
Stopham

Lawn
Fulling Mill
Selham
Ambursham
Turlands
Lodg bridg
Tillington
Crossland Cross
Rother brid
Egdean
Egdean
Common Green
Parsonage
Fittleworth
Heshworth str.
Stopham
Byworth street
Hallgate

Kilsham
Horsebare brid
Conderhall Mills

S T E R

Hyle Place
Parsonage
Heyshot

D H U R S T
Graffham Marsh
Graffham
Wollavington 97
Cocking Race
High ditch Woods

E Dean
Upwaltham

Burton
Burton Park
Engine to Raise Water
Fulling mill
Duncton
Barlavington
Sutton
Parsonage
Horncroft Common
Coates
Coldwalham
Herring

H U N D
Bignor Park
Bignor
Watersfield street
Gritham br
Gritham
Gritham
Wildbrook

Upwaltham Down
Selhurst Park
Red Copp's Lodg
Nemans Land
Cumworth
Trottron
Parsonage
Burton
Bury

R I E

Halnecker Wind
Halnecker Park
Wareheed
HUNDRE
Boxgrove
Cocker hill
Filkinges hole

Part of Aldn
Hundred
Slindon Windmill
Slindon place
Helidon
Madhurst
Eebles Corner
The Mile
Arundel Park

Tangmeer
Aldingbourne
Aldingbourne P.
Knightam 102
Estergate
Walberton
Tortington Priory
Tortington
Binstead

Arundel Castle
ARUNDEL
Badworth
Causway green
Limister

GOODWOOD

DAVID HUNN

GOODWOOD

DAVIS-POYNTER
LONDON

First published in 1975 by
Davis-Poynter Limited
20 Garrick Street London WC2E 9BJ

Copyright © David Hunn 1975

ISBN 0 7067 0170 4

Printed in Great Britain by
Bristol Typesetting Co. Ltd
Barton Manor St Philips Bristol

CONTENTS

ILLUSTRATIONS

PREFACE

This is not the whole story of Goodwood and the Dukes of Richmond, just more of it than has ever been told before. It is not a book for anyone who wants to know what won the Goodwood Cup in 1909, though it will tell you that Roche Abbey won the Singleton Plate that year at such a speed that it went on running past the post, right up The Trundle, and disappeared over the top. It deals in only the outlines of the personal and political history of the Richmond family, which is 300 years old this year, but in greater detail with all their activities at Goodwood, and I hope thoroughly with their very considerable sporting associations. Prime amongst these, as everybody knows, is the racecourse – certainly the most beautiful and probably the most popular in the whole country. How and why it became what it is, and which of the Richmonds really cared, and whether Chichester cared at all, is what this story is mostly about.

ACKNOWLEDGMENTS

Without the immense and always kind help of the Duke of Richmond and Gordon, of his son, the Earl of March, and of many others at Goodwood House, this book could have been neither begun nor ended, I am particularly grateful for the access I was given to the private library at Goodwood House, and to the stupendous collection of family papers now in the care of the West Sussex County Archivist at Chichester, which are the copyright of the Goodwood Estate. My thanks are due to the staff of that office, who were always ready to do more than their duty, and to the unfailing courtesy of the staff of the West Sussex County Reference Library at Chichester.

You will soon see that I have unashamedly drawn on contemporary journalism to illustrate the narrative, because I believe that to be the most accurate and colourful way of establishing the facts: this is particularly true of the reports in *The Times*, which certainly between 1800 and 1940 set a standard that none could equal. Other works from a past age from which I have quoted include the two books written by the eighth Duke of Richmond, *A Duke and His Friends* and *Records of the Old Charlton Hunt*; John Kent's *Racing Life of Lord George Bentinck* and *Records and Reminiscences of Goodwood*; *The Racing Year 1903*, by Edward Moorhouse; Henry Reeve's edition of the *Charles Greville Journals*; the *Chichester Observer*; and many editions of the *Sporting Magazine*.

From more recent times, I found helpful material in *The Duke Who Was Cricket*, by John Marshall (Frederick Muller); *Companion Into Sussex*, by Norman Wymer (Methuen & Co.); *The Buildings of Sussex*, by Ian Nairn and Nikolaus Pevsner (Penguin); *Lord Paramount of the Turf*, by Michael Seth-Smith (Faber & Faber); *Life and Times of the Duchess of Portsmouth*, by Jeanine Delpech (Elek Books); and *Brooklands to Goodwood*, by Rodney Walkerley (Foulis & Co.).

I thank all those on whose labour and talent I have relied to complete a job that I found extraordinarily fascinating – the more so because, with uncanny coincidence, I began my newspaper career in the Chichester office of the *Portsmouth Evening News* on the day of the first post-war Goodwood meeting.

I have read somewhere that perfection is not to be found on this earth; now, with due deference to the uttered judgment, I think I might safely challenge the assertion.

Correspondent of the *Sporting Magazine*,
on returning from Goodwood, 1840.

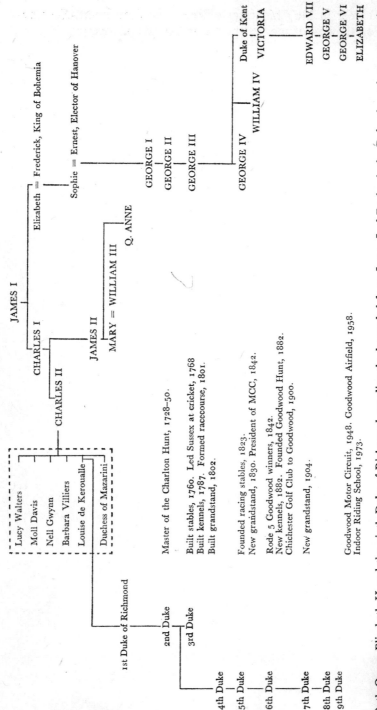

JAMES I

CHARLES I   Elizabeth = Frederick, King of Bohemia

CHARLES II   Sophie = Ernest, Elector of Hanover

JAMES II

MARY = WILLIAM III

Q. ANNE

GEORGE I

GEORGE II

GEORGE III

GEORGE IV   WILLIAM IV   Duke of Kent

VICTORIA

EDWARD VII

GEORGE V

GEORGE VI

ELIZABETH

Lucy Walters
Moll Davis
Nell Gwynn
Barbara Villiers
Louise de Keroualle
Duchess of Mazarini

1st Duke of Richmond

2nd Duke — Master of the Charlton Hunt, 1728–50.

3rd Duke — Built stables, 1760. Led Sussex at cricket, 1768
Built kennels, 1787. Formed raccourse, 1801.
Built grandstand, 1802.

4th Duke

5th Duke — Founded racing stables, 1823.
New graindstand, 1830. President of MCC, 1842.

6th Duke — Rode 5 Goodwood winners, 1842.
New kennels, 1882. Founded Goodwood Hunt, 1882.
Chichester Golf Club to Goodwood, 1900.

7th Duke — New grandstand, 1904.

8th Duke

9th Duke — Goodwood Motor Circuit, 1948. Goodwood Airfield, 1958.
Indoor Riding School, 1973.

Both Queen Elizabeth II and the ninth Duke of Richmond are directly descended from James I of England, the Duke through ten generations (and Charles II's liaison with Louise de Keroualle, later Duchess of Portsmouth), and the Queen through eleven generations. Highlights of Goodwood's sporting history are also shown on the chart.

1

GOOD
FOR NOTHING

A man who can ask the Queen and all her family to his grand-daughter's 18th birthday party, and be sure they will accept, has to be a bit special. The Duke of Richmond is that : his great-great-great-great-great-great-great-grandfather was the King of England. Since that king was Charles II, who probably lost count of the number of infants he sired, that fact alone does not make Richmond unique; to keep Goodwood racecourse in his back garden does.

There is no lovelier racecourse in the world, no more exquisite sporting arena in England. Unlike some others that make good use of a magnificent natural setting, Goodwood is not spoiled by the introduction of people, and has not so far been insulted by the quality of its buildings. 'Nature, in its very kindliest mood,' wrote F. H. Bayles, 'never formed a more pleasant pastoral picture . . . All round is a perfect profusion of invigorating beauty, with an abounding wealth and variety of culture displayed in its loveliness.' It is not quite as beautiful now as it was seventy years ago, when beside its single, pretty grandstand there were avenues of beech trees under which white tablecloths were spread for picnic lunches; and open carriages lined the enclosures, filling the neighbouring air with the delicate percussion of jangling harness and champing bit, the muted trumpet of an impatient snort. Racecourse managements can no longer afford such unproductive luxuries, and the space had to be used to make money. Staging a race week is a costly business these days. The prize money for the five days of Goodwood Week last summer (1974) was £122,510, and well over half of that was put up by the racecourse. It is nearly 20 years now since Goodwood promised itself a new stand, and it is still not much more than an expensive dream.

It is perhaps the only course in Britain where, to vast numbers of its spectators, the racing is no more than a series of mildly amusing interludes in a day that would be blissfully happy anyway. Many of us of that persuasion are not much interested in a new stand. In fact we are deeply apprehensive at the thought of it. If we had our druthers, as the Americans say, we'd put it back the way it was: back to the glorious elegance of the 1830s, and the ensuing era of Goodwood's absolute, universal supremacy. Supreme not just because the quality of the racing was such as had never been seen on any racecourse before – for, honestly, how many of us know the difference? – but because in this unlikely, isolated, rural haven there gathered, for one week each year, kings and queens, dukes and duchesses, earls galore and barons by the score; the place was dripping with generals and cabinet ministers and the loveliest of ladies, and down the hill at Goodwood House the most favoured of them laid their heads and were most sumptuously fed. When it was all over, they snapped their fingers for their servants and the trunks were packed and the postilions summoned and they rose gracefully into their coaches for a thumpingly uncomfortable ride back to London.

Down in Goodwood life went on the year round, though with less excitement. Trees were planted and grass was sown and forelocks touched. Flint walls were raised; estates and yachts were bought and even whole villages here and there. They rode to hounds like mad and bickered with neighbouring dukes and altogether behaved in the sort of way you might feel you can only despise, for its arrogance, expense, depravity and downright idleness. But ah, if we had only had the chance! The estate grew from a couple of hundred acres to a couple of thousand, and then on up to hundreds of thousands, making the Richmonds among the greatest landowners in Britain. Today, three centuries to the very year after the first Duke was created, many of the family's far-flung lands have been sold. Goodwood is being made to work efficiently in the hands of the heir to the title, the Earl of March, a man trained as an accountant. The thought of a future Duke of Richmond actually working, beyond the formality of representing the locality in Parliament, would have caused the first Duke to choke over his brandy. But of course he was Charles II's son, through one of His Majesty's celebrated extra-marital affairs.

Not Nell Gwynn, this one, but a fair maid of France, Louise-Renée de Penancoet de Kéroualle, whom the king created Duchess of Portsmouth. Since Charles left no heirs and was succeeded by his brother, James, you might say that the distance by which the Dukes of Richmond missed being the kings of England was no more than the thickness of a sheet. But that would be to overlook the relevance of several other unscheduled arrivals. In the year of Richmond's birth, 1672, the King was said to have had four children from four different mistresses, though the other three were not among those he acknowledged, and Richmond was in fact the youngest of all the King's admitted children. The royal fertility was phenomenal: he had 13 or 14 recorded illegitimate children, the eldest of whom was born to a teenage whore in Holland when Charles was the Prince of Wales and himself only 19. That son became the infamous Duke of Monmouth, who later attempted to seize the throne and was beheaded by James II.

The King's best known mistress was Nell Gwynn, but before her two sons by him (the elder of whom was made Duke of St Albans), he had three sons and two daughters by the longest-serving of his loves, Barbara Villiers, Duchess of Cleveland. The boys became the Dukes of Cleveland, Grafton and Northumberland, the girls were married to the Earls of Sussex and Lichfield.

Louise de Kéroualle was not introduced to the king's bed (and the event had several witnesses) until the end of October and the boy was born on 29th July. It was such a commonplace occurrence that though Louise was by then firmly established as the favourite mistress, the king barely acknowledged the child for three years. He then made up for it by giving him the English titles of Duke of Richmond, Earl of March and Baron Settrington, and the Scottish ones of Duke of Lennox, Earl of Darnley and Baron Torbolton: they had passed to the Crown in the year of the boy's birth, by the death of James, the last Duke of Richmond and Lennox of the Stuart line.

Louise was a Breton, daughter of a French nobleman, and was a lady-in-waiting to Charles's sister, the Duchess of Orleans, when the King met and fancied her. She was appointed lady-in-waiting to his queen, Catherine, and in 1673 was created Duchess of Portsmouth, Countess of Fareham and Lady Petersfield. From that time to the end of the reign 12 years later, she exercised a rare influence not only on the king personally, but on the nation's relationship with France, critical at that time. Her introduction to the English court had been planned if not by, then certainly with the approval of Louis XIV, who throughout her close alliance with Charles II had in Louise an ambassador most extraordinary. King Louis was not slow to recognize her worth: by the end of 1673 he gave her the considerable estates of the Dukedom of Aubigny, and ordered that they should revert to her own children after her death.

The possibility of the young Duke of Richmond ever becoming king may have been remote, but did become a good deal stronger than the mere accident of his birth might suggest. The Duke of York, the king's brother, was a Catholic, which so incensed the English Protestants that they endeavoured, in the House of Commons, to pass a Bill excluding him from succession. If that had been accomplished, what were the king's options? There seemed no chance of Queen Catherine giving him a son. Would he legitimize the Duke of Monmouth, or would he name as heir the son of his favourite mistress – a woman he respected and trusted long after his passion for her waned? (By the end of 1676, it was said that the king 'gives every appearance of being devoted to her during the day but reserves the right to spend the night with anyone he pleases'.) Richmond's chances might have been greater had his mother not been French, and a Catholic: her biographer, Jeanine Delpech, reports that she was 'loved by a great king, hated by his people, despised by her own countrymen'.

Had the first Duke of Richmond become King Charles III (all Richmond's sons have from that day borne the name of Charles), he would likely have provided history with as many royal scandals as his father, though with rather less charm. Though Delpech says of his early days that he 'deserved all the love he inspired through his beauty, his grace and his precocious intelligence', he soon turned out to be a bad lot, the black ram of the family, and seemingly the only one of the line.

The second Duke was a sportsman and romantic, the third the house builder and art collector, the fourth became Governor-General of Canada, the fifth a cabinet minister, the sixth developed the Goodwood estate and led the Hunt to great acclaim, the seventh built the 'new' racecourse grandstand, and the eighth, twenty years a cripple, wrote books. And of the first, the eighth wrote in *A Duke and His Friends*: 'Good looking, if good for nothing else . . . I fear there can be no denying the fact that, in his later years, lax principles and a love of dissipation formed very prominent features of his character.'

Such defects would not have shown in his earlier years, when the King lavished on him gifts and appointments unlimited. With the dukedoms went Richmond Castle (Yorkshire) and £2,000 a year; two years later, aged 5, the Duke was awarded a duty on all coal shipped from Newcastle; the Order of the Garter at the age of 8, when the young Duke was said to have begun the fashion of wearing that order over the shoulder instead of round the neck. At 9, he was Master of the King's Horse, and at 11, High Steward of the City of York, then the second city of England. And when he visited Paris with his mother, King Louis gave the boy a sword said to be worth nearly £12,000.

Richmond was 13 when his father died. His mother's position was immediately untenable. The hot breath of King James, who swiftly cut off the head of the ambitious Monmouth, melted her security overnight. In deference to the wishes of his brother, and encouraged perhaps by their religious affinity, and the feeling that Louise could still prove a useful ally in the French court, the king did agree to pay her an allowance of £2,000 and her son £3,000, and to keep up the Duchess's vast suite of rooms in Whitehall (they were mysteriously destroyed by fire six years later).

There is little to be gained from alignment with a used mistress, and Louise soon found there were few in London who were prepared to declare themselves as friends. She set sail for France, taking with her the boy and what Delpech called 'a scandalous amount of loot' – furniture as well as much gold and jewellery. By now she was the Duchess of Aubigny, but even in the French court, where earlier she had been received as a queen, she was no longer a welcome visitor. Her old friend King Louis was so uncertain of her intentions that he had a letter written ordering her exile. The same uncertainty persuaded him to destroy it, and when William of Orange took the English throne from James in 1698 and cut off her allowances, Louis settled on her a pension of £12,000 and on the Duke of Richmond, £20,000.

Though his mother was feared and mistrusted, young Richmond had by then won many hearts at the French court. His father, on his deathbed, had admitted his secret devotion to the Catholic faith; at his mother's urging, Richmond too accepted that faith as soon as they reached Paris. Even at that age, he clamoured to be allowed to fight with the French, and at 16 he joined an attack against John Churchill, Earl of Marlborough, at Valcourt. Two years later, King Louis gave him the command of a company of cavalry, but in 1692, when he was 20, Richmond returned to England, became reconciled to William of Orange,

changed his religion, and married Anne, daughter of Lord Brudenell and widow of Lord Bellasis. The following year he took his
seat in the House of Lords and became an aide-de-camp to the
King. It was a volte-face of staggering proportions, and perhaps
the first public sign of the total instability of the Duke's character.

By the time the Duke bought Goodwood he was well on the
road to ruin, physical, mental and financial. He borrowed huge
sums against his property (he had inherited the vast estates of the
Dowager Duchess of Richmond, of the Stuart line, in 1702) to pay
for other extravagances, both of property and of alcohol, and in
1719 cancelled a gambling debt by forcing his 18-year-old son,
the Earl of March, to marry the Earl of Cadogan's 13-year-old
daughter, Sarah, an arrangement that brought with it a settlement
of £60,000. The poor Duchess, a gentle and loving lady, cannot
greatly have enjoyed her 30 long-suffering years as his wife,
though throughout she refers to him in correspondence with
respect and even affection. In her letters to March, who spent
much time travelling in Europe, there are frequent references to
the state of the Duke's health, and even more frequent indications
of the dread she held that her son should stumble downhill on the
same path.

'I find by your last you have thoughts of seeing Venise once
more, I hope you will not keepe Mr Burges company too much, for
I hear he is a violent drinker which is that has killed all our English
youths in Italy.'

In 1722:

'Your poore Papa brought from London an intermiting Feaver and
with it most violent Histerik Fits, that he has been all this Fortnight
that he has favoured Goodewoode most extreamly ill. Mr Peakhame
with the Barke has stopd the Feaver, but his othere Fits were atended
with such convulsions that I sent for a Docter from London, who
assurs Lord Duke unless he intirely leaves of strong watters his
recovery is impossible. I hope this will prevaile else I fear you will
hear very ill news, for indeed I never remember Lord Duke so broke
and decayed as he is at present: in his Fits he raves after you and
says he is sure if he did but see his Dear Boy he should be well.'

And later that year:

'The Dukes of Bolton, Manchester, Earl of Scarborough, Holderness

and Lord Cornwallace are dead, the last kiled himself with strong
watters which none suspected him of; our friend drinks not less
than three Pints a day notwithstanding his late illness. God keep
you from having the same passion.'

In December 1722 the Duchess died, followed in May by her
degenerate husband. 'Worn out with debauchery', the French
diarist Saint-Simon records, 'he had become no longer the hand-
somest creature in the world, but the ugliest.' But however
debauched, however unpleasant a man he had become, he was a
king's son, and the funeral accorded to him in Westminster Abbey
paid full recognition to the fact. Francis Steer's presentation of
the funeral accounts occupies six pages of the *Sussex Archaeological Collection*.

The undertaker, Nicholas Strawbridge, took two days to bring
the hearse from London, and two days to take it back again:
'Hearse and six horses to bring his Grace to Town, £7; two
mourning coaches and six horses, £14.' There were four horsemen in mourning to accompany the hearse (£8 for four days),
and the cortège was decorated with 17 plumes of black 'Ostridge
Feathers'. The body lay in state at Guildford on the way, where
the Richmonds had a house ('deep in mourning, 6 candles all
night, 2 men watching').

The Duke lay in a lead coffin within a 'large Elme Coffin
covered with Crimson Genova Velvett finished with water Guilt
nails 4 pr best handles 9 Crownels and a Flower, all Gilded, £30'.
In the Abbey, the collection of candles was so prolific that the
undertaker had to pay the glazier to remove the upper windows
of the Jerusalem Chamber to keep the room cool: there were 10
large candlesticks round the coffin, 112 sconces with candles
round the walls, and '150 branch lights of wax with men to carry
them, £45'. Fifteen men were needed to carry the late Duke's
banners and standards, his helmet, sword, shield and spurs.

Clearly nothing was forgotten, whatever the cost, that could
add dignity to the occasion: 'Six Mutes in Mourning to attend by
the Corps at 3/6, 58 pr French Topt Gloves for the Choir and
Others of the Abbey, 30 men in mourning that Supported the 15
Gentmn wch carried the Trophies, 6 Conductors in mourning at
the doors to keep the Mob off, 4 managers in mourning to fitt all
the Lords and putt the whole procession in order, 8 pr gloves for
the singing boys, 57 pr gloves for the Lords Gentmn that fitted on
the collers of the order.'

The whole bill for the funeral came to £422.13s.7d., but that was not the end. At Richmond House, in Whitehall, and at Goodwood the principal rooms were completely veiled in light grey cloth – curtains, walls, carpet and upholstery – at an additional cost of £233.10s.6d. And before the account was settled, a sad addition had to be made: £8.19s.0d. for the funeral of the new Duke's still-born child.

Over in Aubigny the royal mistress, the Duchess of Portsmouth, long outlived her son. On the death of King Louis, her pension was increased by the Regent, the Duke of Orleans, and was raised again in 1718 to £24,000. With this, the last years of her extraordinary life were devoted to good works, establishing a hospital at Aubigny and redecorating the parish church. Voltaire said of her: 'Never did woman preserve her charms so late in life. At the age of 70 she was still lovely, her figure stately, her face unfaded.' She died at 85, obscure and alone. Circumstance certainly made her greater than nature had intended, but as a whore she retained remarkable dignity, coming to her king a virgin and remaining faithful to him far longer than he had any right to expect her to. As Jeanine Delpech neatly puts it, 'Ambition never stripped her of her grace, nor scandal of her pride'. Had her son possessed more of her qualities and fewer of his royal father's, the first chapter in the history of Goodwood would, perhaps, have been a less inglorious one.

2

GODINWOOD

Nobody who has visited Goodwood Racecourse will need reminding that there rises beyond the paddock a hill of such phenomenal symmetry that one might be forgiven for wondering briefly if it were a slag heap, pleasantly grassed and gently rounded. This is The Trundle, most famous of racing's hills, most blissful spot from which to survey the most beautiful racecourse in England. In the days that the middle-aged like to believe they remember, you could spend the whole of Goodwood Week on The Trundle for nothing, you and your ecstasies. Even today you can pass through the gates for a pittance, and your children free, but no dogs, and be faced with the delicious problem of how high to stagger with your picnic, balancing the ever-improving sight-lines that the height gives you against the diminishing range of your vision, weighing the charm of space and seclusion near the summit with your need for communion with the bookies at the base.

All day, wherever you sit, you are rich, feasting off the graceful miracle below. Given a dry day and a hefty pair of binoculars, I doubt if there is a more delightful spot in the horseracing world from which to enjoy the sport. You are out of contact, of course, with the snort of the horse and the thunder of his hoof, but the roar of the crowd reaches you well, and the race reader's clarion call; you could hardly say that your hand was plunged deep in the stuff of which racing is made, but the compensations are majestic. The whole of the lush, green coastal plain lies at your right hand, from Littlehampton clear to the Isle of Wight. Even to the naked eye, the Channel and its harbours shine seductively, and Chichester Cathedral stands boldly there only four miles away (from the spire to the summit of The Trundle is precisely 7,115 yards). At your feet, the incredible green baize curve of the course, within which the Downs obligingly drop sharply away on one side and aggravatingly pop up on the other, gives the crowd on the rails a breathtaking view clear through to the edge of Mid-hurst, but deprives them of a slice of the course on the bend.

On those neighbourly slopes, copses cluster and cows contentedly chew and agriculture pursues its dogged way as it has done there for ever more, races or no. Down The Trundle to your left lies Singleton, and closer still, but concealed, is Charlton, now a hamlet unknown beyond the locality but once itself a sporting jewel celebrated throughout the land and beyond its shores. Without Charlton you would, I think, never have heard of Goodwood; indeed, the Dukes of Richmond were not thought to live at Good-wood until the horses first raced there in 1801 – before that, they lived near Charlton. For that, if for no other reason, a lengthy piece of doggerel is included later in this story, the entire *Historical Account of the Rise and Progress of the Charlton Congress*. The original lies in the library of Goodwood House, on which the second Duke noted: 'This was brought to me by a Porter in the beginning of February, 1737. R.'

It is relevant just now, while we are still sitting on The Trundle, to note the opening lines:

> Amidst the South Saxonian hills there runs
> a verdant fruitful Vale, in which, at once
> fower small, and pretty Villages are seen
> (Eastden, Charleton, Singletown, Westden).
> Charleton, from whence so called, no record tells,
> unless that Charles of Richmond Duke, by Fate
> long since determined there at last to come . . .

And of the hill on which we sit, fully 702 feet above the low water mark, the poet writes:

> A vast, high Mountain, to the South doe's bear
> the Name, of one Saint Roke, unknown elsewhere,
> a Roman, or a Saxon, Camp is traced
> on his high Summit.

Today St Roke is unknown not only elsewhere, but right there, except to the antiquarians of the neighbourhood. Nor would the average man of West Sussex be any more familiar with the name by which the hill is properly called, St Roche's; nor with any of the variants which appear on the maps of the past four centuries, from St Roke's Hill (1575), through St Rokeshill (1579), St Rook's

Hill and St Rookeshill (1610), Rowkeshill (1650), St Rocks Hill (1675), Rook's Hill (1725) to St Roach's Hill (1822). According to *Place Names of Sussex*, St Roche's Hill takes its name from a chapel, which formerly existed there, dedicated to St Roch, confessor, a popular saint of France. The *Sussex Archaeological Collection* does contain a reference from 1570 to 'the late chappell of St Rooks', and the John Norden map of 1575 marks a chapel as still situated on top of the hill; but the use of the summit for worship of some kind goes back longer than that.

Smith's *Freeman's Companion*, published in London in 1736, lists: 'No. 65, Lodge of St Rook's Hill, near Chichester, Sussex, once a year, viz. Tuesday in Easter Week, constituted in the reign of Julius Caesar.' A former librarian at Goodwood House, Jacques, wrote a guide to the locality in 1822 in which he too claimed that the Ancient Society of Free and Accepted Masons had met on the hill in some form or other since Julius Caesar. More astute historians point out that there is no evidence at all that Julius was in those parts, and presume it is an error for Claudius Caesar, who certainly was.

How did it become The Trundle? The popular use of the word to denote the entire hill is of comparatively recent origin, probably not beyond this century; properly, it should only describe the ancient camp on its summit, and seems to come from the old English word *tryndel*, or *trendel*, a circle. Though there are now no other trundles in the area, the word was not unknown in the 16th century, when roughly round fields were sometimes, in Sussex at least, called trundlefelds.

It is surprising how deep and persistent the ignorance of archaeological matters used to be. 'A Roman, or a Saxon, Camp is traced on his high Summit,' jingled that 18th century recorder of the scene; and nearly 100 years later Jacques wrote: 'Upon the trundle of this hill will be found the remains of a Danish encampment, supposed to have been constructed about the year AD 992, when this country was infested by the incursions of that race of people' – an even less accurate summary of the situation. Digging was never necessary to surmise that there must have been a camp, or more likely a fort, on The Trundle. The roughly octagonal ramparts are massive and plain to see, and date from the Early Iron Age; perhaps 200 BC, as near as the experts can put it. It was not until the first aerial photographs were taken of the area in 1925 that traces of earlier ramparts were revealed within the 12½ acres of the Iron Age camp.

These were excavated in 1928, when the archaeologists lived under canvas on the site from 7th August to 1st September and did not lose one hour to rain. What they found confirmed the presence of a neolithic camp at least 4,000 years old, in which the inhabitants lived in ditches – homes were scooped out before they were raised up – side by side with their animals. There seemed to be three concentric ditches, the innermost a broken circle enclosing about three acres, into which their stock was no doubt driven for breeding and slaughter, and for safety. Closely without that was another ditch (and the rampart made by digging it) which overlapped itself on one side. Far away, and at some points crossed by the Iron Age ramparts, were signs of an outer ditch, possibly enclosing as much as 18 acres. The complete skeleton of a woman of about 25-30 was found here, and in pits beside the inner ditches were bones of long-horned oxen, horned sheep, pigs, roedeer and dogs, all of the neolithic period. The flintwork finds were thought by some to be poor and scarce, but included a leaf-shaped arrowhead, a roughly-shaped axe, and saw blades polished by contact with wood. There was also some pottery, 17 oyster shells and a remarkable phallus of carved bone.

Excavations were made into the Iron Age hill fort at the same time. There was a large inner and a small outer bank, separated by a ditch. These banks alone occupied six acres of land: the inner bank was 85 feet wide, and its crest was 17 feet above the floor of the ditch. There were two entrances, at the south east and the north west, where the ramparts were turned inwards to form a long passage. Double gates were set within these passages, flanked by wooden towers, and altogether it looks as if The Trundle fort, with its clear and commanding views, could only have been breached by a sizeable army. But for how long could it have withstood siege? The nearest water-well known today is 100 yards outside the ramparts.

Norman Wymer, in his entrancing *Companion into Sussex*, mixes his knowledge and his fancy to produce pictures of different domestic lives of the two ages of man who lived on this pinnacle of Goodwood.

'Here in these pits the Neolithic folk led their self-supporting lives, gathering flint from their nearby mines with which to fashion such tools and implements as they required, tending their beasts and crudely curing their hides to provide covering material for their bodies and perhaps even for their homes, making their earthenware cooking utensils and pots on a turntable composed of sodden leaves, and weaving their cloths on upright looms whose warp they kept taut with weights of downland chalk.'

The flint mines he mentions are now known as Lavant Caves, only a mile south west of The Trundle. The hill city built there in the third century BC had an altogether more important function. It was the largest of its kind in the whole territory of the Regni tribe, and probably served as their capital. Says Wymer:

'In this city the people dwelt in huts of wattle-and-daub, and besides fashioning flint, spinning and weaving, and making pottery, also wrought tools of iron. Unlike the people of the Stone Age, they kept no beasts, but bartered their goods with the inhabitants of the more low-lying districts in exchange for corn, milk and other produce. Thus, The Trundle served as a kind of market town . . . But it was also a fortress, and when danger loomed the herdsmen around would drive their beasts to the hill-top, confident that shelter awaited them behind the ramparts.'

They seem to have deserted it in the middle of the first century BC, just while they were in the process of constructing new and bigger gates to their town. It was at exactly this time that the Romans founded the town of Chichester, then called Regnum, and the inference is obvious: the tribesmen on their isolated hill (which is not on the Downs proper: though as high as any peak for four miles, it is the western end of a lesser ridge that runs south of and parallel to the main line of the Downs) could see clearly the establishment of this new settlement. Though less easily defensible, it was a more attractive proposition. They abandoned the fort and drove their animals down the hill to the pastures below, and it was probably 1,900 years before The Trundle was occupied again, by Victorian picnickers.

During the Roman occupation of Chichester, a temple was built in North Street, the foundations of which were not discovered until 1723, when the ground was excavated for the building of the Council Chamber. Only four feet below the surface the workmen found (and unfortunately greatly damaged) a six foot long marble memorial tablet which is one of the most rare treasures of that period. It records that the Temple of Minerva was there 'erected for the health of the Imperial Family by the authority of King Cogidubnus, the lieutenant of Tiberius Claudius Augustus in Britain'. The stone was presented to the second Duke of Richmond who had been the local MP and was later the Mayor, and rested at Goodwood for many years before being returned to the city. Cogi was a powerful British chief who, in return for his enthusiastic co-operation with Claudius Caesar, became his vice-roy. It may have been he who founded Regnum, though some suggest that he was 'king' of the Regni on The Trundle and came down to join the Romans, since it was clear he could not beat them. Either way, he would nowadays be regarded as a Quisling.

Five hundred years later the town's history advanced significantly, though horrifyingly, when it was stormed and ruthlessly occupied by Ælla, a Saxon warlord. He landed three ships near West Wittering, at what he called Cymen-shore (after his son) and was later Keynor. Repulsed in his first attack on Regnum, he returned with three sons, Cymen, Cissa and Wincheling, put the town to the sword and established the kingdom of Suth-Seaxarnice – roughly Sussex and Surrey. Ælla reigned 36 years and was succeeded by Cissa, who settled in Regnum, which he called Cissa-ceastre. His name was pronounced Chissa, as ceastre was chester. (Cicelhyrst became Chislehurst, and Colchester used to be King Coel-ceastre.) Cissa died, it is said, in AD 577 at the age of 117, just 100 years after he first landed in Britain. He was buried at Cissbury Hill.

So we have had The Trundle occupied and Chichester named, but what signs of Goodwood? Not much, as yet, but we are coming to the origin of its name. Few historians hesitate to attribute it to the Saxon Godwin, who rose from being the son of a local herdsman to be Earl of Wessex, and the most powerful ruler in the land after the king. Before we join that throng, it is necessary to record the objections of the etymologists. They note these 13th century names in the area: Godiuawuda, Goddiuewuda Godivewod, Godeyuewod and Godyeuewod; and in *Place Names of Sussex* go on with some contempt to dismiss other forms as being 'without interest, except to note that they have often been mis-transcribed with an "n" for the "u".' The most likely derivation of Goodwood, they conclude, is 'Godgiefu's wood', that being a common woman's name in late old English, made most familiar in its Latinized form of Godiva.

So be it, perhaps. But Earl Godwin is too good to miss. How the Sussex herdsman's son achieved his early distinction is not known, but by the time Canute landed in England and defeated Edmund Ironside (1016), Godwin (Goduinus) was in a position to offer substantial help to the new king (who, incidentally, promptly married Edmund's widowed mother). Godwin so distinguished himself in battle, according to Horsfield's *History of the Antiquities and Topography of the County of Sussex*, that 'he received from the king the sister of his brother-in-law, Ulfr'. By this lady, Githa, he had quantities of children, one of whom married Edward the Confessor (Ironside's brother) and one of whom became King Harold II of 1066 fame.

By 1020 Godwin seems to have been Earl of Kent, Sussex and Wessex. His lands surrounded the town of Chichester, and his manor was at Bosham, where Canute had a palace at the water's edge. When Canute died (1035), Godwin was at the right hand of the son by Canute's Danish marriage, Harold 'Harefoot', who took the English throne. The arrival in England the next year of Alfred, son of the former king Ethelred the Unready, was evidently interpreted by Godwin as a threat to Harold I, and Dugdale tells the fearful tale in his *Barony of England* :

'Godwyne met him in Canterbury, and having assured him of his fidelity, feasted with him that evening. But soon after, in the night time, when Alfred and his followers were asleep in their beds at Guilford, in Surrey, he rushed in upon them with a multitude of armed men; and binding their hands behind them, set them on a row, causing them all to be beheaded except the tenth man : and not satisfied with that, decimated them once over again, so that few were left alive.'

Godwin then took Alfred to King Harold at Ely, who ordered his eyes to be put out – 'which being performed, he soon died'. As the *Saxon Chronicle* puts it :

> 'A deed more dreary, none
> In this land was done,
> Since Englishmen gave place
> To hordes of Danish race.'

During the reign of Alfred's brother, Edward the Confessor, Godwin and his sons were briefly exiled. They were pardoned two years later, perhaps through the influence of the queen, Godwin's daughter, but were only back in England in time for Godwin to drop dead during dinner at the king's table, in 1053. He was succeeded as Earl of Wessex by his son Harold, who became king of England in 1066, and defeated the Norwegians (for whom his own brother Tostig was fighting) at Stamford Bridge before meeting an early end at the Battle of Hastings. A man of some substance, then, and some renown, was Godwin. Can there be much doubt, when one comes to the first reference to 'Godinwood Manor' in the Burrell Manuscript of 1584, that the name is his?

Till then, the estate at Goodwood had descended as part of the larger one of Halnaker, which in 1540 passed from Lord De La Warr to the Crown in exchange for a nunnery at Wherwell, Hampshire. Queen Mary leased it at £20 a year in 1560 to the Earl of Arundel, an arrangement renewed by Queen Elizabeth in 1565. A survey in 1570 records that 'within halfe a furlonge of Halnaker parke pale on the west side thereof lyeth a park called Goodwoode Parke', and Christopher Saxton's map of 1575 shows a visibly separate estate at Goodwood though he gives it no name. Next door there is 'Halfnaked House,' which by 1584 was Halnaker again and was held by John, Lord Lumley, and his wife Jane Fitzalan (the last of the family who held Arundel Castle for 400 years, till it passed to the Howards): they must by then have bought Halnaker outright from the Crown, for in that year they sold to Henry Walrond 'Godinwood Maner in Hamptonet [Hampnett] with its appendages, and 2 houses, 4 gardens, 2 orchards, 200 acres of Park Lane, 10 of Arable, 500 of pasture, and 300 of wood'. Goodwood is named for the first time on John Norden's fascinating map (1595), when he uses both there and at Halnaker the symbol denoting 'houses of gentry etc.' rather than that for 'houses of noblemen'.

It is astonishing for how long a convenient myth can be perpetuated when historians get their hands on it. As far back as relevant histories appear, and for at least 150 years, it has been supposed that the first Duke of Richmond bought Goodwood House from the Compton family of East Lavant in (or sometimes 'by') 1720 – the date on which he was said to have demolished the 'original' house and built the 'old' house, still incorporated in the present building. Such statements have been repeated with monotonous regularity, even by the Earl of March in 1911, (*A Duke and His Friends*) and the ninth Duke in 1939 (*A Guide to Goodwood House*). In fact it is incontrovertibly clear that Richmond began the purchase in 1695 and completed it in 1697. He had no part in the rebuilding: that was accomplished long before his time.

No room for doubt is left on these points when the staggering array of title deeds now in the care of the West Sussex Archive Office is studied – though it is doubtful if even the most dedicated author would have found his way through it without the meticulous, almost miraculous indexing and interpreting achieved by the staff there. In the hope that the misquoting may now stop, it is worth listing briefly the true descent of Goodwood from the time it was split from the Halnaker estate. The odd variations in price that follow can often be accounted for by the differing quantity of appendages – farms, cottages and so on – included in the sale:

1584, Henry Walrond, £2,400; 1597, Thomas Cesar and Robert Webb, £3,500; 1599, Thomas Bennett, £2,100; 1608, Sir Edward Frances, £2,800; 1614, Earl of Northumberland, £1,800; 1657, John Caryll, £2,400; 1675, Anthony Kemp, £3,500; 1690, Earl of Middleton, £4,000; 1693, Earl of Shrewsbury and William Rowley, £3,500; 1697, Duke of Richmond, £4,100.

When Sir Edward Frances (Frannceyes) bought Goodwood he was the supervisor of the Petworth House estate, whose owner, the ninth Earl of Northumberland, was then in the Tower. In 1616–17 the Earl demolished most of the hunting lodge that then commanded Goodwood Park and rebuilt it at a cost of £556.18.6d. The new house was still obviously intended as a nobleman's 'weekend cottage'; it had two main floors with a cellar and an attic, and was heavily gabled, but was only 76 feet long and 24 feet wide – hardly the proportions required in those days for even a gentleman's main residence.

Two others on the list of owners deserve comment: John Caryll was in 1684 exiled by an Act of Parliament of Charles II for high treason; and in the same year the Earl of Middleton, son of one of King Charles's most famous generals, was made a Secretary of State. Though at last the pieces of this puzzle can be properly fitted together, there is still something odd about the picture. As soon after the event as 1737, the second Duke of Richmond was under the impression that Middleton had bought it directly from Caryll, and that the Duke of Somerset had bought it from Middleton. That much is clear from the extraordinarily confused letter that Richmond wrote to Somerset, his neighbour at Petworth House:

'I have been in searche for ye Deed of Purchase for Goodwood, which Deed I doe now send; by itt Your Grace will see that itt is butt a second Part, signed and sealed by Mr Caryll, the first purchaser of itt.

'I doe suppose you are in possession of ye first Part from the then Earl of Northumberland to Mr Caryll, itt being the Title Deed the Earl of Middleton bought itt from Mr Caryll; and then ye late Duke your Fathere bought it from the late Earl of Middleton, butt notwithstanding by ye Deeds that all writings etc. were to be delivered to Mr Caryll yett I have ordered a searche to be made in all my rooms where evidences are kept.'

Somerset was not much help: 'I wish itt had been more in my power to have retrieved any papers that might have been service-able to Your Grace; but in vaine, wee find none.' How does Somerset come into the picture, when we see by the deeds that Middleton sold to the Earl of Shrewsbury and William Rowley? That remains a mystery, for there is no other reference to the Duke of Somerset owning Goodwood. One clue does wave tan-talizingly in the winds of time: in 1682 that Somerset, the sixth, married Elizabeth Percy, who had inherited the estates of her father, the 11th and last Earl of Northumberland. They included Petworth House, which is how Somerset came to be there; but before his death Northumberland had sold Goodwood to John Caryll.

Another connection between the families, irrelevant to the question of house ownership, is intriguing enough to be men-tioned. In 1679 Elizabeth Percy's grandmother, who brought her up, turned down the suggestion that she should be betrothed to the first Duke of Richmond. She was then 12 and he only seven, but his royal father was no doubt hoping to secure a mighty estate for him. By the time she married Somerset three years later she had already seen out two husbands, the weedy young Earl of Ogle, who died, and the unfortunate Thomas Thynne of Longleat, who was murdered.

It is over the last dozen years of the 17th century that the remaining problem of the first Duke's residence rests. The records of the Corporation of St Pancras, not a civic authority but an ancient social body in the city of Chichester, mentioned 'a fat buck presented by the Duke of Richmond at Goodwoode' for dinner on 4th November, 1689. This would appear to be con-clusive evidence that the Duke was in residence there at the age of 17: but as far as is known, he lived with his mother in France from August 1685 (following Charles II's death) until early in 1692, when he returned to England and married. There were visits to London in that period, but no suggestion of the Duke having acquired a home.

Indeed, despite his royal connections, he was in no position to do so, for there was at that time little sympathy for him at the English court. William of Orange, who in 1689 took the throne from Richmond's uncle, James II, immediately discontinued the pension the Duke had been drawing. It was replaced by one from Louis XIV, in token not only of the French king's respect for the boy's mother, but of appreciation for Richmond's apparent devotion to the French cause. Also in that year of 1689, he had hoped to be allowed to join the abortive attempt by the deposed English king to invade Ireland and win back his throne; and in September 1690, Richmond was given the command of a French cavalry regiment.

All this makes it fairly clear that the lad would not have been househunting in England at that time, and it even seems unlikely that in November 1689 he would have been at Goodwood at all. But that St Pancras record, if it is correct, must have an explanation. Was it simply that he was staying at Goodwood with Anthony Kemp, of whom nothing is known, killed the 'fat buck' in the day's hunting, and presented it to the society? Or could young Richmond have been renting the house before that from Kemp (who himself rented it at £35 a year before he bought it), and the presentation was made by his steward, probably without even the formality of the Duke's approval?

The second supposition would gain strength if only the second Duke were right in thinking that the Earl of Middleton bought the house from John Caryll, or at least bought it earlier than the date of November 1690 that appears on the deeds. King Charles, in the year before his death, did much to ensure the future safety of his favourite mistress and son, for whose treatment he feared when he was no longer there to protect them. In 1684 he asked Louis XIV to allow the boy French naturalization papers, so he could on his mother's death inherit her property there. Another logical and natural step would have been for the King to secure a home in the English countryside for them, and he could well have done that by arranging for Middleton, his new Secretary of State, to buy it and have the boy down there under his guardianship. But Anthony Kemp gets in the way of that theory.

It is certain that King Charles and some of his sons were familiar with the Goodwood territory. The King passed close by on his escape to Shoreham in 1651, the route for which was engineered by a local man, Colonel Gounter of Racton, who arranged for Charles to stop at the George and Dragon at Houghton. Both the King and Richmond were excellent horsemen (the Duke rode a race at Newmarket at the age of ten), and greatly addicted to hunting, of which Charlton was an unrivalled centre and said to be the favourite resort of the eldest royal son, the

Duke of Monmouth. So we have every kind of excuse for bringing Richmond to Goodwood at whatever year suits us; just no corroboration that he was there when St Pancras says he was.

Of the date of purchase by Richmond we can be in no doubt: 20th June, 1695, is on the articles of agreement for 'the mansion house of Goodwood and all lands belonging thereto'; the price was £4,100 'conditional upon his recovering the property by way of mortgage to secure £2,000 with interest at 6 percent to the person who makes the conveyance'. The other £2,100 had to be paid by 24th June, 1697, and the property was finally conveyed to him by the Earl of Shrewsbury and William Rowley on 23rd December.

Whatever the date of the first Duke's arrival, we now run into something of massive importance to the future of Goodwood: the Charlton Hunt. It meant almost as much to racing there as Epsom salts did to the Derby – without the one, the other would never have happened. And without the second Duke of Richmond, one of the great sportsmen of his time, the Charlton Hunt would almost certainly have faded out to a chorus of bickering and backbiting.

3

HAPPILY CONJOINED

All the family stories maintain that the second Duke of Richmond was born at Goodwood House. The eighth Duke, in a biography of his ancestor, opens with an idyllic scene in which the trees there are blossoming and the birds twittering and the estate workers pause on their way across the fields to cast a proud and affectionate eye at the big house where the next master lies in his swaddling clothes. This long and sunny introduction is also used by a much later author, the irrepressible cricket raconteur John Marshall, who found enough evidence of the second Duke's passion for that game, and his influence on it, to write another biography called *The Duke Who Was Cricket*. But with pedantic stubbornness, *The Dictionary of National Biography* insists that the boy was born in London.

That distinguished work may be accurate, but it does paint the account of the second Duke's life in the wrong colours, filling its columns with appointments and promotions and such prosaic matters. He was undoubtedly a man of Goodwood, a man of life, and a man of sport. Though he was an MP for a year before his father's death, that was a perfunctory business and the sort of thing that used to be expected of the eldest son of the local nobleman. He seems to have had no great political, diplomatic nor military ambitions, unlike most of his descendants, and those appointments which fell to him by his rank and position, he accepted not through any burning sense of service, but for the very considerable cash that came with them, a lifebelt for a man who was drowning in a sea of debts from the moment he inherited

B

the title. He was, as his mother put it, 'extremely ratle-headed', but though he became renowned for the size and splendour of his entertaining, he was most romantically devoted to his family and leaves no tainted history, no suggestion of his father's debauches.

The sober view is that he was a man with a defective education and perhaps a somewhat sluggish intellect, but that he did not deserve the epithets later slung crossly at him by Queen Caroline (wife of George II) of 'mulish' and 'half-witted'. He was, after all, a Fellow of the Royal Society, and his interest in natural sciences led to his being given a doctorate of physics at Cambridge University. The eighth Duke's appraisal of his intellect was that he 'has no claims whatever to be deemed a great or exceptional man. His natural endowment was certainly not above average. He was hardly better educated than Louis XIV'. But, he goes on, his 'affability, straightforward honesty and transparent patriotism singled him out as a plain man, abnormally trustworthy and of a solid integrity. The King believed in him, with tolerable correctness, as one of the few genuine disinterested adherents of the dynasty'. The second Duke acted as Lord High Constable of England on the day of George II's coronation in 1727, and despite his wife's opinions, the King appointed him an aide-de-camp and Lord of the Bedchamber. From November to March, however – the hunting season – it is doubtful whether the King saw much of him, in or out of the bedchamber.

But before he had the opportunity to devote himself fully to the pleasures of the chase or the cricket pitch, the young Earl of March had much to go through. Perhaps because his scholastic abilities were not of the highest order, he was 'finished' more thoroughly than most of his time, with three years travelling on the Continent. As soon as his shameful marriage to the child bride had been quietly solemnized (it is said he had not seen the girl before the ceremony, nor did he wait to see her after it) he was pushed off on the grand tour of Europe with a scholarly guardian. He popped home in March 1721 to be commissioned in a strange outfit known then as the Horse Granadier Guards, whose activities were later recorded by Sir George Arthur in *The Story of the Household Cavalry*. The Granadiers, he said, 'dismounted, linked their horses, fired, screwed their daggers, fired and threw their grenades by ranks, the centre and rear ranks advancing in succession through the intervals between the file leaders. They then grounded their arms, went to the right about, and dispersed; and at the preparation or beating to arms they slung their fusils, marched to their horses, unlinked and mounted, after which they fired their pistols and muskets on horseback'. It all sounds like a spectacular exercise for the Aldershot Tattoo, but was probably stunningly effective in battle.

While still on his travels, and theoretically in the army, March was being organized at home to take a seat in Parliament at the next election. Chichester was the obvious constituency, but Newcastle (to which family was connected by those coal duties) put in a strong bid for him, agreeing to elect him not only without his bothering to show his face there (which was not then extraordinary) but without his having to pay for the privilege, which was a startling rarity. With that offer in hand, March's champions in Chichester were under some pressure to come out of the bush with an equalizer; his mother suggested that when they did, he should not do Newcastle the honour to stand. In December 1721 she wrote to him:

> 'Mr Baker Murrie Clowdslys and several others declares if you doe not stand for Chechester theire hearts is broke as yor: Papa is in London, Sabbe is very busie, I doe not much care to medle so he must act for you. The Bishop says all the world must be for the Earl of March that was boarne and educated with them, it is thought this Parlement will soon be at an end.'

'Sabbe' could either have been the Duchess's rendering of the name of March's secretary, Labbé, who was with him for many years, or their familiar name for the Duchess of Portsmouth's faithful old retainer, Monsieur de Carné, who lived in a cottage in the grounds of Goodwood House. He was certainly one of those who played a large part in organizing the election at Chichester after Newcastle had been rejected. Others included both March's wife's father, Lord Cadogan, and his mother's father, Lord Brudenell. Cadogan was so determined that March should be guaranteed a seat in the House that he proceeded to organize him two, as he explained in a letter to the Earl:

'Your Election had been fixed at Newcastle as I formerly acquainted you, but some of your Friends thinking you should rather stand for Chichester, your Lordship is set up there. I conclude you will carry it, but for fear of accidents, I design to get your Lordship chose for Newport in the Isle of Wight, where you will meet with no opposition . . .'

Elections in those days, and for many years afterwards, usually involved the bribing of both agents and electors, with alcohol if not actually with money. Also, apparently, the kissing not of babies but of wives. Lady Anne, the Duchess, wrote to March in January 1722:

'We have no company at present but Lord William [Beauclerk] and Captain Macartney, who follows yor: election at Chechester, ye women complaine Lord William does not kiss them, they think you would be better bread if you were here, all our Sex is for you, and one declares if her Husband will not give a single vote for you he shall not rest by day or night' (a reversal of the customary Lysistratan principle). The dig at Lord William not being well enough 'bread' is delicious, as is so much in the Duchess's letters: Lord William was the grandson of Charles II and Nell Gwynn; the Earl of March was the grandson of Charles II and Louise de Kéroualle.

In February, his sister Anne wrote to him: 'Yor elexion I hope will goe very well, poore Carne takes a great deal of pains, and I beleave if the elexion is not over very soon, will kill himself. Lord William and George Macartney taks as much pains, for they are forst to drink strong bear and smoak with all the voaters twis a week, which you may gus is not very agreable to them, and I beleave would not do it for aney body but you.'

The next letter was from his mother again, with the bad news that 'the Chechester Election must be at our expense but if you carry it now the Towne and Corperation is yours for ever.' She also reports that 'Poore old Carné will kill himself with drinking', and since she goes on, 'he says he cannot dy better than in Lord Marches service', the inference is not that he was taking after the Duke by choice, but that he too was being 'forst to drink strong bear' in the election campaign. To avoid as much expense as possible, the practical Duchess continues: 'Yor: Friends have taken that House that was Mrs Orm's in yor: name and there twice a week you treat wch: is cheaper than running up at a Public House'. The treating went on for five months, which must have been painful to March's allowance, but all in a good cause: in May 1722 he was elected as Member both for Chichester and for Newport. March had little chance to impress with his political skills, for it was barely a year before he was removed to the House of Lords by the death of his father.

His mother had died in December, and right up to his return to Goodwood in August 1722 maintained her charming and affectionate concern for her son, as well as her management of his household: 'I had put a stop to the Lace of yor: Liveries by reason yor: servants must be nine months in mourning for old Mrs Cadogan as grandmothere. Pray take care of yor: health;' 'In yor: last you mentioned yor: being to goe to a Ball though you had set up all the night before dancing wch. gave me many tears therefore pray anothere time keepe yr. irregularities to yourself for knowing them only gives me paine.' She knew much pain, that dear lady: her first husband, Lord Bellasis, had died young; her second marriage was dreadfully hazardous; and both her daughters died before she did – Louise in 1717, aged 23, and Anne at 19 in the year of her own death.

So young March, who had been a husband at 18 and an MP at 21, found himself at barely 22 the master of Goodwood and a large house in Whitehall. But what of his wife? Though he had immediately abandoned her for his tour of Europe (she lived in The Hague with her father, the British ambassador), he had clearly not entirely abrogated his responsibilities, as this extract from his mother's letter in January 1722 makes clear:

> 'Captaine Macartney as a Seecreet tells me when he was at the Hague Lady March had a fall of her Hors which she does not care to acknowledge for feare she shoud be forbid riding, but indeed if she shoud Fall when she ride so violently she must be kild for you can not guess how wild she is when on Hors Back and therefore desire her to be more carefull and discreet, what ever you say is a Law to her so in this case make use of yor: Power.'

'Whatever you say is a law to her': perhaps the abandonment of the child bride was not as complete as was supposed. Or was it just that in the manner of the day, and even in those peculiar circumstances, she was prepared to abide absolutely by her husband's will? Whatever the facts, no truth should be allowed to obscure the unforgettable idyll of their reunion, which is said to have taken place in a theatre in The Hague while March was en route for London in the summer of 1722. 'Who is that ravishing girl?' he is supposed to have asked his companion, or words to that effect. The young beauty, he was told, was the new hit of the season, the target of every proud beau. Her name, of course, was Lady March. They consummated the marriage immediately and never looked back. She was still only 16, and with the least possible delay gave birth to a daughter. Her next two children, both sons, died very early: one at birth and one aged 3, from smallpox, in Paris. Indeed, of their first five babies, only the eldest survived childhood and the heir, one of 12 children, was not born until 1735. All the indications are that the marriage was one of bliss and deep affection, and only a few months after her Duke's death, Lady Sarah died, broken-hearted, at the age of 45.

One or two elections after that in which March won Chichester, there was an extraordinary incident on The Trundle involving a Parliamentary candidate, which is recalled against the year 1725 in Spershott's *Memoirs of 18th Century Chichester*:

'Jno. Page Esquire, native of this City, coming from London to Stand Candidate here, a great number of voters went on Horseback to meet him. Among the rest Mr Joshua Lover a noted School Master, a sober man in the General, but one of flighty Passions. As he was setting out, one of his Scollers, Patty Smith (afterwards my Spouse) asked him for a Coppy, and in haste he wrote the following:

> Extreames beget Extreames, Extreames avoid,
> Extreames, without Extreames, are not enjoyed.

'He set off on High Carrier, and coming down Rooks's Hill before the Squire, rideing like a mad man To and fro, forward and backward Hallooing among the Company, the Horse at full Speed fell with him and kill'd him. A caution to the flighty and unsteady: and a verification of his copy.'

In the same year the second Duke anticipated today's stately home owners by beginning to build up an extraordinary menagerie in High Wood, above Goodwood House. The most notable of the early arrivals was a lion, which did not survive long, but long enough to become such a favourite with the Duke that over its grave he erected a life-size statue of the animal, which is still there today. Before long, and in the lifetime of the lion, Goodwood Park rang to the cries of two tigers, two leopards, a civet cat, a tiger cat, five wolves, three foxes, a jackal, three vultures and two eagles, all of which according to his records consumed 70 lb of meat a day. There were several monkeys and three bears, which are down in the books as eating bread. Spershott notes: 'Now about was brought to Goodwood the Great Novelty of many wild Beast, Birds, and other Animals, and there kept in Dens, with Iron Grates made for them to be seen through, which draw's a great number of People Thither to see them, a Lion, Tiger, man Tiger, Bears, Egles, Ostrich, etc. etc.'

The Duke lost no time in organizing and encouraging the

cricketing ability of his estate employees. Sussex is indisputably the cradle of the game, and the skimpy evidence that survives suggests that Goodwood may have been at the very heart of its development. Marshall says that, after his researches, he became convinced that the second Duke 'perhaps more than any other pioneer was responsible for the spread of cricket and the shaping of the game in the first half of the 18th century'. The county archives contain proof of what is generally regarded as the first known game of cricket involving a number of players, and it took place in May 1622 (a century before the second Duke's succession) in the churchyard at Boxgrove, the parish of which encompasses much of the Goodwood estate. It is contained in a Bill of Present-ment to the Bishop of Chichester from the parishioners, reporting various misdemeanours in their midst. Among them, five men are named 'together with others whose names I have no notice of' for playing cricket in the churchyard on Sunday the fifth of May 'after sufficient warnings given to the contrary'. Not only was that contrary to the seventh article, declares the report, but the players used to break the church windows with the ball, 'and, thirdly, for that a little childe had like to have her braynes beaten out with a crecket bat'. The two churchwardens were also named in the Bill, 'for defending and mayntayning them in it'.

In the early 18th century, says Marshall, there was evidence of inter-village cricket rivalry in the Goodwood-Halnaker-Boxgrove area, and the Duke of Richmond appears to have built up a formidable team by 1725, when they played against Sir William Gage's XI at Firley, near Lewes. Two summers later they played home and away against Mr Alan Brodrick's team from Peper Harow, near Godalming, and it is these two matches that Marshall finds of immense significance. Before them, the two skippers (Brodrick later became Viscount Midleton) drew up an agreement of what constituted fair play and what did not, and what that amounts to is the first set of the laws of cricket. There are 16 clauses, and the similarity they bear to the MCC laws as we know them is remarkable. Even then they played with only 12 men a side, and the wickets were pitched only one yard further apart than they are today. There was also a firm directive on team behaviour which some may be sorry is no longer in force: 'If any of the Gamesters shall speak or give their opinion, on any point of the Game, they are to be turned out and voided in the match; this not to extend to the Duke of Richmond and Mr Brodrick.'

It was not long before the Duke implemented the well-known

'amateur' principles of finding employment for a man who is
going to win matches for you, and his team included Thomas
Waymark, known as the father of all professionals, who was
employed as a groom at Goodwood, and a renowned cricketing
barber, Stephen Dingate. By 1731 the stakes, which had always
been an integral part of matches made between great gentlemen,
rose to a fine height. The Goodwood team went to play on the
Green at Richmond, Surrey, against Mr Chambers's XI for a wager
of £200. The Duke's men notched 79, and the home side were
eight or ten short when play ended at 7 p.m. The result was not
much to the liking of the crowd: 'The Duke of Richmond and his
cricket players were greatly insulted by the mob at Richmond,
some of them having the shirts torn off their backs; and it was
said a lawsuit would commence about the play.'

Less than five miles along the South Downs from Goodwood is
the hillside village of Slindon, one of the jewels in the crown of
West Sussex. By 1740 theirs was one of the great cricket teams of
the country, virtually both Sussex and England in its strength. It
was led by a surgeon who practised in Chichester, Richard New-
land, and one of the star performers was the legendary Richard
Nyren, who later became landlord of the Bat and Ball at Hambledon and captain of that most famous of all clubs. The proximity
of the two Sussex communities, and the unlikelihood of the
second one being able to build up an outstanding team without
the sponsorship of a great landowner, leads Marshall to believe
that 'there can be little doubt that Slindon was the Duke's team'.
Cricket has stayed happily in the blood of the Richmond family:
the third Duke captained Sussex against Hambledon in 1768
(winning £1,000 with a victory), the fourth was a founder of the
MCC and an enthusiastic wicketkeeper who played in Brussels
before the Battle of Waterloo, and also in Canada shortly before
his tragic death there, and the fifth was president of the MCC in
1842. The present Earl of March has played many times on that
enchanting cricket field in front of Goodwood House, where the
cedars of Lebanon are big enough to dwarf the greatest innings.

Though the second Duke is not best remembered for his contribution to the architecture of Goodwood, nor for his nurturing of
the estate, nor for any collection of fine art – in all of which he
was overshadowed by his son – his affection for Goodwood
was evident and his industry not inconsiderable. He increased the
estate to 1,100 acres, chiefly by buying the manors of Singleton
and Charlton (good hunting country). It was he who planted those

marvellous cork oaks in front of the house, one of which bore two crops of acorns in 1911, following a phenomenally hot summer. Collinson, the well-known landscape gardener whom the Duke consulted, noted that 'his Grace intended clothing all the bare hills above the House with trees'. His love of trees is commemorated too in part of a letter written from Goodwood to his wife in London during the last year of his life:

'The team is set out today with a load of charcoal, for London, and it is to bring me a load of trees, butt I beg that nothing else, be it never so small, may come down with it, for the trees are in basketts, and must be in the bed of the wagon and stand upright, so nothing can be under them, and the least thing over them will breake the top shoots, and quite spoil my trees, which will cost me fifteen pounds; so they are every way too valuable to be spoiled . . .'

Aside from anything else, his recognition of beauty and his sympathy with it were shown by his paying in 1746 for a complete restoration of Chichester Cross, that most rare and admirable of architectural adventures. The most notable aspect of that job was the removing of the clock that 22 years earlier had been grievously misplaced immediately under the apex of the building. Under Richmond's patronage, the four clock faces were set as they have so gracefully stayed for two centuries, each one facing one of the four main streets of the city that meet at the Cross. This Duke also distinguished himself artistically by his patronage, comparatively early in the artist's life, of the Italian painter Canaletto, four of whose works he commissioned. They still hang in Goodwood House – one of them being a view of the Thames from Richmond House, the family's London home.

Apart from his devotion to the Charlton Hunt, the second Duke is probably best remembered for the fact that he built Carné's Seat, a huge and elaborate summer house with one of the most enviable views in Sussex. For this he engaged – and obviously – the same architect who had designed the Council Chamber at Chichester, Roger Morris. On the site of the cottage where old Carné had lived, high on the hillside to the north of the House, they built something that lies a trifle uneasily in its setting, not quite a residence and almost a folly. In the words of the experts Ian Nairn and Nikolaus Pevsner, it is 'without either Burlington's certainty of purpose or Kent's decorative charm'. The newly-demolished church tower at Hove provided much of the material for the building, which faces south west and provides an uninterrupted sight of the coast of Sussex and Hampshire almost as sweet and far-reaching as is obtained from the top of The Trundle. Basically, Carné's Seat was an ornate and gilded banqueting room, in which no doubt the second Duke did some of the entertaining for which he was so renowned. In recent years the ninth Duke lived there for a while, but found it more convenient to move into a cottage beside it.

In the hillside behind it, is the most exquisite embellishment: a grotto, a shell house of such perfection it must have been fashioned by the gods, or found intact on Prospero's magic isle. But if you look among the incredibly delicate shell patterns you will find the initials of the second Duke and Duchess and their daughters, for it was the women of the family who made it with shells of pink and white, mauve and blue, collected from all over the world. 'I have a small ship load of shells for the Dukes of Bedford and Richmond,' wrote the captain of HMS *Diamond* to John Russell in 1739. And from the Governor of Barbados to the Duke, 'I am now making a Collection for the Duchess of Richmond of Shells – as we hear her Grace is fitting up a Grotto under one of the finest Roomes in Britain, built lately in Goodwood Park by Your Grace'. It took them seven years to complete, but the search for perfection never ended. In the year of his death the Duke at Charlton, wrote to his wife, in London: 'I am charmed with the middle nitch at Carné's and am now quite clear that the two side ones should be pulled to pieces, and made exactly like the middle one. I never saw Goodwood in more beauty . . .' Sadly, the shell house was so picked to pieces by sightseers that in 1920 one-fifth of it had to be replaced, and now it is no longer open to the public.

When, for reasons of state or sport, the Duke and Duchess were parted, their letters were regular, affectionate and charmingly chatty. One summer, when the Duke was clearly contemplating a mammoth entertainment – or perhaps it was a cricket match? – Lady Sarah wrote from Goodwood House: 'My dear Angel . . . The new bedchamber is finished and the bed up but it smells of paint a good deal . . . Now as to beds for people, there is Lord Midlesexs new room, two good field beds in his outward room, the red bed, the haunted room and one in Sr. Thomas's outward room, six upon that floor. Above there is Carolinas, Mr Hills and Mrs Pitts, at the gardeners house one and St pauls, in all 11 . . .' (The letter was written without any punctuation, which provides an interesting exercise in arithmetic if nothing else).

A later report from his wife gave detailed information on the state of health of the household: 'We are all invalids here. Lady Sophia has got a crick in the neck that she cant stir her head. Lady Pembroke has got cold also and had a very bad sick and fainting fit afterward, in the evening, but was well again in half an hour afterwards. I have a little cold in my gumms, Carolina had the head ake, Paunceferd is afraid of the gout, mis foulkes is dying . . .'

In a stanza of pure McGonagle, that fascinatingly awful verse account of life at Goodwood with the second Duke leaves no doubt as to what impression the marriage made at the time:

> 'Goodwood! the place where all exoticks are,
> from Cooks Exotick, to Exotick Bears;
> but there too, Conjugal Affection shines,
> the finest Duchess, and the finest Duke,
> hail happy Matron, hail most happy wife;
> still blest, still lov'd, though many yrs are past,
> what amorous planett reigned when this fond pair
> were gott, or born, or happily conjoined?'

One is forced to remind oneself that the happy conjunction was a scene of some horror that was welcome to neither party, and that this blissful life began with an absence of three years that the husband ended only by accident. But the sweetest fruit may have a blemished skin, and nothing can spoil the taste of a marriage in which, after 30 years, the wife can receive these words from her husband in the morning mail: 'Observe I seal this letter with a wafer so no broken wax may fall into yr bed and be troublesome to my love.'

4

THE CHARLTON HUNT

There is little room for argument in the West Sussex County Archive Office catalogue of the Richmond family papers, but an eyebrow could be raised at Amanda Venables's note in the preface that, in the time of the second Duke of Richmond, the village of Charlton 'very soon became the centre for the Charlton Hunt'. In 1888 T. I. Bennett more pertinently recorded: 'From time immemorial, the woods and pleasant downs of Charlton have been appropriated to the enjoyment of hunting and the chase.' The first Duke certainly hunted there – a saddler's bill of 1705 shows that for £1.5s. he bought 'a Larg Tand hoggs leather hunting Saddle and flapps stiched with gould wire Sterrups and Leathers and guirths', and 42 other items brought the bill to £19.8s.6d. – and it is inconceivable that he would have bought Goodwood House for any reason but to use as a hunting lodge. No doubt the same could be said of his predecessors there, the Earls of Middleton and Shrewsbury, for as we have seen, the house then was of a size that men of such social stature would have regarded as derisory.

The Duke of Monmouth spent a lot of time at Charlton in the hunting season, and both he and his friend, Forde, Lord Grey, the Earl of Tankerville, who lived a few miles away in the mansion of Up Park, maintained packs of hounds by the middle of the 17th century. Both were managed and mastered by the renowned

Edward Roper. Lord Grey commanded Monmouth's cavalry when he tried and failed to seize the throne from his uncle in 1685. Grey's life was spared for £40,000 and the evidence against his colleagues, which he liberally gave. Roper's relationship with them both was such that he deemed it discreet to disappear to France. They all figure in that jolly saga of the *Charlton Congress*:

> 'Near Compton, where Ropero used to hunt,
> is seen a Castle famed for prospect fine,
> o'er sea and land, the view does far Extend,
> Upparke tis called, thus named from Scite so high:
> here Tankerville, the Friend of Monmouth dwelt . . .'

Though the first Duke of Richmond's sojourns at Goodwood House were spasmodic, the Duchess and her son, the Earl of March, seem to have been quartered there most of the year. March, like his father, took to hunting at a very early age, and with such enthusiasm that all the maternal fears were kept on the boil. At 12 he had a serious hunting accident (1713), and the Duchess wrote one of her most touching letters to her mother-in-law (well, not quite in law, perhaps) at Aubigny, whom the Duke was visiting: 'Madam: After ye Duke of Richmond has given you an account of the danger Lord March has lately escaped your grace will easily I dare say forgive my beging the continuance of your usual compassion towards me in joyning with me to prevaile with Lord Duke to promise his son shall not this year or two venture anny more riding what ye sports men call fine Hunters, for indeed Madam as he is very young, weake, and extremely ratle-headed, his liffe uppon those horses will be in the greatest of dangers, and since he has so lately escaped with liffe and limbs, through god's great mercy, twou'd be presumption to run him in ye like danger again.

'Hunting being a qualification not necessary to make a fine gentleman I thinke a fond Mothere may reasonably aske this favour especially for an only son, which your Grace by experience knows to be a dear creature, besides the danger of it when a youth gives himself up to these kind of sports, it certainly makes them neglect their Booke and Learning, which is of much greater use and consequence (with that of his bin an only Hire to so great titles and estate) will I hope prevaile with your Grace to interest yourself in his affaire, and if your Grace can get Lord Dukes firm promise, twill alay a thousand dreadfull fears attends me constantly.

'I know Lord Duke's haveing bin a very young Horsman himself makes him inclinable to humour his son in trying to be the same, the Lord March's being one of the tallest youths that ever was scene of his age make him most excessively weake in his Limbs, a fault I hope will mend when he has don growing and begun to spread; I had hardly overcome my fears for Lord Duke before this terrible surprise came uppon me, but since God has so meracolously preserved to me the liffe of Fathere and son I should be very ungratefully wicked did I not endeavour being easy, but as first nature will prevaile alike, especially to won so weak and fraile as is, Madam, Your graces most obedient Humble servant, A. Richmond.'

The former Master of Hounds, Roper, had returned from his voluntary exile as soon as James II was out of the way (1689), and resumed the management of the pack, which, with Lord Grey and the Duke of Monmouth gone, seems to have become the property jointly of himself and the Duke of Bolton, for long an enthusiastic follower. Charlton swiftly acquired a unique status in hunting, unquestionably the foremost centre of the sport in England – or as T. I. Bennett put it a century later, 'the Melton Mowbray of its day'. It was not just a matter of the village being a magnet for the hunting gentry of West Sussex: *sine qua non*, anybody who reckoned he was somebody behind a pack did his best to get himself accepted at Charlton. Probably half the aristocracy of England visited the little place at some time during the season, says Bennett, as well as a sprinkling of the best from Europe. So many peers of every class arrived for the meets that the village lane must have looked like the lobby of the House of Lords: 'How these noblemen were accommodated with lodgings is a wonder to the present generation.'

The Dukes of Devonshire and St Albans, and Lord Harcourt, had their own houses in the village, and the Duke of Richmond no doubt had a full house at Goodwood. For the rest, every cottage in Charlton and the neighbouring villages had a distinguished lodger in the hunting season. A splendid banqueting room was designed for the Hunt by the Earl of Burlington, one of the foremost architects of the time. This was known as Foxhall, and there 'these votaries of Diana feasted after the fatigues of the chase'. The ladies were not excluded: Henrietta, Bolton's first Duchess, was a frequent visitor and presented a flagstaff surmounted by the gilt figure of a fox as weathervane. The first Duchess of Richmond used to bring young March to the meet, and in the evening held

receptions there with her daughter. Lady Anne Lennox. It all seems
unbelievable now, when you look at the charming but forgotten
little hamlet, that once it thronged with the cream of London
society – including, on at least one occasion, King William III,
but without his Mary.

Charlton Forest and the 800 acres of downland around it had
been part of the Earl of Arundel's estate. The forest was possibly
awarded to the first Duke of Richmond by Charles II, and most of
the rest of the land became the Richmonds' in the time of the
second and third Dukes. It was great hunting country, and inspired
some of the noble sportsmen to deeds of historic daring:

> 'Northward, and riseing close above the Towne,
> another Mountain's known, by Leving Downe;
> a Pirenean path is still there seen,
> where Devon's Duke, full Speed, did drive his well
> bred Courser down, and flying, leapt five barrs;
> incredible the Acte! but still 'twas fact.'

Roper maintained his Mastership of the pack until the extraordinary age of 84, when at the climax of a hunt, in February
1723, he dropped dead on the field at Monckton Furzes – the end
he would surely have wished for himself ('A Fox just found; gett
on, he cryes! and then that Instant fell, and Life that instant fled').
The hounds became the sole property of Bolton, who devoted
himself to the Hunt until his affections were alienated by the
celebrated actress Lavinia Fenton, the first to play Polly Peachum
in *The Beggar's Opera* in 1727:

> 'A Nutt Brown Wench, with Lightning in her Eyes,
> white teeth her beauty, and a warbling voice,
> outdid herself, in acts of Distress:
> admired by all, but most by Bolton's Grace'

Miss Fenton wanted none of the rural capers, kept Bolton in
London and eventually became his second wife. The Duke
presented the hounds to Richmond in 1728. From that moment it
grew to such magnificence that for more than 20 years it was not
only the most important Hunt of the kingdom, but the most
important sporting event and possibly the most important social
event outside London. Every morning of the hunting season at
Charlton, Bennett tells us, 'a hundred horses were led out, each
with his attendant groom in the Charlton livery of blue, with gold
cord and tassels to their caps'. The new Master liked the hunt to

get away at eight o'clock in the morning, and though Goodwood House was only a couple of miles over the hill to the south, in 1731 he began to build in the village a true hunting lodge, where he and the Duchess slept to be ready for the early start. Long after the other architectural relics of the Charlton Hunt had disappeared the Duke's lodge remained – and part of it does to this day. He was no doubt the envy of those noble huntsmen who were quartered more frugally:

'A warm, but small, Apartement each one has,
the Dukes alone appears magnificent,
conspicuous it stands, above the rest
and uniform, and nearest to the Dome.
The Albian Duke, the next best Pallace owns,
Just in the Centre of the Village.'

('The Dome' was Foxhall.)

The brilliant success of Charlton was not without its somewhat bitter reaction in parts of this hunting county, where other noble gentlemen had to learn to live in the shade and like it. The sixth Duke of Somerset, 'the proud duke', did not like it. Accustomed to being paramount in West Sussex, he could not bear the sight of other horses and hounds riding over his estate. He had kennels and stables built on the Downs near Waltham (later used by the Earl of Egremont as racing stables) and hired the best chefs he could find to provide hunt breakfasts lush enough to lure away some of the Charlton regulars. He failed, and in disgust gave his pack away. Richmond, of course, apart from being an excellent administrator of the Hunt, knew enough about entertaining to outshine any local competition in the catering stakes. He invited William Pulteney, later Earl of Bath, to stay at Goodwood House during the hunting season of 1730–31. Pulteney wrote in September turning down the invitation:

'I am not yet well enough established in my health to do it. Temperance and Regularity are still necessary for me to observe, and at Goodwood I believe no one ever heard of either of them. For my part I am determined not to come within a house that has a French Cooke in it for six months. There is not a Bear or Wolf in your menagerie that shall not live more plentifully and luxuriously than I will, till I am perfectly recovered. Not but that I am in hopes some time or other of becoming a man of this world again, and flatter myself that I shall have the honour of eating many a good dish with you again, and swallowing many a bottle of popping Champagne, but for the present a little discretion is absolutely necessary.'

In due course Somerset got over his pique, for in January 1739 he wrote the most obsequious letter to Richmond, sending over to Charlton some medicine for the Duke's horses (cerstiall balls, whatever they may be). It's an odd fact that spelling in the 17th and 18th centuries seemed to deteriorate as the nobility of the writer rose, with dukes vastly more eccentric than lowlier peers. This, as exactly as it can be printed, was Somerset's effort :

> 'My Lord : The most Exceeding kind visitt the Dutchess of Somerset and I Received yesterday morning from the Dutchess of Richmond and from your Grace, is now & will upon all occasions bee acknowledged with a true sens of it & this day wee desire to have the satisfaction to know that both your Grace's Returned Saffe and well to Charlton, as I did perceive by the lookes of the Dutchess of Richmond horse to bee very well rode by soe noble and soe Great a Huntress to the very death of many ffoxes and soe entirely to Her Grace's Satisfaction.
>
> I doe therefore take liberty to send your Grace the Receipt to make cerstiall Balles to bee given night & morning to this Horse and alsoe to your Grace's Hunters after every chace. the very same Balles I have more than ffivety yeares practiced & my Horses used to receive very great Benefitt by them, as I hope yours will find the same good Effect upon using them. I send your Grace a small Pott of the Balles to be used untill the Receipt dosse produce more by your own Apothecary.
>
> wee wishe both your Grace's good weather which will add to the Pleasure and agreeableness in Every ffox chace now & at your return from London, in the mean time wee doe presume to fflatter our selves with Hopes of the Honour to see both your Grace's here some houres longer than yesterday.
>
> I am with the utmost Respect & Sincerely,
>   my Lord,
>   your Grace's most
>   ffaithfull and most
>   obedient humble servant
>   Somerset.
>
> Wee are all in this House very true & very humble Servants to both your Grace's.'

There was much more at stake than personal prestige as the Charlton Hunt rode triumphantly on. With the Earl of Tankerville at Up Park, only eight miles away, maintaining his own pack, there was a positive danger of the area being over-hunted. Bickering over territorial rights had been going on since Roper's return to Charlton, and in 1729 Richmond's powers of diplomacy and good fellowship effected a remarkable amalgamation of the two Hunts. Richmond and Tankerville drew up a treaty of 'peace, union and friendship' in terms so splendid and yet so patently sincere that it remains a work of some literary fascination:

'Treaty of Peace Union and Friendship between the most High Puissant and Noble Prince Charles Duke of Richmond and Lenox Earl of March and Darnley Baron of Setterington Methuin and Torbolton one of the Gentlemen of His Majesty's Bed Chamber and Knight of the most Noble Order of the Garter and the most Serene and Right Honourable Charles Earl of Tankerville and Baron Ossulstone of Ossulstone. Concluded at London on the Eighteenth day of March in the Year of Our Lord One Thousand seven hundred and Twenty Nine.

'Whereas the abovementioned most Puissant and Noble Peers are disposed towards one another with a mutual desire of making Peace and healing now in their own times the Miseries that have of late years wasted and destroyed the County of Sussex Be it therefor known to all and singular whom it may concern That

'Consulting and providing for (as far as Mortals are able to do) the Advantage Ease and Spirit of their Friends as well as the Tranquillity of the said County have resolved at last to put an end to that War which was unhappily kindled and has been obstinately carried on for many years which has been both Cruel and Destructive by reason of the frequent Chases and the Effusion of the Blood of so many vixen Foxes. Wherefor the said most Noble and Illustrious Lords (after divers and important Consultations had and held in London for that purpose) having at length without the intervention of any Mediator overcome all the Obstacles which hindered the end of so wholesome a Design have agreed on reciprocal Conditions of Peace Union and Friendship as follows.'

The six clauses that followed were of such detail and complexity that the entire document was recorded on a roll of parchment seven feet long. There was to be, it began, 'from this day a True Firm and Inviolable Peace . . . a more sincere and intimate Friendship . . . a Strict Alliance and Union . . .' A pack of at least 40 couple of foxhounds was to be maintained by and between the two men, and was to be kept alternately through the season at Charlton and Up Park, with one visit to Findon. Tankerville was to pay all expenses relating to the hounds, the horses of the hunts-men and whippers-in, the warreners, earth stoppers 'and all other contingent expenses', for which Richmond would pay him £219.1s. annually, in quarters. Richmond would be entirely re-sponsible for the horses, wages and board of his personal hunts-man and whipper-in, and would 'furnish their cloaths'. The treaty was to remain in force 'till the death of one of the contracting parties (which God for many years avert)'.

Six months' notice could be given to terminate the contract, in which case the entire pack passed to the party to whom the notice was given – as it would do to the survivor on the death of the other. A year later they were joined by Gorton Orme, and in 1731 the agreement was dissolved, and Richmond ran the Charlton Hunt on his own for the rest of his life, with the extremely conscientious assistance of Lord Delawarr. Dedicated though they were to the task, the loss of Tankerville must have been consider-able. A few years later that Earl set down his version of the rules and etiquette for hunting men, and some who care about these things say they have never been better expressed:

'The Hounds not to be kept behind the Huntsman in the morn-ing to whatever country they go, except at times when they are obliged to go through covers.

'The Whippers-in to be forward, and if any Hound, or more happens to prowl from the road they go, to call on them but to use no whip, for if they know their names at home, they'll obey abroad.

'When you are come to your beat, the Huntsman only to speak to the Hounds, and the less the better.

'The Whippers-in to have a good look out, stop any Hounds that steals away with a scent, and leaves the body of the Pack behind, unless tis a good one, and has time to give notice for the rest to be well laid in.

'The Whippers-in not to speak by way of encouraging any Hounds in cover, but in case of riot, then they shall gently rate them off.

'As soon as they have found, one Whipper-in to go with the Huntsman, the other to stay behind, to bring any straggling or tail Hound, or Hounds, that may be left behind, which will seldom happen if the two boys knows their business, and does their duty.

'Tis not a part of the business of a Whipper-in at any time to speak to a Hound, otherwise than keeping them together, or rate into the Huntsman, who should always be with the main body of the Hounds.

'Neither Huntsman, or boys, to speak to the Hounds, while running with a good scent. On a middling one the Huntsman to encourage his Hounds at discretion, without any other persons interfering.

'The company always at a distance that the Hounds may not be hurried, which is the loss of many a fox, as well as the loss of a great deal of beauty a good pack of Hounds will show at a half scent.

'When the Hounds from running comes to a check, the Huntsman is not to speak, but allow the Hounds to have their first cast, and if after that, not hit off, the Huntsman to observe the point at which they threw up, and then to help the Hounds to the best of his judgment, but without hurry, for when a fox is sinking, time must be taken, as he then runs short, and is often left behind by clapping down.

'The gentlemen for their own sakes will observe that a confabulation down the wind often heads a fox and endangers the whole day's sport.'

But for all his expertise, Tankerville could not have been an easy man for Richmond to work with. Not long after they parted, the Up Park Earl was upsetting Lord Delawarr, who wrote as follows to Richmond:

'I never wanted you so much in my life as at present. That dear creature the Earl of Tankerville is sending his foxhounds into the forest. Consequently yours must move, for there is not game for three packs. I came to London about it and only desired him to stay till your Grace came over, that you might give orders where yours might go, but to no purpose. So I am returning, to go to Lord Lymington's today. This is hard and I think your friend Tanky uses you but very indifferently, for you will not have a whelp entered; if I knew where I could send them near Bear Forest I would instantly, to Findon would be eternal ruin, because of the sheep in the woods, too great temptation for young hounds. I beg to hear from you, and as soon as I get down I will send to see for some place near Bear Forest.'

By the time the author of the *Charlton Congress* got to work, the hounds were obviously Richmond's responsibility:

'That Care be his, to see them kept all clean,
to view their kennells oft, and see them feed,
to register their names, and how they're bred;
that Incest, foule, may never once intrude
to spoile the race, and vitiate the Blood.'

As soon as he became Master, Richmond wrote to his friend
John Russell, Clerk of the Cheque at Woolwich:

'Dear Bumbo, We want a proper flag for this place, and you
know where such things are made. I would have it a Fox, Red in
a Green Field, with the Union in the corner and about the size
of one of the yacht's ensigns, so pray let me know what it will
cost and be so good as to bespeak it and you will oblige, Richmond.'

The immediate result pleased Richmond neither in estimate nor
execution, and he responded severely:

'Dear Bumbo, The enclosed sketch is most sadly drawn. The fox
ought to be as big again and take up all the middle part of the
flag, and the union little more than a quarter as big in the corner.
The fox's tail must also be straight out and not hanging down like
a horse's; so I beg to have a new sketch of it and the fox must be
yellow and not red, as I said. Surely £3.10s. is a great deal, if it is
but bunting as I would have it; but you are the best judge of that,
however pray let me have a draught before it is begun.'

It is no wonder the Duke quibbled about the cost of the flag.
The expenses of maintaining a hunt of that size and splendour
were considerable. The pack alone in the 1730–31 season cost
£221.16s.9½d, though only £41.12s. of that was for meat (two
horses each week). An idea of the intriguing incidentals is provided by the account book of the huntsman, John Ware (who
later disgraced himself): 'Paid for bringing of a hound home,
1s.0d; for bringing of a teryor home, 1s.6d; for two shows (shoes?)
a honting 1s.0d; for digen of a fox at Findon, 3s.0d; for riting
paper, 1s.0d; for hors hire, 1s.6d; for a bed at Findon 2 weeks,
5s.0d; for a pare of bouts for richard taylor, 12s.0d.'

Ware's subsequent Awful Act was mercilessly chronicled by
the Charlton poet:

'That vilest slave, the Huntsman, Ware his name,
alone, and drunk, went out and let the Pack
kill fourteen Farmers sheep, all in one day.'

The culprits were apparently hanged, which seems a bit harsh, and the remainder of the pack sent to France 'where Farmers ne'er complain'.

That was not the only time Ware was in disgrace. Richmond's assiduous colleague Lord Delawarr went down to inspect the pack in October 1732, and reported thus to Richmond in London:

'I came hither last night, and have this morning viewed your Grace's hounds very carefully, and can assure you there is either very much ignorance, or neglect, in the composition of Jack Ware. Nor do I think Rowell quite to be excused. I separated from amongst the old hounds eight couple thoroughly mangey, they say they have anointed them and given them some Aethiops Mineralis. So I immediately purged them and with the buckthorn gave them some flower of sulphur, both to take off the griping quality of the buckthorn, and to throw the humour out of their blood. When I went from hence I thought such an accident impossible to have happened, for they were very clean, and since that have had seven times whey, and each time two pound of brimstone, which course of physick would have cured the great Devil of the mange, and now these have it, but I hope to set them to rights. This was the manner that made him bring in such apothecary's bills, and to be sure at this rate they will want more physick than meat. With the remaining part of the old ones we shall hunt tomorrow, the ground is soft enough, but if there does not come rain I will not go out again.

'The young hounds are still kept apart, neither have they endeavoured to enter any of them, this piece of laziness may be lucky, for one of them called Ruler, bred by Mr Ormes, did not care to feed last Friday, he was immediately taken from the rest and locked up, he pined away, and I had him despatched this morning. He never offered to bite, as they say, so that it may be anything else as well as madness, however this cannot affect your old pack, they never having kept company together. Neither do I think it possible that madness can without showing itself by 19 weeks in any dog (for so long it was last Friday since any hound has been mad). This I beg you to talk to some of your surgeons, physicians, and philosophers, and send me their opinion. Your horses are very well and in fine order.

'I shall say no more at present on this subject, but assure you I will do my utmost to set things to rights, only if Lovell would recommend two or three couple of truly good hounds to you, I should not be against your buying them, for I do not think three or four of the young ones will do. This is the present state of the case.'

Canine madness (rabies) was a disaster with which any Master of Hounds was then much preoccupied. Another of Richmond's dogs died later that week ('I saw him my self eat his meat at twelve of the clock, and he died at three'), and immediately Delawarr wrote: 'I sent for Harry Woods, and every body agrees it is not madness, for he swelled very much, he did not slaver nor howl, neither would he have chewed his meat three hours before he died had it been madness.'

John Ware was succeeded by the best known of all Charlton huntsmen, and perhaps the most famous professional huntsman in England, Tom Johnson. His life is remembered by a large marble tablet on the wall of Singleton church, placed there by the Duke of Richmond 'to the memory of a good and faithful servant as a reward to the deceased and an incitement to the living'. Johnson, who died shortly before Christmas, 1744, had hunted for some splendid masters, including the Earl of Cardigan and the Duke of Marlborough. According to the epitaph, 'His knowledge in this profession, wherein he had no superior and hardly an equal, joined to his honesty in every other particular, recommended him to the service and gained him the approbation of several of the nobility and gentry'.

It was Johnson who was the huntsman during 'the greatest chase that ever was,' a simply staggering meet in which one fox was hunted for ten hours and for more than 57 miles. Probably nothing like it has been known since, and certainly at the time the members of the Charlton Hunt were in no doubt as to its supremacy. Those who took part sat down later to record the details of the day, and flushed with pride they clearly were. This is how they opened their 'full and impartial account of the late remarkable proceedings at Charlton':

'It has long been a matter of Controversy in the Hunting World, to what particular County or Sett of Men the superiority of Power belonged. Prejudice and Partiality have had the greatest share in their Dispute, and every Society their proper Champions to assert the Preemium and bring home the Trophies to their own County – even Richmond Park has its Dimmock. But on Friday the 26th January 1737/8, there was a decisive Engagement on the plains of Sussex, which after ten hours struggle has settled all future debates, and given the Brush to the Gentlemen of Charlton.'

The start must have been even earlier than usual, for they

found a fox in East Dean Wood at a quarter to eight and away she went. Men and horses fell exhausted as the day went on, and West Sussex was crossed and recrossed, but still the fox kept going and the hounds after her. Every detail is recorded in the breathless report: '. . . to Cobdens at Draught, up his Pine-pitt hanger (there his Grace of St Alban's gott a fall), thro' my Lady Lewkner's buttocks [presumably a local landmark] and mist the earth . . . Thro' West Dean forrest to the corner of Collar down (where Lord Harcourt blew his first horse) . . . up the Hills between Bepton and Cocking (here the unfortunate Lord Harcourt's second horse felt the effect of long legs and a sudden steep) . . .'

Back to my Lady Lewkner's buttocks they went, then through to Warren above West Dean ('where we dropt Sr. H. Liddel') and down to Binderton Farm ('here Lord Harry sunk'). In Goodwood Park the Duke of Richmond sent three lame horses home and 'from thence at a distance Lord Harry was seen driving his horse before him to Charlton'. They went over Halnaker Hill to Sebbige farm ('there the Master of Stag-Hounds, Cornet Honeywood, Tom Johnson, and Nim Ives were thoroughly satisfied'). In Kemp's high wood Billy Ives exhausted his second horse and took the mount of the Duke of St Alban's, who retired. On to Madehurst Parsonage, South Stoke and at last 'to the Wall of Arundell river, where the Glorious Twenty Three Hounds putt an end to the Campaign, and killed the Old Bitch Fox, 10 minutes before six. Billy Ives, His Grace of Richmond and Br. Hawley were the only Persons at the Death, to the Immortal Honour of 17 stone; and three score, and at least as many campaigns'.

Whose the 17 stone were, and whose the three score, and whose the many campaigns, nobody knows. The Duke was then aged only 37 and was unlikely to have been anything like 17 stone, in view of his extremely lanky youth; and of campaigns he is not likely to have tasted many at that time. Two days later, on the Sunday at the Bedford Head tavern in London, the Duke of Richmond proposed before 20 regular members of the Hunt that they should form themselves into a society, the exclusivity of which was guaranteed by the rigorous requirements of membership. No person should ride with the Charlton Hunt, they decided unanimously, who had not been an original subscriber to 'the Great Room at Charlton' or who was not present that day, unless he was admitted in the following manner: he must be proposed at Charlton by a member and his name put up in the Great Room. Not less than seven days later there must be a ballot for his acceptance by at least nine members, and one black ball would exclude him. The Duke of Richmond had the special privilege of being able to bring anybody he liked from Goodwood to dine at Charlton. The meeting also decided that the great chase must be measured 'by the wheel' as accurately as possible. The job took two days, and with allowances of one mile where the wheel could not go, and 20 miles for the three hours the fox spent running in cover, the total distance of the chase was 57 miles 2 furlongs and 15 rods.

By this time the Goodwood estate had been greatly increased by the purchase of the manors of Singleton and Charlton, made possible, at last, by the marriage settlement from the Earl of Cadogan. This somewhat complex agreement required the Earl to purchase on his daughter's behalf, and within three years of her marriage, land in England worth £60,000. He deposited a bond of £100,000 as surety that this would be done, but it had not been done by June 1723, and a further three years was added to the span of the agreement. Before this time had elapsed, Cadogan died, and his trustees were required to sell as much of his property as was necessary to realize the £60,000. The purchase of Singleton and Charlton represented the first £20,000 of that sum, and was the first major addition that the second Duke had been able to make to the estate. Apart from the land his father owned, the Duke had inherited little but debts, including two mortgages on the house of £2,500 and £1,000. As soon as he took over the estate, he had had to raise a loan of £5,000.

He did, as we have seen, build the lodge at Charlton, and three years later some land in the village was surrendered to him so that he could make 'a Beautifull Green before his hunting Seat'. With the death of his grandmother at Aubigny, Richmond had inherited that dukedom, and in 1735 was appointed Master of Horse to George II, a position of sufficient importance to warrant a seat on the Privy Council, and one that he held until his death. Since he was at the same time stepping up through the commissioned ranks of the army, his income must by now have been considerable – enough at least to keep the Hunt going, and incidentally to allow him to buy Sedgwick Castle, near Horsham, an uninhabitable, moated heap that carried with it 150 acres.

The hunting continued to be good, with 143 hunters quartered at Charlton, and the Duke had begun to keep a diary of each day's meet. In the season of the 'greatest chase that ever was', they managed to go out on 45 of the 50 scheduled hunting days, killing

27 foxes and missing 20. November 5th, 1740, appears in the diary as 'the first Blanc day I ever saw in Sussex'. Eighteen months later, with the hounds at Findon, the Hunt went 'down to South Lancing and through the common field to the sea beach. There after a falt a curr dog was seen to course her into the sea and there swam together, and then out of the sea over the beach, where they stood at bay, and the hounds came up and kill'd her . . .' The Hunt was now costing the Duke more than £1,000 a year – £1,300 in 1745, while the Duke, now a lieutenant-general, was away doing his bit for the King in the Jacobite Rebellion – and he was also travelling widely to indulge his interest in game shooting. In one month in the autumn of 1749, shooting at Aubigny, The Hague and St Denis, he bagged 36 partridge, 27 hares, one rabbit, one quail and a cat.

West Sussex was for centuries a notorious smugglers' haunt, and Goodwood saw its share of villainy. John Kent recalled in *Records and Reminiscences of Goodwood* 'one of the most desperate and abominable crimes ever committed', and that great old servant of the family (he and his father trained racehorses for the fifth Duke) was deeply hurt to think that it had been planned on the Goodwood estate. More than 40 particularly ruthless smugglers met in Charlton Forest in October 1747 to plan a raid on the Custom House at Poole, Dorset. They took 40 hundredweight of tea, a precious commodity then, and shed a horrible amount of blood as they returned through Sussex. Many of the gang were caught and hanged, one of them in irons on St Roche's Hill in January 1749. The gibbet remained there until 1791, when it was shattered in the same storm in which two millers were struck dead by lightning.

The Duke died so young that the question of whether he should give up the Charlton Hunt never arose. On 7th March, 1750, he wrote from Charlton to Lady Sarah at Whitehall about payment for some horses he was selling to Mr Bentinck, and added: 'I have seen my last new grey stone horse, and a prodigious fine horse he is.' Two days later, another letter to his wife, and it records that very last hunt of his life, the final exercise of a consuming passion. 'I am just come home from an exceeding fine Chase,' he wrote, 'butt by the excessive dryness of the fallows, wee were forced at last to give it up without killing the fox, so I comfort myself with the thought that it was a bitch fox. This finishes the hunting season in Sussex for the time; and everybody butt myself goes away tomorrow, when I shall go and stay quite alone at Goodwood at least till Wednesday, to see my planting go on.'

A Fleet Street journalist, racing through an appraisal of the Goodwood dynasty for his magazine in 1973, spared only a dozen lines for the second Duke. 'Good though not overinteresting', the man said, and who knows now how wrong he was? Even as Richmond gave life to his new cork oaks, his own was preparing to quit him. And from that moment, as the eighth Duke put it, the sun on Charlton commenced to set.

5

A MAN OF GOOD PARTS

'Nature had endowed him with capacity and good parts,' wrote John Kent of the third Duke. An odd epitaph, but a perspicacious one. This was the Richmond with the mostest of them all: the most renowned, illustrious, ambitious, acquisitive, talented and industrious; he held the dukedom longest, was the richest, spent the most, ended the poorest. Old John Kent said he became one of the most popular men in the kingdom – but only, it seems, with those who did not know him. In politics (which he chose as his career after becoming a major-general at 26) he was the most tactless, difficult and altogether the most utterly disliked of ministers. But he is said to have been generous and affectionate to his relatives, and from what he achieved at Goodwood, we could forgive him anything: he built the house, he made the racecourse. He gave birth to no legitimate children, but his was the embryo from which 'Glorious Goodwood' emerged.

The heir was only 15 when his father died so suddenly, taken ill on a journey from Goodwood to London. He lay in a fever at their half-way house at Godalming, convinced it would pass over in a day or two. The servants who accompanied him thought otherwise, and got a message back to the Duchess just in time for her to be with him at the end. Young March, who had attended Westminster School, was at the time in Geneva, studying under the biologist Abraham Trembley. He returned to England for the

funeral in Chichester Cathedral, when not only the second Duke
was buried in a family vault under the Lady Chapel, but the body
of his father was removed from Westminster Abbey, and six of
his children interred there also.

Spershott, writing towards the end of that century, remembered
the order of events differently : '1749 – The Duke of Richmond's
new vault diged and made in the Cathedral, and his father (the
then late Duke) taken from Westminster and brought into it. And
soon after was his own death and burial there.' But the *Sussex
Archaeological Collection* has the details firmly : at a cost of £105
a vault was prepared 59 feet 6 inches long and 15 feet wide, the
agreement being that burials would cost a further £5 a time. All
the Richmonds to the seventh lie there, the first having been
brought down on 16th August, 1750. (After the last funeral, in
1928, the vault was sealed.) A year later the boy's mother was
dead too, and the whole of the estate and the family fortune
passed to him.

It was an impressive income (about £14,000 a year came from
the Newcastle coal duty alone), but his father left him debts and
mortgages of £17,000. By the time he was 21, the new Duke had
paid all the debts and collected a fortune of more than £18,000.
As a minor, he was not expected to entertain nor to acquire. He
enlisted in the army at 17, where he was highly regarded by
General Wolfe and became a colonel in four years. When the
Seven Years' War ended in 1763 (resulting in the ceding of
Canada to Britain and the foundation of the British Indian Em-
pire), Richmond was a major-general and was appointed Lord
Lieutenant of Sussex. It was a staggering start to his adult life, and
when he moved into politics and, at the age of 30, was appointed
British ambassador to France, there seemed every chance that he
would become one of the most influential statesmen of his time.

He had a dignified, commanding appearance, more than average
intelligence, and a capacity for work that would have overcome
almost any deficiency. At 22 he had married a most handsome
young woman in Lady Mary Bruce, daughter of the Countess of
Ailesbury, and with his wealth, his ability and his personal
reputation it is not difficult to see why the country seemed likely
to fall under his hand before long. Alas, as his political biographer,
Alison Olson, put it : 'By the end of his career nearly every one
of his assets had dwindled into a liability.' Though he so nearly
became prime minister, he remained a minor politician and, in
the end, a discredited one.

Whatever may have been his failings of statesmanship and personal charm, there is no doubt that he was a man of immense vision, in breadth if not in depth. As soon as he had paid off his father's debts, he began to put into operation his plan to turn Goodwood from a third-class rural estate into one of the greatest country seats of England – quite a project at 21. Though in the third Duke's time the Charlton Hunt lost its dominance, there is no indication that he was not an ardent horseman. Far from it: the first major work that he put in hand at Goodwood was the design of stables of breathtaking magnificence, to this day quite the most beautiful building at Goodwood. Indeed, its conception and execution is so superb that its proximity to the house, an architectural disaster, is rather embarrassing. They were designed by Sir William Chambers, who was responsible for Somerset House on the bank of the Thames, and as Nairn and Pevsner put it, hardly anyone in the 18th century could have done as well. The stables form a huge hollow square, just about as big as the house itself, built with Sussex flint and dressed with stone, and awarded a triumphal entrance arch grand enough for the Coronation coach.

Flint was used extensively, almost exclusively, for the bulk of the masonry of buildings all over the Goodwood estate. Most of it was dug out of the Duke's own ground (some of the pits are still open), and the work provided long, if extremely tedious employment for the neighbourhood: 'A number of men, women and children were occupied for a long period of time in collecting and fitting them for the hands of the workmen,' said Jacques. Horsfield noted in 1835: 'All the new part of the mansion is built of squared flint stones, collected from the Downs, broken by a hammer very small, and of the nicest masonry. They are of a lightish hue, and have this superiority over Portland stone, of which the architectural ornaments are composed, that the longer they are exposed to the air, the whiter they become.'

Chambers began work on the stables in 1757, and during the six years it took to complete them he also enlarged the original house so that its southern end, that which is nearest the stables, acquired a more impressive appearance. It does not seem to have impressed the diarist Sylas Neville, who visited Goodwood House in 1781. 'For a Duke's seat,' he wrote, 'it is the meanest I ever saw. The front represents two or three old houses joined together without order or design.' Palmerston stayed there a few years later, and included another unfavourable comment in his *Travels in*

Sussex (1788). At Goodwood, he found 'an irregular old house of the Duke of Richmond with some comfortable rooms, but little worthy of particular notice. The offices form a handsome build-ing near the house and ye Duke is making a dog kennel which is an object from ye house and which both within and without is in a style of elegance unknown hitherto to that species of building'.

More of the dog kennel in a moment. The offices Palmerston referred to were of course the stables, which include provision for much other than horses. The Park, he said, was 'pleasing, and in ye upper part of it at some distance from ye house, which stands low, is a menagerie now going to decay, but originally very pretty, and a little further up is a building called Carney's Seat, from which there is a very fine view of Chichester and all ye adjacent country with the sea, Spithead and the Isle of Wight'. It was to have been Chambers who carried out the building of the new house, which incorporated the old (he was commissioned in 1760 to prepare plans for a mansion of Portland stone), but this work passed to James Wyatt. He seems to have worked off some of Chambers's ideas, and to have had some of his own turned down by the Duke; and in any case the house that we see today is only half what it was intended to be. Wyatt (or was it the Duke?) wanted an immense octagon built round an open courtyard, two storeys high with at each corner three-storey turrets surmounted by saucer-shaped copper domes. It would have looked stupendous from the air, though that could hardly have been the thought at the time. In the event, only three sides were completed, and it seems more correct to put it that way than to suppose that they decided only to use three sides of the original design.

Wyatt used the southern end of the original house within the south front of the new building (the left hand one as you look at it), and proceeded to a much longer main front, facing south-east and embellished with a vast two-storey portico that uses Doric columns below and Ionic above. Round the corner then to a shorter eastern front, which ends abruptly with one of those absurd turrets looking as though the builders had unexpectedly absconded. It is not until you go round the back of the building that you see the original house, much of which remains and forms a north-western wing. Presumably it would have been demolished had the original architectural intentions been carried out. Though the experts in these matters do not rate the interiors much more highly than the exterior, most of the rest of us do, and to walk today through its superbly-preserved delicacy is to step into an 18th century dream.

Goodwood House was built in the last decade of the century, towards the end of the third Duke's life. The east wing interiors, in fact, were completed by the fifth Duke, in 1830. Shortly before doing the house, Wyatt designed the incredible kennels, which now form the main part of the golf clubhouse, half way up that long wooded climb from the south to the racecourse. They are incredible not in design, which is clearly a great success, but that such art and such effort should have been applied to so basic and simple a business as the housing of dogs. 'This building, both from extent and singular arrangement, is unequalled by any other in England destined for the same purpose,' was Dallaway's un-equivocal declaration; and in 1820 Shoberl noted : 'The kennel which the late Duke built for his hounds . . . exceeds in magni-ficence and conveniences of every kind, even to luxury, any structure perhaps ever raised before for the reception of such tenants.' The whole building is considerably longer than the main front of Goodwood House, and its depth is greater than the length of either of the lesser fronts of the main house. In the heart of the operation, the dogs were quartered in large rooms one side of which was lined with iron plates, heated from behind by huge fires in the coldest weather.

This certainly gives the lie to the idea that the third Duke had less regard for foxhunting than his father. What he was obviously determined to do was to turn the Charlton Hunt into the Good-wood Hunt, and in the process it became less a national institution and more a county privilege, less of an obsession and more of a relaxation to a man who spent so much of his time on matters of state and parliament. He was also a hunter of unusual compassion, once sparing the life of a fox that had given them a good chase, in the hope that they might find it again.

John Kent's father used to tell a marvellous story about the third Duke, which was handed down at Goodwood. When the new Earl of Egremont decided in 1802 to give up the pack of hounds that his father had so proudly maintained at Petworth House (in itself a sign that there was plenty of hunting at Good-wood), he offered them to Richmond. The Duke said he did not need them all, but would be glad to have a few, and it was arranged that Egremont's huntsman, who was to have the rest, would bring the pack over so that he could take his pick. Without having hunted with a pack, it is almost impossible to know on

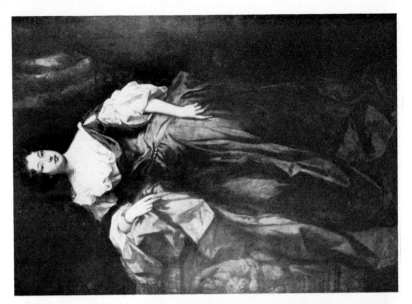

1 Charles II, father of the first Duke of Richmond and of at least 13 other illegitimate children; 'the royal fertility was phenomenal.' *(Portrait by Sir Peter Lely)*

2 Louise de Kéroualle, longest-favoured of the royal mistresses, created Duchess of Portsmouth the year after giving birth to Richmond. *(Portrait by Sir Godfrey Kneller)*

3 Charles, first Duke of Richmond, at about the age of ten: 'Good
looking, if good for nothing else.' *(Portrait by William Wissing)*

sight which are the good hounds and which the bad, and when they arrived at Goodwood, Richmond told the huntsman, Luke Freeman, to take what he wanted and leave the rest at the kennels. But when he had done so, and was on his way back to Petworth with the best of the bunch, Freeman found the Duke waiting for him at Charlton Gate. 'Ah, Freeman,' he said. 'Taken what you wanted?' 'Yes thank you, your Grace, and I'm much obliged to you.'

'And I should be much obliged to you, Freeman, if you would leave me those hounds that you have there. You may go back to the kennels and take away those that you left.' And that man was not a successful politician? *The Times* noted at the end of the hunting season that year, incidentally, that 'the Earl of Egremont's presentation of his fox hounds to the Duke of Richmond has caused a rapid diminution of the race of Reynard in the western part of Sussex, where the Farmers have full liberty to destroy these wily depredators and where (in the neighbourhood of Parham) not less than 20 have been dug out of their earths and killed within the last fortnight'. When the Prince of Wales (later George IV) came down to hunt at Goodwood, he was so impressed with one of the hounds that he offered Richmond the absurd price of 500 guineas for it. The Duke said no dog in the world was worth that money, and gave it to the Prince. Many years later, when the fourth Duke was appointed Lord Lieutenant of Ireland and had to spend most of his time in that country, he gave the whole pack to the Prince Regent. Symptoms of madness were subsequently discovered among them and they were all destroyed. (That was not the end of hunting at Goodwood: the sixth Duke revived it with enthusiasm.)

While the young Duke was still in the army, and indeed while the Seven Years' War was still in progress, he began not only the building of the stables, but his memorable work in the park. Most immediate and spectacular of all this was his planting of 1,000 cedar saplings, procured from Mount Lebanon. Of these, the extent and subsequent magnificence of which were unique in Britain, only 146 remained in 1895. Many of these were lost in a great gale on 3rd March, 1897, and more at the end of February 1927, and now only about 60 remain. The most serious loss in that later storm was of a huge limb on the greatest of all cedars, one of the most famous trees in Britain. Planted on the cricket ground in 1761, it was measured in 1910. The tree was then 100 feet high, and the circumference of the trunk three feet above the

C

ground was more than 28 feet. Five feet above the ground there were 24 branches, many of which had a girth of over 12 feet. Some of them were 70 feet long, and the circumference of the area covered by the tree's branches was more than 150 yards. The rate of its growth was quite phenomenal: after 100 years the trunk was 22 feet round; it then added three feet in 32 years, and more than three feet in the next 20 years. When the great limb crashed in 1927, it provided 800 cubic feet of sound timber, which was cut to planks for Goodwood House in the Westhampnett saw mills.

The cedars of Lebanon, though the most distinctive of his plantings, were by no means the third Duke's only arboreal contribution to the estate. A local historian in the time of his successor noted that 'Many of the knolls and bays, into which the Downs are broken, have been clothed with plantations of fir and beech by the late Duke, who with singular perseverance and success "Has hung with woods the mountain's sultry brow" ' – [Pope].

Before he went to Paris as ambassador in 1765, Richmond paid £48,000 for Halnaker House and its park (to which, before the Richmonds' time, Goodwood had belonged), and straight away set about a daunting proposition: the diversion of the main Chichester–Petworth road. At that time this ran uncomfortably close to Goodwood House before running north to East Dean via Molecomb, the dower house that the third Duke was about to build, and Pilleygreen Lodge. With the purchase of Halnaker, the central portion of the estate was thus divided by a comparatively busy public road, and this was not to his Grace's liking. His prestige and energy combined to affect the shifting of this road one and a half miles further east, so that it ran on the present course of the A285, through the village of Halnaker and Benges Wood, to join the former road at Upwaltham. For a few miles this follows the course of one of the great Roman roads, Stane Street, which they laid from Chichester to London some 1,900 years ago, but which for some reasons of local convenience had been forsaken by the third Duke's time for the route that offended him.

So look at the Duke when he was only 30: already a major-general and about to take up the nation's senior ambassadorial post, he had completed the stables, commissioned the new house, moved a main road and imported 1,000 rare trees. The family's debts had been paid, and his income had risen to about £20,000 a year. Where did he go wrong? At the age of 25 he had made a petulant mistake that he was to regret for the rest of his life: because his brother, Lord George Lennox, had not been given the army promotion that Richmond thought was his due, the Duke resigned his appointment as Gentleman of the King's Bedchamber. For the rest of his political days, Richmond's career was dogged by the knowledge of his superiors that whatever position Richmond was given, the King would not like it. According to the Duke of Newcastle in 1766, His Majesty 'has never once failed to express his own disapprobation of the Duke of Richmond', and the relationship was not calculated to become sweeter when the Duke's nephew and heir fought a duel on Wimbledon Common with the King's brother, the Duke of York. Both were officers of the Coldstream Guards, and Lennox's extremely hot-headed challenge was made after he had overheard a remark on the parade ground. They turned at 12 paces, and Lennox's shot whistled through the Duke's wig. York declined to fire, which is about as far as a man can go in the business of humiliating his opponent.

The hostility between the families, not surprisingly, remained to the end, and it was the Duke of York's appointment as Commander-in-Chief of the army five years later (in 1794) that brought about, as it was obviously intended to, Richmond's resignation as Master-General of the Ordnance. Other things apart, York reckoned that he had been professionally, and nearly fatally, let down by Richmond the previous year, when the artillery failed to arrive to support York at the siege of Dunkirk. George III accepted the resignation with alacrity, explaining in his letter to Richmond: 'I thought it but justice to say that Mr Pitt yielded to the arrangement to prevent a want of concert in the Cabinet which the Duke himself must allow would be highly detrimental to the conduct of affairs at so critical a time as the present.'

Richmond had expected that the threat of his resignation would persuade Pitt, the Prime Minister, to think again about having York at the head of the army, and was most hurt at the turn of events. In a letter to his nephew ten years later he recalled: 'After owing me a great deal at a time he stood in much need of my assistance, and being served by me with all the fidelity of the warmest friendship, he turned me out of office and in the most shuffling manner, without alledging any cause but evidently to sacrifice me to the Duke of York and Mr Dundas's jealousy.'

It was almost inconceivable in those days that power could be granted or success won without the royal favour, and this Richmond lost almost before he had begun. Unpleasant though it seems to us now, it was also extremely difficult then to climb the ladder of politics without controlling by patronage some positions of influence. We were still in the days of the pocket boroughs, ancient parliamentary seats that were filled by the nomination of the major landowner – remember the Earl of Cadogan giving Newport to the Earl of March in 1722, though he was already contesting Chichester? Richmond's brother George, and then his nephew Charles, sat as MPs for Sussex from 1767 to Richmond's death in 1806, but beyond that and his local influence in the city of Chichester, the third Duke showed little interest in acquiring control by the devious means that were customary in his time. In view of such obstacles, and his disagreeable personality, it says much for his ability that he reached such political heights.

Edmund Burke, the Irish politician and writer who joined the Commons in 1765, said that Richmond was 'very full of rectitude, zealous against abuses, a little teizing in his disposition, and of little management with the world'. A less discreet colleague re-marked that 'if there were two Dukes of Richmond in this country, I would not live in it'. He was an unsociable man, of retiring and introverted disposition, who abhorred London society. But his patronage of the arts was genuine and far-reaching. At an early stage he arranged for his Whitehall house to be open to 'any painter, carver, sculptor, or other artist and youth over 12 years of age, to whom the study of statuary might be useful'. He also offered an annual prize to the artists who worked there, but when one year he failed to come up with it (he was with the army in Europe at the time), the young artists posted placards of com-plaint around the house and the Duke was so annoyed that he shut down the studio. The celebrated English portrait painter, George Romney, spent much time living with the writer William Hayley at Eartham, only a mile or two from Goodwood, and the commissions which Richmond gave him hang still at Goodwood House.

The treasures in the house bear witness to his artistic taste, particularly the extraordinarily beautiful collection of Sèvres china, the result of his years in France. But perhaps the most fascinating aspect of his aesthetic delights was his building of a theatre within Richmond House, off Whitehall, and his super-intending of the building of the forgotten little theatre in South Street, Chichester, in 1767, which he furnished with scenery from his private theatre. The theatre still stands in Chichester, long since put to cruder commercial use, but retaining its unmistakable upper storey. It became, in the early 19th century, an integral part of the entertainment for visitors to the Goodwood races.

As if this extraordinary man had not extended himself in enough directions, he became an enthusiastic yachtsman. He bought 300 acres at Itchenor, on Chichester Harbour, where he built another house and kept another staff, to whom he was able to signal from Carné's Seat (eight miles as the light flashes) when he wanted the boat made ready. As the *Sussex Weekly Advertiser* informed readers in August, 1777, even this sport was not free from the passion for gambling that possessed the gentlemen of the day:

'We are credibly informed that on Friday next His Grace the Duke of Richmond's yacht is to sail against Sir Alexander Leith's from Brighthelmstone round Worthing Port to Beachy Head, and from there back again to Brighthelmstone, it is said for 1,000 Guineas. A great number of nobility and gentry, beside the many who at this time honour the place with their company, are expected to be present there at the decision of this grand bet.'

As well as Itchenor, the third Duke bought manors and other land across much of the southern part of West Sussex. Not content with the neighbouring estates of Halnaker and Lavant, which with Singleton and Charlton gave him a central territory of about six square miles, he moved south and east of Chichester to buy in North Mundham, Birdham and Barnham, then further down Chichester Harbour to West Wittering and right along the coast to take in the manors of Atherington (south of Climping) and East Preston, the other side of Littlehampton. The coast obviously exercised a peculiar fascination for him, and as Master-General of the Ordnance he dedicated himself with surprising passion to the fortifications of the south-east. 'Some of his plans to effect his object', records John Kent, 'were so extensive and costly that the House of Commons took alarm . . .' Even many of his own party voted against them, but the fruits of his intentions ripened after his time, when the 74 Martello towers were built from Hythe to Seaford to repel Napoleon's threatened invasion.

Some of the pockets of Richmond's estate were now 18 miles apart, and 13 miles from Goodwood, and he was paying the wages of 1,200 workers spread over 17,000 acres. Small wonder that financial difficulties at first crept up on him, and by the last decade of the century were hitting him from every direction. He had spent some £120,000 on buying land and houses, which were costing £4,000 a year to maintain. In addition hunting, yachting, the militia and Richmond House (which uninsured, burned down in 1792) cost another £1,600; he had borrowed £95,000, on which he was paying interest of £3,300 a year; rates cost him £2,300, and he paid £3,000 in tax. He was promoted to Field Marshal in 1796, at the age of 61. By then he had been cast out of politics and was nursing his wife (who bore no children) at Goodwood. She died later that year. In 1800 he surrendered his Newcastle coal duties to the government for £19,000 a year, and estimated that he could discharge all his debts in 26 years – by which time, had he lived, he would have been over 90. One might have expected that at this stage the Duke, one way and another, would be considerably depressed. But this was the moment that he chose to turn his attention to laying out a racecourse in Goodwood Park.

Though there is little record of the third Duke's early interest in horse racing, there is evidence that he built racing stables at Itchenor in 1783, near his yachting headquarters. Racing was by then established in the other half of the county, at Lewes and Brighton, and at places like Newmarket, Doncaster, Ascot and Epsom had been popular for a century or more. But in West Sussex there seems to have been nothing but occasional meetings, probably built around private matches and restricted, of course, to gentlemen. Midhurst had seen a good deal of it in the 1730s, Chichester had a meeting now and then, and on the Earl of Tankerville's estate at Up Park 'private and aristocratic' gatherings were so well known that in 1785 the Prince Regent attended, and saw Sir H. Fetherston's Epaminondas, 'rode by himself', win a 120 guinea cup.

At Epsom, by the time Richmond was thinking about his own racecourse, the crowds had been pouring on to the Downs for 20 years to watch the Derby. But mainly they were Londoners, eager for battle and excitement. What's more, nobody could charge them for a day on Epsom Downs – it was common land, a slice of which had been leased by the Lord of the Manor to the consortium that built the grandstand. The atmosphere was very different in the depths of West Sussex, where the population was sparse and unsophisticated in the extreme. Not only were they unlikely to attend a race meeting, but they were unlikely to be invited to do so. The roads in the county were so awful that only the strongest coaches and the best teams of horses could get through in acceptable time, so Goodwood, even if His Grace had at that time opened it to the public, would not have attracted much popular attention. And indeed His Grace, when he planned the course in 1800, may have had little intention of arranging a public spectacle, but rather a private entertainment.

Dr John Burton came to Sussex in 1751, and left a detailed account of his impressions of the people and their habits:

'The men there, as not being accustomed to quit their homes for the sake of traffic or any other purpose, generally live by themselves, and being born on the soil continue unrefined. . . . Their manners are not the most gentlemanlike or agreeable, but neither are they quite barbarous. In their persons not corpulent, but rather spare or thin-shanked, in their diet generally frugal; and in their cookery being neither dainty nor expensive, they care most for pork. Which indeed they prepare skilfully by steeping in brine. After being thus pickled, they slice it off when cured, as the family may want. They also cook a certain lump of barley meal, looking much like mud and hardened like iron, offering it at meals instead of bread.'

With that background, it is not surprising that he goes on to point out that the Sussex people 'do not concern themselves with literature or philosophy, for they consider such things to be only idling; but they persevere in paying attention to the whole art and practice of breeding cattle, and being greedy of gain, and terrible overreachers, they despise everything else'. The condition of the roads comes in for some caustic treatment by the roving doctor, who asks: 'Why is it that the oxen, the swine, the women and all other animals, are so long-legged in Sussex? May it be from the difficulty of pulling the feet out of so much mud by the strength of the ankle, that the muscles get stretched, as it were, and the bones lengthened?'

He refers to Chichester as 'the metropolis of all Sussex', for his travelling was done before the Prince of Wales discovered Brighton. Indeed he describes Brighthelmstone, as it still was, as 'a village on the seacoast . . . not indeed contemptible of size, for it is thronged with people, though the inhabitants are mostly very needy and wretched in their mode of living, occupied in the employment of fishing, robust in their bodies, laborious, skilled in all nautical crafts, and, as it is said, terrible cheats of the custom house officers'. Burton obviously did not encounter the races there, but to Lewes races, he said, 'all people of the county flock from every quarter, and there is much competition among the fashionable'.

Goodwood was soon clearly to outstrip Lewes as an arena for the fashionable, but it is not possible to say with any certainty when racing first came to the flanks of St Roche's Hill. Goodwood Park itself is shown on late 18th century maps to have a northern boundary approximately where the road now runs behind the racecourse. Four gates – from west to east, Rooks Hill Gate, Little Pond Gate, Charlton Gate and Counter's Gate – led out to a track known as The Harroways, and beyond that was a fine stretch of level turf, probably where the racecourse buildings are now, before the hill dropped down towards Charlton. No doubt it had often been the practice of visiting horsemen, particularly in the more sociable times of the first two Richmonds, to hold matches up there, but the first time the Duke seems to have organized any sort of racing occasion was in the spring of 1800, when he had the officers of his Sussex militia up there for an afternoon's sport. That was obviously such a success that he decided to do the thing properly, and many of the labourers of the estate were diverted to lay out a course under the supervision of his overseer. In April 1801 the *Sporting Magazine* reported that 'the new Racecourse on the Harroway near Goodwood' was now completely formed for sport and much admired by the amateurs of the turf, and he held his first private meeting at the beginning of May. *The Times* reported on 8th May: 'The Races set on foot this year by the Duke of Richmond at Goodwood have been very well attended, and afforded good sport. Next year they are to last three days.'

The man from *The Times* had obviously not been there. A much more intimate picture comes from the representative of the *Sporting Magazine*: 'The company was splendid and numerous, and, for the accommodation and refreshment of whom, by order of the Duke of Richmond, five or six roomy tents were pitched, in each of which collations, consisting of every dainty in season, were profusely served up. Ice, even, was not prohibited.'

Though the Duke must have been satisfied with that first great occasion on the course, since by the end of the first day he had decided to hold a three-day meeting the next year, he could not much have enjoyed it himself. 'He appeared extremely ill from the effects of the gout', an eye-witness noted, never left his tent all day, and returned to bed as soon as the races were over. The other disappointment of the day was that the Prince of Wales, who was staying at Up Park for the purpose of attending the races, did not show up. At the last minute he was summoned by express coach to return to London, the beginning of a long run of bad luck that the Dukes of Richmond had with their royal invitations.

The first winner of that historic first day's racing was a black mare owned by Mr Halsted, which started at 6–4 favourite for a £50 Hunter's Plate with two-mile heats. There were seven runners, 'rode by gentlemen only', and the only extraordinary note on the race card was that they were carrying 17 stone, a phenomenal weight that gives a better idea than anything else of the kind of meeting with which Goodwood began. The afternoon ended with another similar event for horses carrying 10 stone, and between was a sweepstake of 10 guineas each for horses 'the property of gentlemen who have hunted with his Grace the Duke of Richmond's hounds'.

It is usually thought that the 1801 meeting, which some historians ignore altogether, was only a one-day affair. Not so : the *Sporting Magazine* for May records that, 'on the second day, in turning, one of the horses started, and bolted out of the course, by which three men were knocked down and rode over, one of whom was slightly bruised, but the others escaped without the least hurt'. On the first evening, the Chichester theatre was crowded with highly-fashionable patrons, and on the second, there was 'a splendid ball at the Assembly Room'. The reporter also notes that the unusually high social standing of most of the visitors at the races ensured 'an abundant harvest to the nimble-fingered fraternity of the metropolis, who, perhaps, never more successfully practised their dexterity of hand.'

The stewards of the meeting, 'who paid such strict attention to the regulations recommended by the Duke that the course was kept as free of obstructions as any of the races at Newmarket', were Mr Blake and Mr Poyntz. The unfortunate Col William Poyntz, from time to time Member of Parliament for Midhurst and for Chichester (both then returned two members), is worth a line or two. Before her marriage, his wife had been Elizabeth Browne, sister of the young and foolhardy Viscount Montague, owner of Cowdray House at Midhurst and all its estates. In September 1793, that magnificent Elizabethan mansion and everything it contained (including William the Conqueror's sword and coronation robe) were totally destroyed by fire, in the absence of both the Viscount (on holiday with a friend in Switzerland), and his mother and sister, who were at Brighton.

Only a few hours before the fire, which happened at night, the steward of the estate had written to Viscount Montague to tell him that the long repairs and redecoration of the house were at last over and it was once again ready for occupation. On the next day, he had of course to write another letter telling of its destruction, and this in his agitation he addressed to Lausanne instead of Lucerne. The letter, thus delayed, arrived at the Viscount's hotel one morning just after he and his friend had left for an extraordinarily rash expedition on the Rhine, some rapids on which they were determined to negotiate by boat despite the urgent warnings they were given of its danger. The boat over-turned and both were drowned.

The Viscount left all his property to his sister, though she did not inherit the title, and when she married Col Poyntz the follow-ing year they lived in the keeper's lodge. Nineteen years later the couple took their two sons and two unmarried daughters to spend the summer at Bognor, where they occupied Pavilion House, overlooking the sea. One calm July afternoon the father and sons, their tutor, two young daughters of a friend, and a boatman and his son, went out in a sailing boat. It capsized in a sudden gust of wind and all except Col Poyntz and the boatman were drowned, within sight of Mrs Poyntz and her daughters as they watched from the house.

The decision that the 1802 meeting should last three days com-mitted the Duke of Richmond to establish Goodwood as a racing centre, though, like Ascot, it held only one meeting a year until recent times. Though as the *Victoria History of the County of Sussex* puts it, that first three-day meeting was 'organized for the recreation of neighbouring landowners and hunting folk' and probably had more of the character of hunt races than flat racing as we now know it, the Duke launched it with all the energy and flair at his command. During the summer of 1801 he built a small wooden stand to accommodate his most distinguished guests and the ladies. No record of it remains, but it appears to have been situated further along the course to the east than the present stands, which suggests there was much less of a finishing straight than there is now, the racing perhaps being concentrated on the long Charlton arm of the course.

The Duke's sense of public relations was acute, and on 30th March *The Times* carried the line: 'The commencement of the Goodwood Races is fixed for Wednesday the 28th of April.' A fortnight before the event he announced through the Press that five races would be held on the first day, four on the second and six on the third, and that 'the Prince of Wales has signified his

intention of honouring the meeting with his presence'. That the
Duke did not neglect the representatives of the local paper is clear
enough from an embarrassingly sycophantic editorial that
appeared after the event:

'To the efforts of equestrian skill is to be added the princely
and almost unprecedented munificence of the noble founder of
Goodwood Races, in providing the new-erected stand with a
collation which might be entitled a general refrigarium, for the
access was as easy as the reception was elegant and hospitable.

'The thanks of the county in general, and of this city and its
vicinity in particular, are largely due to His Grace the Duke of
Richmond for having thus munificently and liberally instituted
an establishment of most material local benefit in every point of
view, both as a source of pecuniary advantage to the inhabitants
and as a means of forwarding to notice and increasing the consequence of this western part of the county. We can only add our
wish that the illustrious founder may for years enjoy in
health and happiness this promising scion, planted by his own
hand, a wish in which we shall be joined by all true Sussex
patriots.'

The man from *The Times* was there this time, and though his
report was short it contained one interesting comment. The meeting, he said, had been uncommonly well attended, among the
visitors being the Prince of Wales, the Duke of Norfolk, the Lords
Egremont and Chichester, and many other families of distinction.
All the matches, of course 'were rode by gentlemen' – though his
use of the word match was incorrect in racing terms, that being
more properly used to describe the event on the third day when,
in a match for 100 guineas, the Prince of Wales's Rebel beat the
Duke of Richmond's Cedar. The report went on: 'This is the
second year of the meeting, and from the great number of persons
that attended from all parts, it bids fair to rival the famous Club
at Bibery.' The 'famous Club' can only be the Jockey Club at
Newmarket, and the consumption of alcohol at Goodwood must
have been remarkable to put it immediately into such a league.
The Duke was obviously pushing the boat out in all directions
at once.

The first race on the first day of this first three-day meeting, on
28th April 1802, perhaps reflected the character of the whole
meeting: it was restricted to members of the Goodwood Hunting
Club, subscribing 20 guineas each. The horses, which had to be
ridden by the subscribers, had to race over two-mile heats. This

form of racing had been universal for races of any consequence until, in 1776, Lieutenant-Colonel Anthony St Leger inaugurated his one-run classic at Doncaster, shortly followed by the Oaks and the Derby. At courses with a long straight run, like the notorious four miles from Banstead to Epsom Downs, running such heats was so gruelling a business that no thoroughbred today would stand it. There were customarily three heats, with half an hour between each for rubbing down and returning to the start, and the prize went to the horse that won two out of three. A runner that was 'distanced' (not within 240 yards of the winner as it passed the post) was not allowed to compete in any further heats, and if no horse won more than one of the heats, a fourth heat was run between all the winners. At Epsom, where there was usually a long break for carousal at midday, this could involve the best horses in racing 16 miles and cantering 16 miles in one day, so it is not surprising that breeding in those days was designed to produce immensely strong horses with infinite stamina and no sprinting ability. On Goodwood's more confined course, that first Hunting Club race could not have required more than eight miles racing, which for the hunters of West Sussex was nothing to worry about.

It was eventually won by Mr Newbury's Pantagruel, and gave way to a two-mile sweepstakes for maiden horses carrying ten-stone gentlemen riders (won by Richmond's Cedar). Another hunter's plate followed, and on the second and third days the principal races were £50 plates put up by the City of Chichester, the second of which was won by the Duke of Richmond with You Know Me. All the races seem to have been over two miles, and this equates neatly with starting and finishing at the wooden stand and racing round something like the same narrow loop that still extends towards the Downs.

In 1803, by which time England was at war with Napoleon, the Goodwood meeting was altogether less successful, though the local Press, by now most conscious of the commercial benefits Chichester was deriving from Goodwood, was as ecstatic as ever. *The Times* confined itself to remarking that the Duke entertained his friends with the most splendid hospitality, but that the races 'in consequence of the badness of the weather, were not attended by so large a company as was expected'. Nevertheless, several excellent horses started, and each day afforded good sport. The ball was 'very splendid', and the theatre crowded every night. On the third day there were only three races, two of them matches and one involving three heats of a ladies' plate; also, that afternoon, 'a foot race of two miles performed in 12 minutes and 20 seconds, occasioned much minor betting, and engaged the attention principally of Lilliputian sporters'.

The stewards of the meeting had already announced that, 'from the great failure of subscription', they would not be able to give £50 for a handicap sweepstake, owners to subscribe 10 guineas each unless they had won a race at the meeting, in which case they could enter free. At the same time it had been announced that the stewards would attend at the Waterbeech Inn at noon on the day following the meeting 'to settle accounts and answer any demands on the General Fund'.

The *Sussex Chronicle* went to press on a Wednesday afternoon, which was unfortunate when the high-spot of the Chichester year lasted from Wednesday to Friday. Though they were not able to provide a report of the proceedings that week, they did their best :

'Chichester, Wednesday 3 o'clock : The fascinations of the Race Course have not permitted the return of any of our reporters at the last possible moment of delaying the press. The influx of company, which still yesterday had been moderate, has we think quite equalled last year – we speak of those resorting to this city for accommodation. The number repairing to Goodwood is quite beyond the most sanguine expectation, as the Newmarket Meetings have crossed us quite *mal a propos*. All lodgings and beds are in a state of close siege, and provisions have very handsomely risen in price, as duty bound.'

Duty bound! 'Twas ever thus, and still is. The following week the *Chronicle* noted that 'notwithstanding the interference of the Newmarket Meeting, the Prince's Arabian Match at Winchester, and the unsettled or rather repelling weather', the races drew not only a large attendance, but a large selection of rank and fashion. 'The sport in scientific estimation was extremely good, and some very close racing was exhibited.' The Duke of Richmond, of course, 'repeated his munificent hospitality upon the Race Course, entertaining innumerable visitors with every desirable and elegant refreshment'. The social peak of the week was undoubtedly the ball and supper on the Thursday night ('Gentlemen's tickets 15s., Ladies' tickets 7s.6d., to be had at the Post and Printing Offices, Chichester'). The *Chronicle* correspondent wished his readers to know that the event 'was (what is here reckoned) numerously attended; the company amounting to near two hundred', and then went into the delicious details :

'The dancers were in two sets, at twelve o'clock the supper rooms were opened, where about 100 persons were accommodated at one time; the decorations (among which was a temple of Minerva in very pretty style) as well as the provisions in both quality and abundance did infinite credit to the exertions of Mrs Combes and Mrs Carlton, the established *arbiter elegantarium* upon this and other festal occasions. The dances were resumed after supper, and finally concluded at about two o'clock.' The requirements of local paper editors have not changed much over the years, though the style of their contributors has hardened a little. Oddly enough, the paper did not mention where the ball was held. It obviously was not a Goodwood House affair, and was possibly in the Chichester Assembly Rooms. The city, concluded the report, 'retained the bustle of departure until Sunday evening, when it became pretty much restored to the old order of things'. The Goodwood pattern was established.

6

A FATAL
JOURNEY

The third Duke was indeed a curate's egg of a man, but his good parts were unforgettable, and the obituary in the local paper remembered them handsomely. He was 'acknowledged to have been one of the greatest men of his day, and to have derived this greatness neither from his rank nor his fortune . . . but by his talents and abilities alone'. He died a widower in December 1806, with no legitimate children, but supposedly four illegitimate daughters. The closest of these was so recognized that her portrait hangs in Goodwood House. It was she who was left the priceless treasure of her father's personal papers, and it was she who, tragically destroyed them. The Duke's heir, his brother's son, was born on the Goodwood estate, at Molecomb, and by the time he succeeded his uncle at the age of 42, he was married to the Duke of Gordon's daughter, Charlotte (who inherited the Gordon estates but not the title), and had a 15-year-old son – the boy who grew up to mean more to Goodwood racecourse than anyone else in history.

The new Duke was, as Kent put it, 'one of the most fearless of men', though his duel with the Duke of York smacked of rashness rather than bravery. His brother officers passed a resolution that Lennox had 'behaved with courage, but from the peculiarity of the circumstances, not with judgment'. He subseqently exchanged his captaincy in the Coldstream Guards with Lord Strathnairn, for a colonelcy in the 35th foot, stationed in Edinburgh. Before leaving to join his regiment he fought another duel, in a field off the Uxbridge Road, west of London. This was with Theophilus

Swift, second cousin of the more famous writer, who Lennox thought had libelled him in a pamphlet. Swift was hit, but not fatally.

This Duke was to spend less time at Goodwood than any other, and though there were two significant advances at the racecourse in his time – the founding of the Goodwood Cup and the moving of the meeting to July – it is almost certain that they were attributable to the Earl of March rather than his father. Neither March nor the Duke were hunting men, and they disposed of the foxhound pack to the Prince Regent, causing the local historian to move into top gear:

'So end the glories of Charlton and the Goodwood Pack. Fox-hall was pulled down, Noblemen's residences disappeared (the Duke of Richmond's lodging only remaining). The villager, as he hears the distant cry of Lord Leconfield's Hounds occasionally in the neighbourhood, may wonder at those changes in the world which have given to that nobleman what all the rank and power of his great ancestor could never command – the privilege of hunting West Sussex.'

Richmond also let Halnaker House decay, and seemingly embarked on a policy of what would now be called rationalization of the estate. He had, as usual, inherited vast debts from his uncle, and was soon paying out more: to William Ridge for the funeral, £537.7s.11½d; to Richard Hookey for putting the coach in mourning, £6.0s.6d; to Charles Arnold Esquire for proving the will, £650; to every servant for mourning, £10.10s; to William Gilbert for entertainment, 12s.3d; Dr Hunter, a fee etc., £210; Sarah Dailey for cleaning the bath, £1.7s. In January 1807 the wages for the previous year were paid, a system that would not find much favour today, and in the stable they amounted to £490. 15s.8½d. Some idea of the number of staff involved is given by the fact that when, in August, 24 were discharged with a year's wages (among them, no doubt, the kennel staff), the amounts varied from £70 down to £8.

In October the Duke obtained a loan of £30,000 on a mortgage from the Duke of Portland, but nevertheless by the end of the year his accounts were out of the red: expenses £53,000, income £59,000 – to which a considerable contribution was made by the sale of timber, the first time this had been mentioned. Though he later became a Vice-Admiral of Sussex, commanded the 48-strong Goodwood Troop of Horse Artillery, and, as a freemason, was Provincial Grand Master of Sussex, Richmond from this year on

saw little of Goodwood. He did buy into the estate the peak of
St Roche's Hill, and Jacques assured us it was his avowed intention, had he returned to England, to gather his freemasonry
brethren together on The Trundle, where they had last met under
the mastership of the first Duke a century earlier. But, says
Jacques, 'the ways of Heaven are inscrutable and it is not for
mortals to repine at the will of Omnipotence'.

It was certainly a dreadful death that the Almighty had in store
for this duke, a man who had so impressed George III, or perhaps
his son, that within four months of his father's death he had been
appointed Lord Lieutenant of Ireland. Six years later he moved to
Brussels, where he acted as a special envoy during the Napoleonic
wars. By the time of the battle of Waterloo, Richmond was a full
general, though not on active service. Three of his seven sons (he
also had seven daughters) were actively employed on the Duke of
Wellington's staff, though the Earl of March was removed from
the scene by a severe wound in the battle of Orthez in 1814, and
the fourth son, Lord William Pitt Lennox (Pitt was his godfather)
saw little of the battle because of a riding accident.

March had already fought against the French under Wellington
(then Wellesley) in Portugal, to which he had taken three chargers.
He brought one of them back to Goodwood, a mighty beast that
he named Busaco after the bloody battle at that place. The horse
was peppered with gunshot wounds, and bore about his head and
neck, said Kent, the scars of heavy sabre cuts that he had withstood while carrying the Earl through the battle (in which the
French lost 3,000 men). Busaco was put peacefully out to pasture
in Halnaker Park, where it lived to a great age before being buried
near the ice house. A tree was planted over the grave.

At Orthez, the Earl had left Wellington's staff to join the 52nd
Light Infantry, a company of which he was leading when he was
struck in the chest by a musket ball, receiving a wound which was
expected to be fatal. He was carried to the rear of the lines, where
the field surgeons found him slowly bleeding to death from an
internal haemorrhage. There was one small chance of saving his
life: to open a vein in his foot and set up an external flow of
blood, which might be sufficient to stop the internal flow. 'If he
were one of the rank and file,' the surgeon-major is reported to
have said, 'I would do this at once; but he is heir to a duke, and
the responsibility is great.' Knowing that if the gamble did not
come off, the young Earl would die almost immediately, the senior
surgeons were reluctant to attempt the operation.

A junior surgeon, Archibald Hair, stepped forward with a scalpel. 'If nobody else will do it,' he said, 'I will.' He cut the vein without further ado, and within a few minutes the haemorrhage ceased. Dr Hair joined Busaco at Goodwood, not pensioned off in Halnaker Park, but as the fifth Duke's personal doctor. He was with him when he died, 46 years later.

The musket ball was never removed, and ultimately contributed to the ill-health that the Duke suffered in the last 20 years of his life. This was the man who, in his youth, had ridden a hunter down the precipitous slopes of Bow Hill, a feat equal in daring and folly to flying a plane under London's Tower Bridge. When the wars were over, musket ball or not, he resumed hunting with his customary recklessness. Galloping down another of the Goodwood hills in pursuit of a fox, his horse fell with the Earl underneath it. The accident caused the ball to shift, and March was so severely injured that he was advised never to hunt again. He later turned to shooting instead, for which he trained a pony of remarkable equanimity, named Pigeon. It seldom even needed a bridle, and its back was so broad that the Duke could turn this way and that with his guns without fear of falling off. But back to his parents, the fourth Duke and Duchess.

It was these Richmonds who gave the famous ball on the eve of the battle of Quatre-Bras (three nights before Waterloo), when Wellington received the news of the French advance – a scene relived often on screen but perhaps more memorably by Byron, despite his being under the mistaken impression, as many are, that the ball was held on the eve of Waterloo :

> 'There was a sound of revelry by night,
> And Belgium's capital had gather'd then
> Her Beauty and her Chivalry, and bright
> The lamps shone o'er fair women and brave men;
> A thousand hearts beat happily; and when
> Music arose with its voluptuous swell,
> Soft eyes look'd love to eyes which spake again,
> And all went merry as a marriage bell;
> But hush! hark! a deep sound strikes like a rising knell!
>
> Did ye not hear it? – No; 'twas but the wind,
> Or the car rattling o'er the stoney street;
> On with the dance! let joy be unconfined;
> No sleep till morn, when Youth and Pleasure meet
> To chase the glowing Hours with flying feet –

But hark! – that heavy sound breaks in once more,
As if the clouds its echo would repeat;
And nearer, clearer, deadlier than before!
Arm! Arm! it is – it is – the cannon's opening roar!'

The absence of the Duke, and often of all his family, naturally
detracted considerably from the appeal of Goodwood races, since
without the hosts, the guests were less likely to appear. Transport
from London became less hazardous with the inauguration, in
1803, of a coach service at 6.30 every morning, picking up
travellers at the Golden Cross inn at Charing Cross, and the Bolt-
in-Tun, Fleet Street. At 7 a.m. a coach left Chichester (the Swan
and the Dolphin) in the opposite direction, inside seat 22s. outside
seat 12s. These prices dropped encouragingly until, in 1809, they
were 12s. in and 8s. out, a fair proposition.

Nevertheless, racing was not what the third Duke had hoped
it would be, despite the attractions of *The Battle of Hexham* and
The Lake of Lausanne at the Chichester theatre, and an 'ordinary'
– a race dinner presided over by the stewards – for the price of
half a guinea at the Swan. The meeting came down to two days,
with three races a day, and in 1810 there were only five events in
the two days, three of which were walkovers. Something had to
be done to save the situation, and circumstances combined to give
it a double fillip. The third Duke had launched a race for a silver
cup, and in 1811 this was won outright by Bucephalus. It was
replaced by one of the most famous of Goodwood races, the
Goodwood Cup: a 100 guinea gold trophy awarded for a three-
mile race, later to drop to 2 miles 5 furlongs. It became, and still
is, an important target for trainers of staying horses of classic
pretensions. This, and the moving of the meeting in 1814 to the
end of July, close to which it has stayed ever since, breathed just
sufficient life into the body to keep it going until Lord George
Bentinck and the fifth Duke gave it a complete transfusion and
new heart in 1830.

When Richmond was appointed Governor-General of the British
settlements in Canada in 1818, his elder son did more than just
mind the shop. An agreement appointing two gamekeepers for the
estate at West Stoke and East Lavant is signed 'by me his attorney
March'. It charges the men 'to kill any hare pheasant partridge or
any other game whatsoever for my sole use and immediate benefit
and also to take and seize all such guns bows greyhounds setting
dogs lurchers or other dogs snares or other engines' that were

being used to take or kill the Duke's hares, conies or other animals. March seemed well able to cope with the administration of the estate in his father's absence, and it was Lord William who accompanied the Duke to Canada as his aide-de-camp. He was not, however, with his father on the last long journey that ended with his death from one of the most terrible diseases known to man. It was a sickening irony that the fifth Duke should die of dropsy, a surfeit of water in the body, after his father had died of a manic aversion to it – hydrophobia.

Among the ragbag of canine detail in *Records of the Old Charlton Hunt*, there is a section headed 'Amusing Receipts for the bite of a mad dog'. They include Dr Mead's cure, which involves making four doses out of a mixture of two drams of black pepper and half an ounce of *lychen cinerens terrestris*, to be taken before breakfast each morning in half a pint of cow's milk, warm. An even less likely prescription requires the patient to take a cold bath before breakfast every morning for a month, then three times a week for a fortnight. 'He must be dipt all over, and not keep his head above water more than half a minute.'

Dr Mead was for many years the second Duke's medical adviser. But the frequency of rabies and the consequent fear of hydrophobia two hundred years ago was such that every household that kept hounds made sure it had a 'receipt' against it. The Charlton hound book also contained one recommended by Prince Rupert (son-in-law of James I, commander of Charles II's fleet). Some of the ingredients might be hard to find in an emergency, and you might think its preparation so lengthy that it would be too late by the time it was ready, but perhaps it was worth the effort:

'A large handful of Rue, a handful of red Sage, a handful of ground Liverwort, two heaped spoonfulls of scraped Pewter, six heads of Garlick, one pound of Venice Treacle or Mithridate, three quarts of strong Ale.

'Put all into a well glazed earthen pot, stop the pot very close with paste, set it over the fire, and as soon as it has boiled, take the pot off the fire, and set it to infuse by a gentle heat for 24 hours, then press it, and strain it off for use.

'To a man give five spoonfuls, morning and evening, for three days, and repeat it at the next full and new moon. The same quantity once a day to a dog.'

Certainly, although one of the fourth Duke's companions through his long death was a doctor, there was no chance of making up such a prescription where they were. Indeed, in the account of the fatal journey there is no reference made even to attempting to cure the Duke's condition.

It was a major part of Richmond's job to show the flag among the pioneers of Upper and Lower Canada (Ontario and Quebec), and it was typical of the man's determination that he should do so regardless of the appalling conditions for travelling out there. There were few roads, and in some areas it was even impossible for horses to be used, so wet was the land. He had to cross some of the worst of it on his way to open a new settlement somewhere south of the Saint Lawrence River, near Richmond. The Governor-General and his small party left York by boat on 17th August, staying at the military post at Kingston on the nights of the 18th and 19th. It was here that the Duke, finding a dog (possibly his own dog) and a pet fox fighting, is said to have tried to separate them and was bitten for his pains, though the injury itself was of no consequence. The Duke's senior companion was Colonel Cockburn, who at the request of the Richmond family, chronicled the events of the next ten days in painful detail. His bound manuscript still rests in the Duke of Richmond's private library at Goodwood House, a stunningly effective document that is probably unique not least as a medical case history.

They took two days to cover the 20 miles to Perth, by wagon, on horseback, and on foot. On the first evening, Cockburn noticed that the Duke 'appeared a little fatigued', and that the next morning he took very little breakfast. But during the day he asked anxiously for refreshment, 'and some bread and cheese being produced, he partook of it very heartily'. On the third day of the journey, the party were soaked in heavy rain, but after drinking some hot wine and water, the Duke ate heartily again and appeared in good spirits, not going to bed until midnight. There were no problems the next day, and the Duke enjoyed two or three cigars after dinner that evening.

On 24th August they were up at 6.30 for the remaining 15 miles to Richmond, and it was then that the first symptoms of the illness touched the Duke, though little did any of them then guess what it was: 'Perceiving that he did not eat much breakfast, we enquired if he was unwell. He replied that he had a pain in his shoulder, and that he had not slept very well, which was rather an unusual thing for him . . . however, he made light of his indisposition.' From here on the road was impassable for a wagon, and the plan was to go about half-way on horseback, leave the horses at a settler's house, and walk the rest of the way to Richmond. By the time they reached the house, the Duke did not look well enough for the rigours of that sort of journey.

'We prevailed on him on his arrival there to lay down for an hour or two: here we endeavoured to persuade him to return to Perth, and to take the Brockville road to Montreal; in this however we did not succeed.' He took some chicken broth and an hour's sleep, then insisted on going on to the next settlement, Beckville, which they reached at 6.30.

'The Duke immediately went upstairs and laid down, nor did he join us again until just as we were setting down to dinner, when he remained a very short time, ate very little, and then went up again to lay down: during this day's journey the Duke drank constantly of weak brandy and water.' He slept scarcely at all during the night, ate little breakfast and left the table suddenly to lie down. On that day, the 25th, Cockburn completed the journey to Richmond, but the Duke with his doctor and the servants, stayed four miles short at a settler's house.

The next day they had to negotiate the long swamp before Richmond, which they did not reach until 10 o'clock at night. The Duke, who had less pain in his shoulder but was having some difficulty in swallowing, 'struck me as looking unusually ill, and I observed he was walking unusually fast', said Cockburn on his arrival.

'At dinner, the sight of the wine produced a convulsion in the first instance, and so great was his difficulty in drinking it that he was obliged to raise the glass sideways to his mouth, after which he appeared to swallow it with the greatest difficulty, remarking "It is fortunate I am not a dog or I should have been shot some time ago." ' That night Cockburn awoke once or twice to hear the Duke talking in his sleep, and in the morning his dislike of water had become so intense that he could not put his towel in it to wash.

They were due to make a short journey by canoe, and the Duke was persuaded to take his seat in the boat. He took his dog in his arms and kissed it, but he could not bear to pass through the water. They had instead to walk a considerable distance, and once, perceiving a little water in the bottom of a ravine, the Duke refused to cross it. He began to talk, Cockburn went on, of the possibly speedy termination of his life, and to give directions accordingly. Soon he would not walk even within sight of the river, and at one point jumped a fence to get away from it, and walked so fast they could hardly follow him. When they got near a house where they could stay, the Duke saw there was a barn some 50 yards further from the river than the house was, and insisted that he should stay there, scrambling over railings at least six feet high on his way to it.

'The paroxysms came on soon after with increasing violence; during these his sufferings were dreadful, but between them the pain and the delirium both seemed to subside and it was in these intervals that he made known such communications as he thought would be consolatory to his family . . . At about four in the afternoon nature appeared to have exhausted herself and he became more tranquil. It was about this time that he took a laudanum pill and on our asking him if he would endeavour to take a little broth he replied in the affirmative: he accordingly swallowed without much apparent difficulty two or three tea-spoonsful of it; on our afterwards offering him some bread, his mode of taking it appeared to me almost to amount to snapping.'

During the evening, it being clear that the Duke's life was near its end, they moved him into the house. 'About one o'clock in the morning the difficulty of getting rid of his saliva was much increased and from this time I do not think he recognized anyone. At seven o'clock there was an appearance of a slight paroxysm; nature however seemed unequal to any further struggle, and precisely at 8 he breathed his last so tranquilly that though anxiously watching him at the moment, I was not certain till I called Dr Collins whether life had quitted him or not.'

The manner of the Duke's death was a profound shock not only to his family at Goodwood, who could not have heard of it for several weeks, but to the whole of the British community in Canada, to whom his appointment and brief tenure of office had brought such pride and excitement. 'This mysterious dispensation of Providence hath caused a most grievous mourning and sore lamentation through both Provinces', declared the *Christian Recorder* the next month, 'for we felt ourselves deeply interested in his welfare, and entertained the most sanguine expectations of the success of his administration. When it was announced in the public journals that this distinguished nobleman was to become our Governor-in-Chief few would believe it. That a person of his illustrious rank, who had filled the most splendid offices which the Crown has to bestow, would condescend to accept an appointment in this distant region, appeared somewhat incredible.'

When the news reached Quebec, a sermon was preached in the

cathedral church there without delay by the Reverend G. J. Mountain, the Bishop's official in Lower Canada, and Rector of Quebec. The following day his churchwardens delivered to him this communication:

'Having participated with the rest of your Congregation in the feeling excited yesterday by your excellent Discourse on the subject of the late deep and heavy calamity, the death of His Grace the Governor-in-Chief, we trust we shall be indulged in the wish we entertain, that you would favour us with a Copy of your Sermon, that it may be delivered to the Press for publication.'

Mr Mountain was of course delighted to oblige. A copy of the publication was sent to the Dowager Duchess Charlotte, and remains to this day at Goodwood House. So does the Duke's last message to his heir, dictated to Colonel Cockburn in one of the lucid moments of Richmond's final day:

'Tell March that I know he will regret being Duke of Richmond, but that I am satisfied I leave my estate and titles to one of the best and most honourable men in England.'

7

ON COURSE

There may have been something of a hiatus in the development of Goodwood racecourse during the fourth Duke's time, but there was never much doubt that his son would be much occupied with its prosperity. A horseman of great dash and daring until he was wounded in battle, it was this Richmond who turned the Goodwood meeting into a social occasion of such splendour and appeal that nobody who was anybody, but nobody, could miss it and be sure it did not matter. At the same time, with the expert guidance and encouragement of Lord George Bentinck, he contrived to run it with such admirable efficiency that even the critics cheered: 'It should be held out as a model', wrote the man from *The Times*, who was never slow to chastise when he felt it necessary, 'in every respect the accommodation and amusement of the public is consulted without regard to expense and trouble, insomuch that we every year find something new to admire.'

The man who deserved such compliments remained master of Goodwood for 41 years, but there were aspects of his life in which he was regarded as rather less of a paragon. Like the third Duke, he took to politics, though not quite with his great-uncle's passion and perversity, and in this field his limitations, some thought, were cruelly exposed. The waspish political diarist Charles Greville considered the political future of the Duke in April, 1829, a time when Richmond was being spoken of by some as a successor to the Duke of Wellington as Prime Minister:

'He happens to have his wits, such as they are, about him, and has been quick and neat in one or two little speeches, though he spoke too often, and particularly in his attack on the Bishop of Oxford the other night . . . He lives in the country, is well versed in rural affairs and the business of the quarter sessions, has a

certain calibre of understanding, is prejudiced, narrow-minded,
illiterate, and ignorant, good-looking, good-humoured, and unaffected, tedious, prolix, unassuming, and a duke.'

Prolix, a word seldom used today, suggests that Greville found
Richmond boringly long-winded. A footnote by the author points
out: 'It is of the essence of these memoirs not to soften or tone
down judgments by the lights of altered convictions, but to leave
them standing as contemporary evidence of what was thought at
the time they were written.' However, four years later, Greville's
convictions do not seem much altered. He then wrote 'of the
Duke:

'He is utterly incapable, entirely ignorant, and his pert smart-
ness, saying sharp things, cheering offensively, have greatly
exasperated many people against him in the House of Commons,
and these feelings of anger have been heightened by his taking
frequent opportunities of comporting himself with acrimony
towards the Duke of Wellington, though he always professes
great veneration for him, and talks as if he had constantly
abstained from anything like incivility or disrespect towards him.
It is remarkable certainly that his colleagues appear to entertain
a higher opinion of him than he deserves, and you hear of one or
another saying, "Oh, you don't know the Duke of Richmond".
He has, in fact, that weight which a man can derive from being
positive, obstinate, pertinacious, and busy, but his understanding
lies in a nutshell, and his information in a pin's head. He is, however, good-humoured, a good fellow, and personally liked, particularly by Stanley and Graham, who are of his own age, and have
both the same taste for sporting and gay occupations.'

One should mention that Greville, who elsewhere refers to
Richmond as 'my excellent friend', was close enough to him to
be invited to stay at Goodwood during the races; and that the
diaries were not published until after the deaths of both Richmond
and Greville. The editor of the first edition of *Charles Greville's
Journals*, Henry Reeve, nevertheless appended a firm note: 'I have
not thought it consistent with my duty as the editor of these
papers to suppress or modify any of the statements or opinions
of their author on public men or public events; nor do I hold
myself in any way responsible for the tenor of them. Some of
these judgements of the writer may be thought harsh and severe,
and some of them were subsequently mitigated by himself. But
those who enter public life submit their conduct and their lives
to the judgement of their contemporaries and of posterity, and

this is especially true of those who fill the most exalted station in society.'

A hard-line Tory who was opposed to Peel's free trade and even to Catholic emancipation, Richmond rather oddly became a Cabinet minister in Earl Grey's Whig government, a move that did not endear him either to his friends or his enemies. Like his ancestor, he was first made Master-General of the Ordnance, but since he was only an inactive lieutenant-colonel, this annoyed the army and the appointment was withdrawn. He refused the Mastership of the King's Horse, and ended as Postmaster-General.

This Earl of March was born in London, sat as MP for Chichester and seems to have had little in the way of a formal education. When he came back from the war against Napoleon, he married Lady Caroline Paget, daughter of the Marquis of Anglesey, and lived at Molecomb until his succession. The first of their ten children was born in 1818, the year in which, as an owner, March won his first race at Goodwood with Roncesvalles. The debts he inherited were largely those of his mother, in her lifetime. She had a taste for the tables, but not much luck at them, and the first years of his dukedom were notable for an almost passive restraint.

The Dowager Duchess inherited all the Gordon estates in Scotland on the death of her brother in 1836. This took the Richmond lands up to nearly 300,000 acres (470 square miles), which is approximately what the royal family owns today, and placed the fifth Duke fourth on the list of the country's great landlords. It was obviously this Duke and his two Duchesses who were the subjects of an anonymous and undated verse found amid the family scraps. No doubt the work of some worthy and ecstatic civic dignitary from Chichester, rather than one of the house party, it is headed *The Goodwood Ball*:

> Now first it does become us most
> To sing the praises of our host;
> Not only host, but hostess too,
> We owe our gratulations to.

> See Richmond how graceful, how youthful her mien
> As she treads a soft measure, like blushing sixteen;
> And the Dowager Duchess, with energy – fire
> Proves the blood of the Gordons will never expire.

And our gratulations to the poet, who a century earlier might have written the *Charlton Congress*.

At this time, racing and the racecourse were occasional and pleasant adjuncts to life at Goodwood, and by no means a focus for it. In Jacques's little book of 1822 he says no more about the racecourse than that the races there 'are in general respectably and well attended, yielding frequently very excellent sport; the course is protected from accidents by a strong railing, which extends on both sides for a considerable distance, and has also a commodious stand, or lookout building for the accommodation of ladies.' But a year later Richmond began to expand his modest racing stable, a venture in which he was greatly encouraged by Viscount Dunwich. It was he who urged Richmond to get hold of a trainer who knew his business, and on his recommendation Richmond hired John Kent (the elder version), who was then working at Newmarket for Dunwich's father, the Earl of Strad-broke. The racing partnership of Kent and more notably his son with Richmond and Bentinck was one of the most remarkable in the history of 19th century racing and fills a large and distinguished part of Goodwood's great canvas. It also has a more personal relevance to this book, since with *Records and Reminiscences of Goodwood and the Dukes of Richmond* in 1896, John Kent the younger was the only previous author to have attempted any kind of history of Goodwood.

'During the period I was upon the Goodwood estate,' he wrote in his preface, 'extending over a great number of years, I had exceptional opportunities for observing much, which few now living can have seen . . . I may not have done justice to the subjects dealt with, but it has been more than a labour of love to write what I have.'

Grandfather Kent was a builder in Newmarket. The famous Subscription Rooms and the Rutland Arms Hotel were his work, and he built himself a house on Mill Hill, near the stables of Richard Prince. Prince trained for the third Duke of Portland (Bentinck's grandfather), and 'old' John Kent became his head lad. Young John was only five when they moved to Goodwood in 1823, the year the Duke of Richmond launched the Goodwood Stakes, still one of the most popular of races there. In the first year there were only two runners, and its running in 1824 was notable for one of the grossest judging errors in the recorded history of racing: the Duke himself was the victim, and it is odd that the judge should have been his excellent friend Charles Greville. Operating from a high little box on the north side of the track, Greville was concentrating so hard on the battle between

Vitellina and Ghost, neck and neck on the far side, that he completely failed to notice Dandizette passing two or three lengths ahead of them right under his nose. When Lord Verulam received the stakes as winning owner, neither he nor anyone else could understand it. He immediately offered them to Richmond, but they were declined. The race had been judged, he said, and that was that.

Greville was at that time the Duke of York's racing manager and a man of some influence on the Turf. He was the cousin and close friend of Bentinck, and later his racing associate. Bentinck's father, the fourth Duke, was so opposed to racing that he would not allow his son to run horses in the family name, forcing Lord George (who was probably more immersed in and devoted to affairs of the Turf than any man in England) to run them with the co-operation of friends such as Greville and Richmond. Both his friendship and his partnership with Greville foundered during the Goodwood meeting of 1836, following a bitter incident on the course.

On the opening day of the meeting a filly they jointly owned, Preserve, won the first race, encouraging Lord George to back it heavily for the Goodwood Stakes the next day. Greville also had a runner in the Stakes, Dacre, an outsider that made the early running. A furlong from the end, Preserve, as expected, came up to overtake. Dacre leaned heavily into the challenger, forcing Preserve to swerve, lose ground, and let another horse through to win the race. As one reporter had it, 'Halfway up the distance Preserve endeavoured to go to the front, but Dacre hung upon her, and drove her out of line'. Bentinck was convinced Greville was responsible for the action, and it was many years before mutual friends were able to bring the two men together again. Greville, of course, recorded his side of the story for posterity:

'Till then not an unkind word had ever passed between us, nor had a single cloud darkened our habitual intercourse; but on this occasion I opposed and thwarted him and his resentment broke out against me with a vehemence and ferocity that perfectly astounded me, and displayed in perfection the domineering insolence of his character. I knew he was out of humour, but had no idea that he meant to quarrel with me, and thought his serenity would speedily return. I wrote to him as usual, and to my astonishment received one of his most elaborate epistles, couched in terms so savage and so virulently abusive, imputing to me conduct the most selfish and dishonourable, that I knew not on reading it whether I stood on my head or my heels.'

The precise moment at which Bentinck became actively involved at Goodwood is not easy to spot. It has been generally thought up to now that he did not begin to influence the Duke of Richmond's management of the racecourse until the 1830s, but there is conclusive evidence that his was the guiding hand long before that. It was Bentinck who superintended – and probably devised – the relaying of the racecourse in the winter of 1829, which included the immense and splendidly-conceived job of extending the plateau of the finishing straight right over the hillside that fell away from it towards Charlton.

Bentinck's racing career is believed to have begun at Goodwood. At the age of 22 he stayed during the meeting with Colonel Poyntz, the Goodwood steward, at Cowdray Park, and rode the colonel's mare, Olive, to win the Cocked Hat Stakes. As that was in 1824, he would no doubt have seen Greville's monumental *faux pas*. That may well have been enough to ripen within him the seeds of determination that he carried throughout his life; the determination that racing should be good, clean and well-managed and be seen to be so, that racecourses should be used for the benefit and enjoyment of racegoers and not just of owners, and that villainy should be kicked off the Turf.

These things seem so obvious to us now that they are hardly worth mentioning. But in the early 19th century, things were very different. As the *Illustrated London News* racing man put it in 1835: 'Up to the first quarter of this century, you went to Newmarket, where the existence of the animal you staked your money on could no more be known to you till he came to the starting post (and not then, unless you had a good telescope) than the state of the Emperor of Morocco's bile. You went to Epsom, and found the jockeys starting themselves; or to Doncaster, and saw them deciding how they came in . . .'

Even as late as 1844, the Derby was won by a ringer – a four-year-old, Maccabeus, dyed and disguised to look like a three-year-old, Running Rein, and called by that name. The deception, which had been suspected at Newmarket the previous year, was uncovered personally by Bentinck after lurking in shop doorways and shadowing the owner as faithfully as any private eye. He became the senior steward of the Jockey Club – 'Lord Paramount of the Turf', as his biographer has it – coming between Sir Charles Bunbury and Admiral Henry Rous in that most autocratic position.

To Bentinck more than to any other man in racing history, followers of the sport today owe an immeasurable debt. He re-shaped the whole pattern of racing, persuading (even blackmailing when it was necessary) clerks at the classic courses to do things his way. It was he who brought first to Goodwood and Epsom the pre-race parade and the public saddling, which gave an enormous boost to on-course betting; it was he who let it be known that members of the Jockey Club would not be inclined to support meetings at which the management were not adding sufficient money to the stakes, and at which the efficiency of either the starting or the judging was in question.

It is clear that at Goodwood he soon recognized the immense, unfulfilled potential of the course, and the rare desire of its owner to improve it. It was an ideal subject for Bentinck's plans and experiments, not least because there were no tiresome committees of management or boards of directors to contend with : like Ascot, Goodwood was and still is privately owned. Decisions however great could be taken over the breakfast table or in a corner of the club and none could oppose them, and in the hands of Richmond and Bentinck (ten years the Duke's junior), Goodwood became a model racecourse, if an overwhelmingly upper-class one.

The major work with which they began their reform of the meeting was the re-laying of the finishing straight and its extension by more than two furlongs. Until then, anyone on The Trundle would hardly have been in touch with the racing, which finished about half-way along the straight as it is today. This was no problem to the occupants of the stand, since that also was much further to the east – as near as one can tell, about where the children's playground now starts. The reason for that was simple : until Bentinck began to move mountains, there was no room for a longer finish. The natural geography had left too narrow a strip between the Harroways and the hillside, but between mid-September and early December, 1829, Bentinck got the better of nature. For 500 yards across the hill he deferred the slope until he was ready for it, by bringing in hundreds of tons of soil and relaying 16,000 yards of turf, and giving Goodwood that superb wide green finish that now faces the enclosures. While he was at it, he had them re-lay the course for eighty yards round the bend so that too was almost level.

The surveyor's account was brief and his charges slight: 'To surveying measuring marking out different lines for a new race course at Goodwood, taking elevations, making calculations for estimate, drawing plans etc, numerous journies and other expenses attending the scene, £13.16s.od.' It is in the details of the contractor's estimate (£660.17s.10d.) that we begin to form a picture of that part of the course as it was then, and it is here too that Bentinck's early involvement is confirmed :

'Statement of expence of mooving earth filling and raising ground on the lower or north side of Race Course at Goodwood, from the present Wining Post to the proposed new wining post the distance of near five hundred yards by twenty-six yards wide and to cut grub and form the lower line of course marked by the direction of Lord Bentinck, to be formed twelve yards wide with the exception of the nearest corner to the stand which is to be made fifteen yards wide and to be made nearly level for a distance of eighty yards round the turn of the course. (NB this estimate do not include any part of carriage of turfs not knowing from whence to be taken.')

The estimate proved remarkably accurate. An account book kept by the contractor, Josiah Higgs, shows that by December he had spent £639.8s.7d. the men being paid at the rate of between 1s. 6d. and 2s. a day. As it turned out, there was some disagreement between the Duke and Higgs over the final account, which Richmond declined to pay as it stood. Higgs died before the matter was settled and it was December 1834 before his widow 'Jane Higgs of Summers Town in the suburbs of the city of Chichester' and the Duke agreed to abide by arbitration over the 'divers disputes and differences' that had arisen, the arbitrators being Harry Silverlock, a Chichester seedsman, James Howard, a Liphook surveyor, and an unnamed third person.

The Duke's progress as a racing man, regardless of the improvements at Goodwood, had by 1829 been quite spectacular. He had many successes with a young horse called Link Boy, which Viscount Dunwich persuaded him to sell in 1825, and with which Dunwich won the Goodwood Cup in 1827. That year, with only seven horses in training under Kent, Richmond won 23 races including the Goodwood Stakes. Two years later he had a sensational meeting at Ascot, winning all seven open races in the three days – two on the first day, the Gold Cup on the second and all four on the third. He had become a leading member of the Jockey Club, as were Bentinck and Greville, and the diarist recorded a Club dinner with George IV at St James's Palace. About thirty members of the Club attended, 'several not being invited whom he did not fancy'. The dinner, wrote Greville, was in the Great

4 Hunting continued to be a passion with the third Duke, seen here
following the Goodwood Hounds in 1759. 30 years later he built the
unique centrally heated kennels. *(George Stubbs)*

5 The third Duke, with his wife and sister-in-law, watching racehorses
training at Goodwood. 'The Richmond with the mostest of them all,'
he built the present Goodwood House and founded the racecourse.
(George Stubbs, 1759–60)

6 Cricket was as important as racing to some of the Richmonds. This one, the fourth, was a founder of the MCC and an enthusiastic wicket-keeper, who played in Brussels on the eve of Waterloo.

Supper Room and very magnificent. The King sat in the middle, with the Dukes of Richmond and Grafton on each side of him.

'I sat opposite to him, and he was particularly gracious to me, talking to me across the table and recommending all the good things; he made me (after eating a quantity of turtle) eat a dish of crawfish soup, till I thought I should have burst.' The Duke of Leeds, who presided at the dinner, made the loyal toast, the King twice toasted the Turf, and the Duke of Richmond again toasted the King, who then spoke:

'He thanked all the gentlemen, and said that there was no man who had the interests of the Turf more at heart than himself, that he was delighted at having this party, and that the oftener they met the better, and he only wanted to have it pointed out to him how he could promote the pleasure and amusement of the Turf, and he was ready to do anything in his power.'

Richmond had hoped that the King would attend the Goodwood meeting in 1830, but it was not possible – particularly unfortunate in view of the successes the royal horses were to enjoy. In answer to his invitation he received a letter from the King's secretary, Lord Erroll: 'I laid your letter this morning before the King and His Majesty desired me to inform you with his kind regards that he is very sorry it will not be in his power to accept your kind invitation for Goodwood Races as the Duke and Duchess of Cambridge are to arrive at Windsor on the 10th. His Majesty really seemed quite disappointed at not being able to go to Goodwood. Most sincerely, Erroll.'

The 'very elegant and commodious new stand' that Richmond had built while the course was being altered was a great hit even without royal patronage. It was 120 feet long, capable of holding 3,000, and contained refreshment and retiring rooms on the ground floor, and glass-fronted saloon and betting rooms on the first floor. The stand followed the pattern then customary of being topped with a large and steeply-raked, benched terrace, which apart from being completely open to the elements was not unlike the gallery of a Victorian theatre. 'The Duke seems determined', wrote 'Observator' in the *Sporting Magazine*, 'to leave no stone unturned to make this eventually the very first meeting in the kingdom. Even now, indeed, there are but few superior to it; but by this day five years I prophesy, barring accidents, that there will be nothing excepting Doncaster in the list of country races at all to be compared with it.'

On all three days of the meeting, he wrote, the sport was

D

excellent and 'there was a most magnificent display of all that is most lovely and noble in the land'. It is amusing to see that in the same magazine of 1842, a later correspondent incorrectly recalls: 'A dozen years ago we went to see a couple of paltry days' racing, with a company almost entirely confined to the neighbourhood of Goodwood House.' There were in fact 14 races and some matches in 1830, with a sensational result in the Gold (later Goodwood) Cup: the first three home were all owned by the new King, William IV.

That event alone, the magazine reported, 'brought thousands from their homes to witness . . . the almost unprecedented sight of the three best horses in Europe, belonging to Royalty, about to start for it. Beautiful and magnificent in the extreme indeed was it – knowing the orders issued by His Majesty – to behold this race; and never were orders given by a master, for each one of his horses to do his best, more strictly and implicitly obeyed. From end to end the race belonged entirely to His Majesty's three; and, to borrow a simile from his own profession, the others had about as good a chance against them as half a dozen schooners would have against three first-rate three-deckers of the line. Each one of them, however, decidedly intended winning, and here was the beauty of the struggle.

'The pace throughout I should say was most awful, and altogether as a race the one of last year bore no comparison to it in any shape or way. I need scarcely add that His Majesty's success was received by all ranks on the ground with the greatest and most lively enthusiasm; and all I hope and pray for now is that he may be stimulated by it not only to keep up the whole of his lamented brother's racing stud, but to add to and increase it with liberality and judgment.'

William IV had served in the navy and was Lord High Admiral of England before succeeding his brother, George IV, to the throne. The winner of the Cup was Fleur-de-Lis, second was Zinganee, which had triumphed at Ascot, and third The Colonel, the horse that dead-heated in the 1828 Derby and lost the run-off.

It is hard for us now to understand the extravagant and incessant praise that the racing writers of the day heaped upon almost every Goodwood meeting for the next 12 or 15 years. Despite the lushness of the Duke's entertaining, there is no reason to believe that the gentlemen of the Press were much influenced by it, since they were not even given a room to work in until 1847, and then it was only a roped off area of the betting room. The truth has to be that nobody had seen racing so beautifully staged and so efficiently organized, nor indeed a meeting that attracted (by the size of its prizes) so much racing talent. And so, over those years and from a selection of journals, phrases of this kind crop up again and again: 'The racing has ever been surpassed and very rarely equalled on this or any other course'; 'the most brilliant programme ever known'; 'surpasses all other meetings in rank and splendour'; 'Goodwood is without a rival in Turf annals'; 'no meeting comes so near perfection as Goodwood'; 'the most glorious meeting that ever man attended.'

Even the women seemed to get better and better. In the same report, one correspondent wrote of a ticket for 5s. introducing the racegoer to 'a hundred of the very prettiest ladies in all England', and of 'vast numbers of the prettiest peasantry in the kingdom'. There were 'days of jocund hilarity and evenings crowned with the banquet', and ultimately: 'I have read somewhere that perfection is not to be found on this earth; now, with all due deference to the uttered judgment, I think I might safely challenge the assertion. This was the most magnificent racing meeting I ever beheld' (*Sporting Magazine*, 1840).

It should have been enough to turn the head of its proprietor, but no doubt he had Bentinck at his elbow to remind him of what needed next to be done. And even he must have been somewhat impressed by the symphony of superlatives that they read in the *Sporting Magazine* in August, 1831. Having delivered himself of the eulogy to the Duke that was quoted at the beginning of this chapter, the anonymous writer went on to consider the quality of the turf, of the whole course, the situation, the buildings and all the conveniences, which altogether formed, he said, 'a perfect display of exquisite taste'. If you could forget the incorrectness of the race cards and the high price of beds in the neighbourhood, then, he declared, casting off all restraint, 'Goodwood is the most beautiful place on earth.'

That year all had been fixed for a royal visit when there was an even more dramatic disappointment than before. The King's father-in-law, the Duke of Saxe Meiwingen, arrived unexpectedly at Windsor and caused the King to cancel his trip to Goodwood. It was a sad blow to Richmond and to the whole local community, but they went ahead and put on the most impressive meeting ever. *The Times* had been so geared up for the full treatment that it had sent its man down a day early:

'For some time past active preparations have been made in all parts of the county to give *éclat* to the expected Royal visit, and divers speculations have been hazarded upon the route to be taken by His Majesty, the formula to be observed in presenting loyal addresses, and the other details consequent upon so rare and exciting an occasion. The arrival of the Earl and Countess of Munster at the seat of Lord Egremont, and the subsequent arrangements directed by the venerable Earl, added to the still more extensive accommodations provided at the hospitable residence of his Grace the Duke of Richmond, encouraged the belief that the long-promised visit would actually take place : the Chichester lieges were especially on the *qui vive* – speeches were manufactured, processions arranged, and everything else duly ordered that might beseem a spirited and loyal city; the prices for lodging, horses, stabling and provisions (at all times dear enough) rose in proportion to the occasion, and there was a general and joyful anticipation of a glorious harvest in all the towns and villages within 10 or 15 miles of the place.'

There is a phrase in Fleet Street used to describe the withholding, to a dangerously late stage in one's story, of what one would expect to be its salient feature : the delayed drop. Clearly the correspondent was not going to be done out of those well-rounded sentences he had been polishing in the coach. But at last he can hold out on us no longer :

'Up to the latter part of the week all was sunshine, when a death blow was given to the hopes of all the parties interested, by the unexpected and (to them) untoward arrival of the Duke of Saxe Meiwingen. Bad news travels a "racing pace". It soon, therefore, became known in the vicinity of Chichester that His Majesty could not, under existing circumstances, participate in the festivities of Goodwood; it is almost superfluous to add, that the disappointment is severely felt by all classes. The absence of His Majesty is not likely to have any very prejudicial affect on the meeting; indeed we have abundant reasons for believing that it will be one of unrivalled splendour, and that it will surpass any other in the excellence and importance of the racing.

'Very little betting has yet taken place.'

The difficulties for a journalist of getting his material back to London from the depths of the country were such that the descriptive reporting was always a day late, and even the race results, sent later 'by express', only took in half the day's events, the remainder of which were recorded in the paper two days after they had occurred. So on the morning after the 1831 meeting had opened, *The Times* could only carry a preview:

'In the course of the last 24 hours the arrivals have been so numerous that every place within ten miles of Goodwood is crowded; at Chichester, Midhurst, Bognor, Arundel etc. not a lodging is to be procured, although large prices are offered. Equal difficulty is experienced in procuring stabling, an immense number of saddle horses having been sent down from London; in short, everything bespeaks a brilliant meeting. Long before the commencement of the races this afternoon the ground presented a very animated scene – carriages, gigs, carts, pedestrians and horsemen were observed approaching in every direction, and by 2 o'clock the assemblage was at once numerous and respectable.'

Every year, the most respectable were listed, and there were many occasions when the reporter's contribution consisted solely of something like 'The weather was good and the sport excellent and the following were observed in the stand', and after it: 'The above list forms but a small portion of the fashionables congregated within a few miles of Goodwood Park.' The massive list of this glittering occasion was headed by the Duke of Argyle, the Marquesses of Tavistock and Exeter, and ten earls. Protocol was always strictly observed, and quite often on the following day the man had to make additions to placate affronted noblemen who had been overlooked. This was done quite shamelessly and with *The Times*'s unnerving tradition of absolute accuracy, so that one might have read on a Monday morning a report headed 'Goodwood, Saturday' which opened: 'Among those mentioned in our report on Thursday as having been present in the grand stand on Wednesday, there should have been included Viscount This, the Hon. Sir Algernon That; and so on.' At this period, the meetings were in fact always held on Wednesday, Thursday and Friday, so that it was Monday before the papers could carry the last of the results and the correspondents' summing up of the races:

'In every respect they came up fully to our expectations. The sport was of the finest description, the company infinitely more numerous than at any former meeting, and the weather favourable. The prospects for next year are of a still more flattering nature.' Among the bouquets which the reporter then handed the management was one which obviously reflected Bentinck's careful attention: 'It would be well if the same method of starting horses adopted at Goodwood was practised at other meetings. There was not one false start, though there were 15 horses in one race and 13 in two others.'

That this was an achievement of note is clear from the fact that the 1830 Derby, for instance, suffered 14 false starts. At Epsom it was another seven years before the science of starting became so advanced that a flag was used instead of a shout. There was no such thing as a starting gate, or even a tape across the course, and the runners milled about in the area hoping they would be facing the right way when the starter shouted. Many of the jockeys were there with the deliberate intention of perpetrating the equivalent of what is now glibly referred to in soccer as a 'professional foul', as John Kent makes clear in his *Racing Life of Lord George Bentinck*:

'The starting of the horses was generally performed by the clerk of the course or some other official quite unused to the work, and the jockeys took every advantage of him. Jockeys then, as now [1892], would use every device in their power to obtain an advantageous start, and to this end some would deliberately cause false starts until they attained their object. Sometimes a favourite would be kept at the starting post for an hour in a state of frenzy until he was more than half exhausted before the flag fell. As the horses were started by word of command, the jockeys were often unable to understand what the starter meant, and sometimes ran the race right through when it was no start.'

As he went on to illustrate, starts by a shouted command could have hilarious consequences, even in such well-ordered spheres as the Goodwood racecourse:

'The person deputed to start the horses at Goodwood in 1830 had an impediment in his speech, and when he became excited it was with great difficulty that he could articulate a word. For the Duke of Richmond's Plate that year there were a number of false starts, which delayed the actual start for a very long time. After the race William Arnull, the oldest jockey who took part in it, and one upon whose word full reliance could be placed, was summoned by the stewards to explain the cause of the long delay. He replied: "Some of the horses were no doubt restive, but in my opinion the fault lay chiefly with the starter. He is just like an old firelock which fizzles ever so long in the pan before it goes off, and when he did get the word out, there was no knowing whether he said 'Go!' or 'No!' " '

Arnull, then 45, was the youngest of three outstanding jockey brothers, who between them won the Derby twelve times. That false-starting Derby of 1830 is particularly relevant, since it was won by Priam, one of the greatest horses of all times, and Priam won the Cup at Goodwood in 1831 and 1832.

Lord Chesterfield had bought Priam after the Derby, and sent it to Goodwood to be trained by old John Kent. His son was then 13 and often rode the horse in exercise; in 1896 he was able to write: 'I question whether there is any other man now living who ever crossed the back of the beautiful and incomparable Priam . . . the horse par excellence of the 19th century.' Many other experts shared his view, and rated the perfections of Priam in that century almost as phenomenal as those of Eclipse had been in the previous one. Though there was hardly a man who could have seen both horses run (Eclipse was foaled in 1764) it is more sensible to compare the two than it is to hold Priam against Brigadier Gerard or Mill Reef, for both the earlier champions were in an era when the ability to gallop with unflagging speed for four miles two or three times a day was the stuff of which winners were made. A good many mounts 100 years ago would be laughed off the course today – including, no doubt, the Duke of Richmond's colt Hyper, the outstanding quality of which, according to one reporter, was its extreme stoutness. But not the only one: on the day of Priam's second Goodwood win, Hyper achieved a dead heat in another race despite being in evident distress at the half-way mark. 'His blood, however, was of the right sort: he struggled nobly and managed to make a draw of it.'

Charles Greville left a note in his diary which captures the essential appeal of Goodwood, as well, of course, as cutting firmly at the wider pretensions of his host:

'Goodwood, August 20th 1831 – Here I have been a week today for the races, and here I should not be now – for everybody else is gone – if it were not for the gout, which has laid me fast by the foot, owing to a blow. While on these racing expeditions I never know anything of politics, and, though I just read the newspapers, have no anecdotes to record of reform or foreign affairs. I never come here without fresh admiration of the beauty and delightfulness of the place, combining everything that is enjoyable in life – large and comfortable house, spacious and beautiful park, extensive views, dry soil, sea air, woods and rides over downs, and all the facilities of occupation and amusement. The Duke, who has so strangely become a Cabinet Minister in a Whig Government, and who is a very good sort of man and my excellent friend, appears here to advantage, exercising a magnificent hospitality, and as a sportsman, a farmer, a magistrate, and good, simple, unaffected country gentleman, with great personal influence. This is what he is fit for, to be

> With safer pride content,
> The wisest justice on the banks of Trent,

and not to assist in settling Europe and making new constitutions.'

By the next summer, Bentinck and Richmond had extended the finish even further towards The Trundle (much as it is today, but rather straighter), giving the course a potential of nearly three-and-a-half miles when raced from the finish down the straight, round the loop and back to the finish as the Goodwood Cup is now. But the King's Plate course was nearly a mile longer than today's Cup course, since the loop was very much wider and deeper than it is now. 'Very curiously formed', one anonymous jotter rightly regarded the course at about this time, 'inasmuch as in a race along the whole of it, the horses pass very nearly over the same ground twice.' But the turf, he declared, was 'little if anything inferior to the best of Newmarket', and in other respects Goodwood had a decided superiority over racing's headquarters 'save in the eyes of those of the regular Turf devotees who see in the flat, uninteresting Newmarket plains a beauty surpassing the finest feature in mountain scenery'. The extension to the straight met with much approval from *The Times*, whose correspondent's praise for the whole meeting was almost overwhelming :

'Of the management of the meeting too much cannot be said in praise, it should be held out as a model; in every respect the accommodation and amusement of the public is consulted without regard to expense and trouble, insomuch that we every year find something new to admire. Amongst others, two striking improvements ought not to be omitted; one consists in the extension of the course full half a mile beyond the judge's chair, increasing the King's Plate a distance to 3 miles 3 furlongs; the other in enclosing within a neat iron railing a large space in front of the grandstand, for the exclusive use of those who had paid for admission into the building.'

'All the alterations are improvements', was the *Sporting Magazine*'s welcome in 1833. 'The first and most striking is the removal of the Judge's chair to the opposite side of the course, now looking towards the north; on former years it stood opposite to the Grand Stand – enough to dazzle the eyes of any man, without the aid of a blazing midday sun.' That rearrangement was belated, nine years after Greville's judging error.

'The course, too, is made longer by nearly two miles, extending towards the village of Singleton . . . The horses are now made to believe they are running all the way on fresh ground for nearly four miles, though they pass the Stand twice, instead of making a double circle in a remote part of the course, almost out of sight, as heretofore.'

That was a bit of Bentinck, for sure. Starts had been made on the far, north-reaching loop of the course, of which sometimes a complete circuit was made before running down to the finishing straight. By making the loop even bigger and starting at the winning post, the grandstand customers could now have an excellent view of most of the race. *The Times* also drew the attention of its readers to one item in the race management that was, as the reporter put it, 'deserving of notice on account of its novelty':

'On the last day of the races, or sooner if required, the amount of each stakes is sealed up in a neat canvas bag, with the name and amount written on it, and handed over to the winner, who has not the trouble of hunting up clerks of the course or secretaries, or perhaps kept out of it for years as has been the case at more than one place we could name. This plan ought to be adopted at all places.'

A canvas bag may seem an odd way of presenting the winnings, but in those days bank cheques were not much in use. Entry stakes were handed over in cash by the owners on the course, and often enough in the first half of the 19th century there was nothing else to be won. The practice of added money, from sponsors or particularly from the course management, was something much encouraged and eventually insisted on by the Jockey Club under Bentinck, who was determined that racecourse owners should not continue to pocket the entire income from visitors to their stands and contribute nothing to the racing prize money. The man from *The Times* this year did not let the occasion pass without criticism. He found one serious fault, he said, though he declined to blame it on the management: the lists (programme of racing) were 'absolutely disgraceful, full of inaccuracies and omissions'. We would not hesitate today to blame the management for a faulty card, but at that time the lists of runners were published as a freelance speculation by a local printer, who could only do his best to get the necessary information from the clerk of the course as late as it was practical to do so. At Goodwood, this no doubt involved riding up to the course the previous afternoon from Chichester and delivering the lists in the morning. A fairly thankless chore, but it is worth noting that from such humble connections with Epsom Racecourse sprang the whole dynasty of Dorlings, who ruled racing there for more than a century.

8

WILY NATIVES

Chichester had existed securely enough for many centuries before the Richmonds came to Goodwood, but thereafter the family and the city grew and prospered if not exactly hand in hand, then at least with a certain amount of mutual respect. Enclosed by Roman walls and focused on the unique glories of its medieval stone-work, Chichester remains an archaeological paradise; but its heart-warming beauty lies less in those ancient edifices than in the strength and pride of its domestic architecture, street after street, alley after intriguing alley of Georgian bliss. The city had reached its peak, as Goodwood had, by the time Victoria was so suddenly summoned to the throne. The beauty of Goodwood has never faded, though its social pre-eminence has; that of Chichester, though it can be no less transient than masonry, has largely survived in the face of some appalling commercial degradations. It is still one of the greatest 18th century treasures of England. And still there is no more dramatic occasion in its calendar than Good-wood Week, when the pumpkin of Chichester becomes a porcupine. Bedrooms and bars, tables and taxis, seem eternally occupied as the citizens of the city go about their annual money-making fiesta. Judging by a magazine account of the 1830s, they used to be a shade less scrupulous about it than they are now :

'Though Chichester is a cathedral town – ergo, one of the dullest holes in Christendom – still the inhabitants are no fools, at least they are keenly alive to the value of the circulating medium, and we think we durst match them against any provincial sharks in the kingdom. When we tell our readers that they charged five shillings a night for stalls for horses, the like sum for beds (or rather apologies for beds) for grooms, we shall give them a clue whereby they may calculate what the other charges would be like.

'The past meeting gave promise of a good harvest, and the wily natives were on the alert to improve the opportunity. On the Monday afternoon both the high and low bred sportsmen began to arrive, but not in any overpowering numbers – and though not all the beds at the hotels were engaged, there were plenty of low lodgings to let at high prices in all parts of the town – we beg its pardon, city – many of which continued unoccupied up to the day previous to that on which the Cup was run for. Monday night passed over without much incident. Tuesday morning was hailed with satisfaction by many whom the fleas – and others, bad betting books – had kept on the *qui vive* throughout the night.'

The biggest inn at Chichester then was the Swan, which one correspondent thought should be renamed the Shark. It was, in appearance at least, a magnificent building, standing on the north side of East Street, quite close to the Cross – the site now occupied by the National Westminster Bank. The Market House in North Street was built on what used to be a lane that led to the Swan's back door. The inn seems to have been built at the beginning of the 18th century, and was devastated by fire 100 years later. It was rebuilt and reopened in 1819, when 600 people attended the celebratory dinner held in the brewer's cellar, the only room in the district big enough to hold them and the band of the Sussex Militia. As we have seen, it was one of the two main coaching houses of Chichester, and its trade suffered severely as the railway line crept nearer the city. In 1844 it closed as an inn and was used as shop premises by a draper, and later jointly by a house furnisher and a tailor. In 1897 it was totally destroyed by fire early one Sunday morning.

(It was a bad period for fires in the city: much of Henty's brewery at Westgate burned down in 1865, and there had been an even worse fire in East Street in 1871. This destroyed the town's leading ironmongery, and began when an assistant took a candle to help him draw half a pint of petrol. The business was owned by Mr Halsted, whose father had won the first race at Goodwood in 1801, and as well as petrol he stored on the premises gunpowder and cartridges, making fire-fighting a somewhat hazardous process.)

The Swan's relevance to Goodwood was considerable. Not only

did it house many of the middle-class visitors to the races, and usually stage the 'ordinary' during the meeting, but its front porch was the recognized centre of off-course betting in the area. When the inn closed, an official betting room was set up in the city, but proved nothing like as popular as the doorway of the Swan. The Dolphin was the Swan's leading rival (it later joined with its neighbour, the Anchor, and is still there, in the shadow of the cathedral), and in the early 19th century was probably the only other inn at which respectable Goodwood patrons would have cared to stay.

Lord and Lady Sefton were there for the 1828 meeting with their friend Thomas Creevey, and in Creevey's *Life and Times* he recalled that the bill for their three nights was £40, 'but £10 of that was for post horses, and as we brought away £700 that Bobadilla won us, it was all very well'. The Duke of Richmond, concerned that such distinguished visitors should have to slum it in the city, sent along half a buck to bolster the landlord's fare. Creevey, incidentally, found the racecourse 'the prettiest possible, just outside the Park wall, and a delightful, cheerful, commodious stand just the reverse of that at Chelmsford' – and he was talking about the 1802 stand.

Goodwood at its best is one long houseparty, and there is no doubt that those who enjoyed Goodwood most were those who did not have to find digs in the neighbouring towns. Goodwood House itself accommodated 20 or 30 guests throughout the meeting, with another dozen up at Molecomb. West Sussex is thick with noble mansions, and all their noble owners endeavoured to have their houses full of the *crème de la crème* for Goodwood Week, and most of them still do – Stansted, Up Park, West Dean, Cowdray, Petworth, Slindon, Arundel, there could have been few in the upper layer of London society who could not claim friendship under one of those great roofs. For the masses who could not, life that week was rather less desirable, as 'The Young Forester' reported in the *Sporting Magazine* in August, 1832:

'The only drawback is the uncertain and, in the majority of cases, wretched accommodation to be met with in the vicinity. Chichester, which ought, and might with a trifling share of businesslike energy, be made capable of supplying the demands of nearly all the company who visit Goodwood, is, through the imbecility of "mine hosts", unable to satisfy anything like half; and Midhurst and Petworth share with their imposing city the honour of "doing for" as many simple souls as are necessitated to place themselves in their clutches : they may well indeed exhibit the old phrase, so long the ensign of the profession of Boniface, of "Travellers taken in"! Bognor, which is really the most inviting place during race week, and delightfully situated on a fine open part of the coast, and within very moderate distance of Goodwood as the crow flies, is, by the most tortuous windings of a bad road, ingeniously spun out to more than double the number of miles that there is the smallest occasion for; and to keep pace with that, with the finest materials, the roads themselves are among the worst in England.'

Year after year some racing writers returned to the attack, determined to expose both Chichester's inadequate facilities and the extortionate prices asked for them. 'A party of us dined together after the races at the grandstand', reported 'Craven', 'where things are conducted upon a system that should shame the Shylocks of Chichester, but that Nature has kindly spared them the pain by stinting them of sense.' That was in 1836, and the following year it was no better : 'If Shylock were sent to Goodwood races, before he is an hour in Chichester they shall do him as brown as a rusk. Imagine a county town (with a cathedral in it) where dry lodging is charged at the rate of £300 a year!'

The citizens of Chichester would perhaps not like it thought that the suffering in this matter is entirely one-sided. There is no attraction in having a major racecourse on your doorstep unless you are a devoted follower of the sport – and even then what it leaves on your doorstep may tarnish your devotion. When the century turned and Goodwood had given up its absolute exclusivity in favour of making a greater appeal to the customers on the rails, the dignity of Chichester suffered, for one week a year, a severe twist in the nose. Perhaps the writer of this letter to the *Chichester Observer* was laying it on a bit in 1904, but the drift of his message is inescapable :

'Goodwood is over and all the life and bustle which for five days have characterized the little city of Chichester has terminated as quickly as it began. And Cicestrians are not sorry, for although it is but the one week in the year that money appears to come unbidden to their pockets, the inconvenience which this influx of visitors puts them to is not slight.

'Years agone, however, things were different. In the days of the "top hat" meetings, Chichester was the one great centre for the genteel portion of racegoers, now none but the lower fraternity of the great influx pass their days in Chichester. Foul-mouthed cabmen, filthy louts and lynx-eyed thieves associate together and constitute the greater part of Chichester's Race Week crowd. No self-respecting girl can cross the town after the race meeting without male escort, and even then the remarks passed by these undesirables are sometimes none the less filthy.

'Drink is their one great object, and throughout the five days the quiet, peaceful little hotels of this equally quiet little city are transformed into veritable hells. The men of the city who gather there for an evening's convivial are thrust into the corner of the bar parlour, until the bloated bullies paint the atmosphere with filth and blackguardism.

'Nor does this suffice, their grim ideas of practical jokes resulting in much discomfort to the inoffensive local. Blind supports outside of shops suffer and are bent back to such an extent as to be dangerous to the unwary pedestrians. A peaceful household too may be awakened in the small hours by a ringing of bells and a knocking of knockers, while the letter box is a favourite receptacle for all conditions of filth.

'And yet there is some talk of two Goodwood meetings a year. May God forbid.'

Goodwood has always suffered from some degree of inaccessibility, and by road alone there was, in the early 19th century, no hope of returning to London each night after racing. But the iron horse was on its way, and what a welcome it received even when the facilities it brought were not what we would call conveniently placed. 'All the difficulties that heretofore existed in reaching this delightful locality have been removed,' reported *The Times* in 1843, 'and the vicissitudes of road travelling, so frequently experienced by persons of the highest rank, altogether obviated.' Goodwood was by then within what the writer called a moderate distance of two railways (it was 22 miles to Fareham station and 23 to Shoreham, which could be reached respectively from Southampton and Brighton, each of which were connected by rail to London).

Thanks apparently to the 'active exertions of the ever-vigilant and pre-eminently successful reformer' Lord George Bentinck, a link had been arranged by road to Fareham. The proprietors of the South Western Railway at Southampton were conveying coaches and horses free from that town to Fareham, to take the racegoers on to Goodwood. This publicized fact vastly increased their business on the line from London Bridge, and early morning specials were run throughout Goodwood Week. 'Trains of immense extent were quickly filled', continued *The Times*. 'That at 11 o'clock, consisting of 36 first-class carriages with a large proportion of private drags and horses [drag : a private four-horsed vehicle, like a stage coach], was so unusually heavy that although three engines were employed, it was nearly an hour and a half behind time at Fareham.'

It took as long, and sometimes longer if the weather had been bad, to get from Fareham to Goodwood as from London to Fareham. The journey could not be done in less than three hours, nearly half of which was devoted to the long climb up from Chichester. The King of Holland's timetable, when he visited the races in 1845, was to leave London at 2 p.m. and arrive at Fareham at 4 p.m. (you could not do it any faster in 1974), but even in his lightly-filled coach he did not make Goodwood House before ten to six. In the first years of this arrangement, it was not unusual for the travellers to miss the first two or three races, which somewhat damaged their amiability. Despite those hazards, the system had the insuperable attraction of freeing racegoers from the clutches of the Chichester landlords.

Their greedy hands, indeed, were driving visitors further and further out in search of pleasant surroundings and a decent bed for a few nights. Despite the rotten road to Goodwood, Bognor had great appeal. It was still only a small village (outclassed by what have since become its suburbs of Bersted and Felpham), and was the property of Sir Richard Hotham. He was in the process of converting it from a jumble of fishermen's huts – and a noted smugglers' haunt – into an elegant watering place, which he hoped would remain genteel and exclusive. The roads and houses he built were extremely elegant, but few now remain. Bognor's commercial attraction, and the beginning of its slow death as a town of any aesthetic virtues, came ironically with the convalescence of George V at Craigweil, the success of which prompted him to award it a 'Regis'. By 1940 poor Sir Richard's hopes lay buried under the pier, an ice cream cornet staked through their heart, and with the post-war establishment there of a Butlin's holiday camp, the last nuggets of Bognor's charm were shattered.

But 100 years earlier it was a place that society was quite anxious to cultivate. It consisted, according to *The Beauties of England and Wales*, of 'several rows of elegant brick structures, but so detached that the place is at least a mile in length, erected with the professed design of making Bognor the resort of more select company than is to be found at other bathing places'. There was one hotel (the Norfolk), a chapel, a library, a warm sea bath, and a dozen bathing machines. In deference to the status of its residents, it also had a coach that left the hotel at eight each morning and called at Little Hampton and Worthing on the way to the railway station at Shoreham. Thus, by the London, Brighton and South Coast Railway, the capital could be reached from Bognor in a mere five and a half hours.

Its visitors for Goodwood Week, of course, were the sort to bring their own coaches. In view of the social position of an army officer in those days, it would not then seem at all surprising that two Guards regiments, the Coldstreams and the Royal Horse, actually took houses in Bognor for the races on behalf of their officers, and provided a coach to get them there. 'As far as I can remember,' wrote the Duke of Portland 55 years later, 'we all had a high old time.'

Reporters down for Goodwood Week no doubt found the Norfolk Hotel prices too much for their expense accounts, and favoured the hamlet and port of Little Hampton, another seaside jewel that has been sold to satisfy man's blind desire for what he calls prosperity. Visitors who laid their 19th century heads on pillows there found it convenient to take a coach to the course, stopping for a leisurely breakfast at the Water Beech inn (now the Richmond Arms hotel) just outside the gates of the park. Short of an invitation to stay at Goodwood House, that is still probably as pleasant a way as any to move up to the races, though we are not now likely to find breakfast available at noon. The railway at Shoreham, by the way, had no organized coach connection with Chichester, but it was edging nearer. It reached Drayton, a neighbouring village to the east from which the station has of course since been removed, and then nosed into the city to a halt near the canal basin. There it stayed while Chichester station was being built, and 1847 the lines from Brighton and from Portsmouth met there and accommodation worries were over.

Meanwhile, having passed his first night in 'one of the dullest holes in Christendom', that writer prepared to forget his tribulations, summoned his carriage and set off on the road for the races. He, too, would have passed the Water Beech, driving then through the park in front of the mansion on his way up the hill to the racecourse. The glimpse that he gives of the way things were arranged for the Duke and his guests seems no more real now than Cinderella's arrangements for going to the ball, and less relevant to a day's racing than to a state opening of parliament. But we are talking of an age of supreme elegance, when status was contentedly accompanied by servitude and a man like the Duke of Richmond was, in more than just fancy, monarch of all he surveyed:

'Three miles of twisting, dusty lanes brings us to the gate of Goodwood Park, which being open we drive through the grounds directly past the house, in front of which is placed a marquee, under whose friendly awning the Duke of Argyle and Colonel Udney may be seen taking shelter from the burning sun, while His Grace's bay and grey are stamping their feet under the neighbouring trees.

'At the door is a green landau with four bays, the postilions in red and white striped jackets, and the footmen in rich white and red liveries turned up with silver and turned down with yellow, while two other carriages and pair, with the coachmen and footmen in similar liveries, are waiting to convey the noble party to the stand.

'Goodwood is not a picturesque mansion, therefore we will pass on to the grounds and neighbouring country, which will vie with all England for magnificence and natural beauty.'

As he and his notebook proceed to the course, the reporter's style changes abruptly, to something like a parody of a Victorian traveller's French phrasebook: 'We have now passed Goodwood House and our horses' heads are turned towards the hill. How steep and dusty it is! Let us get out and walk and give the poor brutes a chance this sultry day! Postboy, get off and walk, and we will meet you at the top of the hill. What splendid turf this is, to be sure! Now we have reached the summit, and what a scene lays extended at our feet!'

On one of the evenings of his stay, the writer attended a Stewards' Ordinary, the traditional but now defunct dinner that accompanied most race meetings of substance. It pleased him little:

'There was an ordinary after this day's racing at the Dolphin, in Chichester, and a very ordinary affair it was. It was called the Stewards' Ordinary, we suppose upon the old principle of contrariety, because they did not dine at it. Two bedrooms knocked into one formed the banqueting room, which, from the bareness of the apartment, the quantity of the viands, and the number of guests assembled to partake thereof, would not have furnished a bad prototype to the famous Black Hole at Calcutta.

'The repast, however, was rich and rare. Turtle soup and venison in abundance, flanked by rounds of beef, saddles of mutton, and other little entrements, while the remainder of the sheep did duty in the candlesticks, in the shape of thick-wicked flaring candles, which threw a lurid light upon the dingy walls, and the greasy faces of the guests and perspiring waiters.'

Neither Sussex, nor Chichester, nor even the Duke of Richmond emerge from this experience with much credit. It seems to confirm the writer's impression that the county could not 'lay claim to much aristocracy of character, though there are many very excellent, opulent and ancient families residing within its limits'. It was customary, the writer pointed out, for one of the stewards of the racemeeting to chair the dinner, and for the others to attend it. Here they did not do so, though there were grounds at this meeting, he thought, for tradition to be changed:

'The races being in fact the Goodwood races, and the town of Chichester abundantly indebted to the promoters of them, without any extraneous tax upon their good nature, the proper thing would be either to prevail upon some gentleman of influence to act as chairman, or abolish the ordinary altogether; for as it is now arranged, or rather mis-arranged, it is calculated to produce a very erroneous impression on the mind of a stranger . . . The provender was kept cooling and the temper of the guests heating, until half past seven, when some 30 or 40 sat down without chairman or deputy, and apparently without much acquaintance of each other.'

When the chairman did arrive, he did not impress that observer of the scene, who ended his account sternly indeed. He would like, he said, to 'call the attention of the Duke of Richmond and the neighbouring gentry to the fact that upon inquiring the name of the chairman of the Stewards' Ordinary of the Goodwood races, we found it was the keeper of the saloon in Piccadilly (a very respectable man we make no doubt), but not exactly the sort of person that we should like to see presiding at the Ordinary of a great race meeting in any county with which we are connected.'

9

BENTINCK AND KENT

Goodwood proceeded through the 1830s with ever-growing glory, its race meeting yearly setting new standards in perfection. Was there ever such a reputation built on the achievements of only three days; such praise heaped on but one bat of the year's eyelid? As yet, the Duke's training establishment had not won such fame, though that was to come. John Kent the Great was still only a lad, though his father was doing well enough with 25 or 30 horses, all belonging to a handful of Richmond's friends. One of them, Rubini, won the Cup there in 1833 and so impressed Bentinck that he wanted to move all his horses to Goodwood and race them in Richmond's name, an idea that the Duke resisted.

Rubini had in fact beaten into second place Whale, a horse that was ostensibly the property of Charles Greville but actually belonged to Bentinck. In his diary, Greville did not let on: 'August 7th, 1833 – At Goodwood from Saturday se'nnight to Saturday last. Magnificent weather, numerous assemblage, tolerable racing, but I did not win the great cup, which I ought to have won, a most vile piece of ill luck, but good fortune seems to have deserted me, and the most I can do is not to lose.'

Bentinck too was remarkably depressed at this time. In September he wrote to Richmond from Welbeck: 'I have got dreadfully low in the world, all our prospects are gone to the devil. Our two-year-olds are truly execrable and I verily believe the best thing we could do would be forthwith to cut the throats of the whole lot we tried the other day. . . . I think you want a new stock as well as we.' And in the same month, from Harcourt House: 'Don't forget to take care of the Racecourse and to get an estimate of the expense of a balcony made as I proposed and let me know what was the expense of doing the new Course last year.'

Despite his temporary misfortunes, Bentinck was a rich man – probably even richer than Richmond, and it seems likely that he personally underwrote the cost of some of the improvements at Goodwood. Even at this most splendid time in the racecourse's history, the Duke, plagued by generosity and suffering from his determination to have at Goodwood the best of all possible racing worlds, was running the meetings at a loss. An analysis of his racing accounts for the 14 years from 1829 to 1843 shows that he spent the tremendous sum of £17,400 on the course; receipts from the meetings, after deducting racing costs such as subscriptions to the prize money, were £10,400.

The chief source of revenue was the sale of tickets for the stand, which over that period averaged £522 a year (for a stand that held 3,000). The management's share of the catering profit was £95, and the rent of ground for the standing of booths, carriages and horses brought together an average of just less than £200. The only decreasing segment of income was that from the carriages, which in 1830 brought £168 on their own, averaged £88 over the 14 years, and had dropped to £66 by 1843 as more and more visitors used the slowly improving public transport. All other income continued to rise, till in 1843 the stand alone brought in £878 a year.

The balcony that Bentinck suggested was added to the stand in 1837, a year in which an imminent general election and bad weather immediately before the meeting did little to spoil it. On the last day, reported *The Times*, the company was 'the largest and most fashionable ever seen on Goodwood racecourse'; the stand, 'enlarged as it is, was full of elegant females and had a very brilliant appearance'; and even 'the attendance of the lower classes was unusually large'. The balcony was built at first floor level on three sides of the stand, making a most attractive promenade outside the windows of the saloon, and a convenient haven for the patrons who preferred to be on the lawn. As *The Times* put it: 'The noble proprietor of the stand has surprised his numerous visitors by adding to it an elegant and commodious balcony which, supported on pillars, with a neat flight of steps at either end of it, is capable of holding 300 or 400 persons, and besides being a great convenience to those in the stand, affords a shelter from rain and heat to those without it.'

The previous year there had been a racing landmark at Goodwood, and again it was Bentinck who raised it. One of the most famous of the Bentinck-Greville mounts was Elis, whose dam had been foaled by the great Priam. As a two-year-old, Elis won the Molecomb Stakes in 1835 (the first four-day meeting), and in 1836 came second in the Goodwood Cup and first in two other races, an achievement that attracted a good deal of attention. Two weeks later, Elis was walked over to Lewes (walking was the only form of horse transport then known: Priam walked from Newmarket to Epsom to win the 1830 Derby, and it was rare for a horse to race in both the north and the south of the country) and won a good race there, returning to Goodwood, where Kent was training it. The racing fraternity had expected Elis to contest the St Leger at Doncaster, but when it became known that, on top of all that activity, the horse was still at Goodwood four days before the Leger, it was ruled out as a serious contender. No horse could walk 200 miles in that time and then keep up with a classic field.

In the circumstances, Bentinck was able to get 12 to 1 against the horse, far longer odds than Elis deserved. When it arrived at Doncaster fresh, lively and in peak condition, it was, said its trainer, 'to the undisguised amazement of thousands of beholders'. Bentinck the innovator, Bentinck the racecourse reformer, and not least Bentinck the better, had struck again. Elis won the Leger and Lord George won £12,000 from the bookies. But how did he do it?

He recalled that a little earlier a racehorse had travelled a short distance to a meeting in the Midlands in a bullock cart. Bentinck worked on that idea, and persuaded a puzzled and suspicious London coachbuilder to construct him what turned out to be the world's first horsebox, but which Kent said at the time was more like a movable stable. It was not unlike a tall and narrow Romany caravan, roofed and totally enclosed (apart from any other considerations, Lord George didn't want anybody on the road to know what was inside). It was very high off the ground, the full size carriage wheels being underneath and not outside the bodywork, which meant elaborate banks and ramps being constructed to get Elis and its stable-mate, Drummer Boy, inside.

The walls and even the floor were thickly padded, to lessen the chance of injury through the lurches and stumbles that were bound to accompany such a journey on those roads. Six post horses were harnessed, changed on each of the four days the trip took, and a policeman was installed to accompany Kent and the driver. The food and equipment that Elis was used to went with the horse, and at Lichfield racecourse they stopped for a gallop. It was a triumphant invention, and it transformed the potential scene for trainers from parochial to national.

Richmond's racing confederate at this time was G. W. Gratwicke, a well-known owner who won the Derby twice – in 1829 with his first horse, Frederick (which had never raced before), and in 1845 with The Merry Monarch. He shared the Goodwood training facilities until a dispute with the Duke ended the partnership after a few years. Bentinck moved in with his tremendous string in 1841. This natural culmination of their friendship and mutual success in course management would probably have happened earlier but for the fact that, according to his cousin Greville, the noble gentleman (who never married) had fallen in love with Richmond's wife. There is no confirmation of this in the Duke's available correspondence, but that is no surprise. Greville's journal lingers over the matter in 1837:

'He fell desperately in love, and addicted himself with extraordinary vivacity to the Turf. At this time and for a great many years we were most intimate friends, and I was the depository of his most secret thoughts and feelings. This passion, the only one he ever felt for any woman, betrayed him into great imprudence of manner and behaviour, so much so that I ventured to put him on his guard. I cannot now say when this occurred, it is so long ago, but I well recollect that as I was leaving Goodwood after the races I took him aside, and told him it was not possible to be blind to his sentiments, that he was exposing himself and her likewise; that all eyes were on him, all tongues ready to talk, and that it behoved him to be more guarded and reserved for her sake as well as his own. He made no reply, and I departed.

'I think I repeated the same thing to him in a letter; but whether I did or no, I received from him a very long one in which he confessed his sentiments without disguise, went at great length into his own case, declared his inability to sacrifice feeling which made the whole interest of his existence, but affirmed with the utmost solemnity that he had no reason to believe his feelings were reciprocated by her, and that not only did he not aspire to success, but that if it were in his power to obtain it (which he knew it was not), he would not purchase his own gratification at the expense of her honour and happiness.'

It could of course have been for purely racing reasons, but it may equally well be significant to their personal relationship that in 1836 Richmond asked Bentinck to remove from the Goodwood training stables those horses that Kent had been training for him there for the past two or three years. This was just at the time that Lord George wanted to increase his representation at Goodwood, and to have more horses running in Richmond's name. The Duke used his objection to that practice (strictly illegal, by the Jockey Club rules) to get Bentinck out of the stables altogether. The hiatus in their friendship, if there was one, seems soon to have been mended, and at least their voluminous correspondence went on without a break.

Lord George was an indefatigable letter writer (Kent said that in later years sometimes three arrived from him by the same post), and they were in constant communication. The vast majority of the letters were purely political (Bentinck was for many years a prominent MP, and Richmond was by then a Cabinet Minister), but now and then a racing message crept in to the packed pages. A colt that Richmond was buying from him had arrived at Bentinck's stables quite unfit to travel any further; he suggested that the Duke should not pay the agreed £150 until he had had the animal four months and was quite satisfied as to its fitness; after the 1838 meeting, a peremptory note from Bentinck of the kind that can only pass without offence between friends: 'Write forthwith to Weatherby [the Jockey Club secretary] in your capacity of Steward of Brighton Races, authorizing him to hold back the Brighton Stake until the objection taken to Lotherbourg's pedigree and identity at Goodwood is decided.'

One should not think that the Duke of Richmond was immersed in racing, particularly in the years before Bentinck persuaded him that Goodwood could become the country's finest training centre as well as its greatest racecourse. His political interests and duties were far more time-consuming, and he probably spent little time in the country outside the summer season. Too little, one of the neighbouring gentlemen clearly thought. A letter from the Reverend Hockett, rector of Petworth and Duncton:

'My Lord Duke: After much hesitation I venture to call your Grace's attention to an irregularity on the part of your servants, of which you are probably not aware, and the nature of which I humbly hope you will pardon, as arising solely from a feeling of duty on my part.

'During the time your Grace's family is in London, I am in the habit of meeting a tilted cart *on a Sunday* and *during the hours of divine service, in the morning*, passing through my two parishes of Petworth and Duncton, with your Grace's name upon it, and this has been the case for, I think, two or three years.

'My own humble opinion is that (even if religion were put out of the question) all travelling and unnecessary work on a Sunday tends much to demoralize the lower orders, and I cannot help feeling grieved at its, even in appearance, being so publicly sanctioned by a name we so highly respect and reverence. I am, my Lord Duke, with the greatest respect, your obedient and humble servant,

Hockett, Rector of Petworth and Duncton.'

All the Duke's correspondence, of which there was an almost unbelievable quantity, was written by a secretary at his dictation. The reply to the rector's humble impudence was immediate, brief, polite and devastating: 'The Duke of Richmond presents his compliments to Mr Hockett, and begs to acknowledge the receipt of his letter of the 11th instant.'

Richmond was in fact renowned for the brevity of his replies, perhaps because he had to make so many of them. He sometimes devoted as many words to a subject as Bentinck did pages. On the strength of a two-word letter that his land agent, Rusbridger, once received from him, the man made a bet with old John Kent that he could produce the shortest letter in existence. Kent accepted the bet, and won it: he drew out of his pocket a reply he had just had from the Duke. It read: 'Kent – Yes. Richmond.'

Even in the summer, racing was not all that occupied the attention at Goodwood. Cricket remained a pastime on the estate of the utmost importance, and it is clear from the account book of the Goodwood Cricket Club that some of the matches were so long that the umpires and scorers (who were paid) were obliged to stay in the locality overnight. 'Super and bed' cost the club 1s.3d. a head, with breakfast another 1s.3d. Dinner for the team was 2s.6d. a head, but umpires' dinners were 3s. Fifteen shillings covered the fees for the four officials.

From time to time both the play and the subsequent celebrations warranted the properly bucolic treatment that remains such an admirable part of village cricket life : 'Pint wine in the play, 2s.6d.' reads one entry; and elsewhere, '18 bottles wine, £4.10s.' and '36 gallons beer, £3.12s.' The band, when they played, warranted only eight ginger beers, 1s.4d. What the match was in July 1840 that entitled a Mr Edwards to this supply of 'winning liquer' is not recorded, but he and his team must have had quite an evening : '12 bottles shampane, 2 bottles brandy, 2 gin, 4 sherry plus shuger, tobacco, ribbons, cigares . . .' At the end of the season of 1841 there was a splendid dinner in the tennis court 'layed for 166 gentlemen and 120 labourers', which was presumably something a bit more special than the annual binge, though it appears in the club accounts. The menu was likely written by one of the 120 labourers : 66 sammons, 15 cupel chicken, 8 tongues, 4 hames, 1 round of beef, 2 rumps, 2 pies, 5 pieces of rold beef, 6 pigon pays, 7 targets lamb, coucombers, cheese and butter, disert.' Truly a phonetical feast.

There were of course everlasting local duties for the Duke to perform whenever he was in the area. Among the many foundation stones he laid was that at what is now the Royal West Sussex Hospital, but at the time (1826) was the West Sussex, East Hampshire and Chichester General Infirmary and Dispensary. Ten years into its life the attractions of the July race meeting were too much for one of the medical staff, and the committee of management recorded these findings on the matter : 'That the House Surgeon in absenting himself from the house during the three days of the Races, and taking with him the Senior pupil – leaving a junior pupil alone to take care of the house – who was necessarily absent at mealtimes (the Matron also being absent on leave at the same time) neglected the duties of his office in so doing, in the opinion of the majority of this Committee. The House Surgeon having justified his conduct to the Committee upon this opinion being expressed to him, renders it necessary that a minute of the above should be placed upon the books.'

The racecourse has provided the hospital with a good many customers over the years, though there have been mercifully few incidents as serious as that in 1856, when a horse went out of control near the Craven Stakes starting post and brought down six others, severely injuring three jockeys. The Duke of Richmond showed his appreciation of the hospital's prompt ministrations by presenting them, according to the odd way the *West Sussex Gazette* reported it, with £100 less £10 expenses.

By the time Bentinck moved his stable from Danebury to Goodwood in the autumn of 1841, old Kent was 60 and young Kent was 23, and was well into his father's training business. He had been sent to study chemistry with a relative at Stratford (London), but before that project was much advanced his mother died and John came home to be with his father: 'He carefully explained to me the various systems of training adopted by the different professors of that difficult art.' Young Kent and Bentinck each had a superb natural talent for the two arms of their business, and the greatest respect for each other. 'There was no doubt', wrote Kent many years after Lord George's death, 'that he saved Goodwood from going to the wall at a time when the meeting was struggling to maintain its position, and except for him there would be no tableland racecourse in Sussex for the public to climb up to next week.'

Those who had climbed there that summer again found something new on the course: a neat little stand faced the grandstand from the other side of the finishing straight, containing basically the weighing room, jockeys' room and printing room. It enabled the printers to have the result of each race in type three minutes after the decision, a service the significance of which might escape the racegoers of this age, who take for granted instant trackside broadcasts. The man from *The Times*, what's more, said the new building was 'a great ornament to the course', though from ground level it must have made it still more difficult to see any racing on the loop. But, for a change, that correspondent was not altogether happy about the meeting: it went on too long, and for the first time for many years, heats were reintroduced.

'In consequence of the extraordinary number of races, it was originally intended that they should commence each day at 12 o'clock; subsequently, however, it was decided they should start an hour later. This arrangement may probably suit those who by the adoption of fashionable usages sit down to their dinner about the time reasonable people are thinking of their pillows; but protracting the racing until late in the evening will be found generally inconvenient. The change is made still more objectionable by the introduction of heats, abominations to be tolerated only at places where it is necessary to make a little money go a great way, but quite out of character at so aristocratic a meeting as Goodwood, where the quantity of sport each day is more than sufficient to gratify the most inordinate appetite; the sooner they are abolished the better.'

The Times had spoken, and Goodwood listened. The next year all was well: the arrangements then were 'conceived in the best possible taste, and carried out with a precision and completeness that leave nothing to be desired; everything, in short, is quiet, regular, business-like, and in the highest degree enjoyable'. Nothing to be desired, at least, except the blessing of a royal visit – but then Queen Victoria was never much of a racegoer, and her son Edward, being barely one year old, was not yet in his stride. Other than that, most of the customers, or at least those in the stand, must have been satisfied:

'That Goodwood is the first meeting of the kind in the kingdom is an established fact that no one who has had the evidence of his eyes will gainsay . . . It is not from one important race, or one peculiar feature, that Goodwood derives its reputation, but by the combination of many – from the extraordinary number and value of its two- and three-year-old stakes, its magnificent cups, its handicaps, its profusion and variety of prizes, its excellent course, and the delightful scenery by which it is approached and surrounded. The company, wanting the single charm of royalty, surpasses all other meetings in rank and splendour, is generally large and always without the annoyance of a mob.'

The actual move of the equine ménage from Danebury was no small operation. Ever since his success with Elis's horsebox, Bentinck had been so convinced of the value of such transport that he would move a horse no other way. Single boxes cost about £120 to build, and doubles £150, but he had soon secured two of one and three of the other. Young Kent would rather have walked the entire mob the 106 miles from Danebury to Goodwood, over two or three days, but Lord George was having none of that. Every day for four days Kent had to leave Goodwood between four and five in the morning, collect as many horses as the vans would hold, and drive back to Goodwood, which he reached at about ten in the evening.

From that time on, Bentinck's horses were taken to meetings all over the country. Kent reckoned that in 1842 alone he travelled with them 6,155 miles at a cost of £3,600. Such activity was not only physically arduous, but wore out his wardrobe so fast that Bentinck told Kent to charge him £200 a year for wear and tear on his clothes.

Under Kent's care the horses of both the Duke and Lord George flourished as never before, and though Bentinck in particular, whose zest for racing recognized no limitations in himself or in others, was not an easy man to work for, Kent affirmed in his *Reminiscences*: 'I don't believe it ever fell to the lot of any other trainer to serve two such masters.' For the rest of Bentinck's sadly short life in racing, Kent was sometimes responsible for as many as 120 horses at Goodwood, and there was nothing that the owner did not want to know about them.

'My positive instructions', wrote Kent, 'were never to come to London without seeing Lord George, let the hour be what it might. Frequently I arrived at Harcourt House, in Cavendish Square, very early in the morning, and the hall porter would immediately call his lordship's valet to announce my advent. Without a moment's delay, Lord George would summon me to his bedside, and after I had talked to him for two hours or more, would order breakfast for me . . . On one occasion I sat with him from 2 a.m. to nearly 6 a.m., when he bade me hurry down to Willesden to inspect some yearlings before I returned home by the coach from Piccadilly at 9 a.m. His lordship never made any allowance for fatigue in himself or in others.'

As soon as his horses were settled at Goodwood, Bentinck began to apply his relentless energy to turning the stables there into the best in the land. When trainers elsewhere could not exercise their horses because of frost or snow, Goodwood remained clear. Bentinck used 100 labourers and 28 carthorses to lay the famous Halnaker Gallops, superb clearings in the woods of the Goodwood estate that with the protective help of the trees and the six inches of mould he had laid on them, were never unusable. As they were three or four miles from the stables, the whole of the track to the gallops was covered with bracken and other foliage, so there could be no accidents on the way. It cost £3,500, but it paid off many times over: wherever the meetings, at whatever time of year, the Goodwood horses were in training. 'No other place', said Kent, 'possessed such excellent training grounds at all times of the year, however variable and exceptionable the conditions might be.' Between them they began to sort things out at Goodwood, and after the meeting of 1842, Bentinck had an important suggestion to make to the Duke:

'Kent is at a dead lock for want of stable room and suggests that the two coach houses at very little expense would make four incomparable boxes. He tells me they are never wanted as coach houses except for the carriages of the company during the races. If so, I dare say you will be of the opinion that the carriages of the company could very well bear during a race week to submit to stand out in the open air and that you will agree to have them made into boxes; if you will find wood I will find labour.' But Richmond was not to be pushed around all the time. If there isn't room for all your horses, he said, you'd better get rid of some of them. And Lord George was persuaded to sell fifteen at Tattersalls.

In the same letter, Lord George made clear that he did not regard Kent's talents for stable management as by any means the equal of his skill as a trainer:

'I have another subject on which I wish to write to you; under Kent's management my men and carthorses at the outside do not do more than literally half the work they ought. I question if they do one-third; he allows two horses to work in carts that half a horse would draw and there is no method or management or energy in anything he does, he just lets the men do exactly as little as they like. I am anxious therefore to have a man of my own over from Stockbridge who understands my ways, if you have no objection and if you would allow me to furnish a couple of rooms at Molecomb or could let him hire a cottage anywhere near. I am quite sure since Kent has had the management of my carthorses, he has been losing me by waste horsepower and human power not less than a guinea a day.'

With both Kents active in the stables, it is difficult to know which one he meant. Since the indications are that the son had by then taken over the training, it may be that the old man was saddled with the less interesting chores. Bentinck, who spent as much time as possible at Goodwood, obviously remained on good terms with them both despite the criticism. When the Duke was away, Lord George slept at the Swan in Chichester, but came to the Kents for his daytime meals. In his *Racing Life* of this employer, young Kent records:

'It was impossible to witness the zest and appetite with which he invariably partook of breakfast and luncheon at my father's house after walking about on the Downs, and breathing their elastic and invigorating air, without feeling that his mind and body were at their very best. He repeatedly avowed that he never enjoyed food so much as the simple viands put before him on my father's table, and expressed a wish to know where they were obtained, so that he might procure some of the same sort and send them to Welbeck Abbey. Even the common fruits and vegetables at Goodwood he thought superior to those he tasted elsewhere.'

By the summer of 1844, only two seasons after Bentinck's arrival, the stable was enjoying an unrivalled success, with 13 winners at Goodwood alone. Richmond and Bentinck won £6,000 of the £25,000 prize money offered for the 40 races. Of the 244 starters, Bentinck fielded 49 and won the Goodwood Cup, the Goodwood Stakes, the Craven Stakes, the Anglesey Stakes, the March Stakes, the Bentinck Stakes, the Innkeepers' Plate and a £200 subscription race.

The following year the Goodwood stable had 82 wins across the country, to a value of £31,502. This may seem a trifle now, when you can win £80,000 on one race, but in those days such success was absolutely unparalleled. There can be no questioning the fact that from that day to this, no other training establishment in the country has exercised such supremacy over its rivals, which makes it all the more sad that not only is there no racing stable at Goodwood now, but that there has not been one for so long that there is nobody living to remember it. To maintain such an establishment at such a pitch, the Goodwood household no doubt had to suffer a little – particularly since the stables themselves were well within earshot of the house. But it was so clear that Bentinck loved Goodwood and loved his racing life there, that the Richmonds could not find it in their hearts to be annoyed by the clatter of dozens of stablemen and boys. Kent himself was constantly apprehensive about the nuisance caused by his young staff, but the Duchess assured him that the family enjoyed hearing the sounds, at work or play, of so happy a lot of lads.

Typically, the 1844 meeting was attended, according to *The Times* count, by one prince, two dukes, a marquess and nine earls. But, the reporter stressed, 'the accommodation and pleasures of the humbler classes were assiduously consulted.' The pleasures of trainers, however, were not regarded as of great consequence : they were shut out of the stand, and thus had no possible chance of seeing their horses run. As one critic mentioned a year or two earlier, 'perhaps Goodwood may have a shade too much of the exclusive in its colouring'. He expressed the wish that the mighty in the land would occasionally leave their seats in the stand and 'walk a little more about'. There was no harm in it, he assured them, for Goodwood had taken great pains to keep undesirables off the lawn. And in any case, 'the further you get from London, the more refinement you meet in the lower classes'. A comforting thought for those of us who have abandoned the big city.

The Duke of Richmond had his share of success that year too, winning the Queen's Plate and the Maidstone Stakes at Goodwood with his massive horse Red Deer, which then went on to Chester to win the coveted Cup there. In the $2\frac{1}{4}$ mile race, Red Deer led from the start and finished, as far as could be judged, 50 lengths ahead of the next runner. 'Upon the return of the horse to Goodwood', recalled Kent, 'the rejoicings were universal upon the road from the Fareham railway station, and when he reached Chichester the van in which the horse travelled was met by a concourse of persons displaying the yellow and scarlet colours in every form and device, from flags to rosettes and ribbons.' At the park gates, the post horses were detached and the stable lads drew the van in by hand to the stables, 'where they were met by the noble owner of the horse and a large portion of his family, who were welcomed and cheered to an extent that would vie with the rejoicings after any great victory'.

The Duke had his greatest year as an owner in 1845, winning the Oaks with Refraction and the 1,000 Guineas with Pic Nic, and in October of that year the Jockey Club honoured him by passing this resolution: 'That the unanimous thanks of the Jockey Club be rendered to his Grace the Duke of Richmond, for his Grace's indefatigable exertions and eminent services in the House of Lords, whereby many obsolete statutes which threatened destruction to the best interests of the Turf have been repealed, and the remaining laws in regard to horse racing put upon a safe and satisfactory footing.'

Some of the keenest public interest was in the repeal of an Act which prohibited any person from running more than one horse in a race, or from running any horse otherwise than in his own name. As Richmond pointed out in the Lords, his late Majesty (William IV) frequently ran three horses in one race in the name of his Master of the Horse, and so both were liable to penalty and the forfeiture of the horses.

By now even the Jockey Club, which should long since have been giving a lead to the nation's racecourses, had begun to follow the example of Goodwood in race management, and to urge those who had not already done so to note the way a meeting should be conducted. Bentinck, who was a steward of the Jockey Club, had been engaged in a bitter battle with some of its members over what became publicly known as the Thornton case. It began when

7 'The beautiful and incomparable Priam, the horse par excellence of the 19th century,' wins the 1831 Goodwood Cup.

8 Lord George Bentinck's Elis and the first horse-box ever made, by which it travelled from Goodwood to Doncaster and confounded the bookmakers by winning the 1836 St Leger.

a bookmaker named Gurney found he did not have enough money to pay his debts – largely, he said, because he was owed so much. The Jockey Club appointed 'three persons of high respectability' to try to settle his affairs for him, but some debtors (including at first Bentinck himself) refused to settle with these nominees.

One of them, Thornton, was taken to court over his debt. But the court decided that, since no ruling of the Jockey Club was legally binding, Thornton was not obliged to pay the money to anybody but Gurney. The Club felt that Thornton deserved their traditional and ultimate punishment, to be 'warned off' Newmarket Heath, which means in effect that you can no longer place a bet on any racecourse. They instructed their tenant at Newmarket to carry out the warning off, but the tenant was the Duke of Portland and, much influenced by Bentinck, his brother, he declined to do so. Racing's ruling body was in a turmoil, and Bentinck naturally looked to Richmond for support. He wrote:

'I propose calling upon you tomorrow morning at ten o'clock, if that will suit you, for the purpose of considering the course to be taken at the meeting of the Jockey Club on Saturday. It is very important that anything we do should be previously well considered, for I understand that never was half the Whip made for any Government or Opposition that has been made on this occasion by the Stewards – and I hear on all sides and have heard for some days past from people unconnected with racing that there would be far more excitement about the meeting of the Jockey Club than about the meeting of Parliament, so we must mind what we are about. I believe the Publick out of doors is with me, the members of the Jockey Club against me.'

Things did not go Bentinck's way at the meeting, and he followed it by writing to the *Morning Post* a long letter that was extremely critical of the way the affairs of the Jockey Club were being conducted. The next day he wrote again to the Duke:

My dear Richmond: The thing is done, I sent my protest to the *Morning Post* last night and I have no doubt it is in type by this time. Whatever I might have been disposed to do under other circumstances the blackguard conduct of Rous and George Anson in making the comments they did upon Thornton and all those who appealed to Courts of Law (which they well knew applied equally to, if not meant for, me) after the conciliatory tone I had taken towards them would utterly prevent my sparing them and those who asked with them in any way.

E

In regard to the Jockey Club, if it proceeds in the course in which it has of late been proceeding, the sooner for the sake of the Turf it is abolished the better. There is no good in such an assembly, in fact it is an absolute nuisance.

This is the third time that Rous by deciding matters in his own favour in which he had a pecuniary claim has raised a general war amongst the members of the Jockey Club. His vicious example instead of being avoided has been imitated – where then do you gather your hope that by submitting to these proceedings of the Jockey Club you will obtain any reform in their general conduct?

Yours ever most sincerely,

G. Bentinck

The meeting of 1845 is generally held to have been the absolute zenith of Goodwood's existence. 'With magnificent scenery, first-rate racing, and the cream of England's best society to inspirit and gratify him,' wrote one anonymous journalist, 'a stranger would indeed be fastidious who did not consider the Goodwood course the perfection and paradise of racegrounds.' Though the people kept coming, and the profits from the meeting kept rising, nothing was ever quite the same again. *The Times* reported huge crowds the next summer, 'but neither the racing, the betting, nor the company were quite up to par'.

Early in 1846 Bentinck made his sensational decision to give up racing and devote himself to politics. It was clear that he had become far more involved in the business of the House, and he wrote to Richmond on 25th July to tell him that he could not get down to Goodwood until the first morning of the meeting, and that he would have to leave for London as soon as the races were over that afternoon. He caught the 7 a.m. express, reaching Drayton station at 10 ('I believe there will be a great many others doing the same thing. Will you send some sort of conveyance to meet us and bring us to breakfast?'). He was back again on the third day, and stayed at Goodwood House that night, when without warning he exploded his racing blockbuster in front of Richmond's guests. In his fragmentary portrayal of the best-known personalities of the Turf in the 19th century, T. H. Bird rewrites John Kent's faithful record of the occasion with this more dramatic account:

'It was Lord George's custom in those days to drink four glasses of wine at dinner and no more – he never smoked – and to doze afterwards, but slumber never so mastered him that he would not come to attention if anyone in the room mentioned a bet or a match. On the evening of the third day's racing, he appeared to be half asleep, when he suddenly roused himself, rose, looked at the men in the room and said: "Will anyone give me £10,000 for all my lot, beginning with Bay Middleton and ending with little Kitchener [his jockey], and take over their engagements?" '

When they had recovered, the absurdity of the price soon hit the company, and George Payne was the first to take up the challenge. He offered to pay a £300 forfeit if he did not complete the deal by noon the next day, and after talking to him for a long time, Bentinck went to bed. Payne's first move in the morning was to ask John Kent to leave Goodwood with Bentinck's stud and train them for him at Michelgrove, outside Worthing. Kent declined, after consulting the Richmonds, and Payne paid the forfeit. That afternoon Bentinck's horses won the Nassau Stakes, the March Stakes, and the Bentinck Stakes, but his mind was made up. He was waiting only for £10,000 and the certainty that his racing commitments would be honoured. The next morning *Bell's Life* prematurely reported Bentinck's retirement, incorrectly assuming that the deal with Payne had been clinched:

'We cannot help expressing our regret at the circumstance, for although his Lordship may have his peculiarities, which to some may be unpopular, there never was a nobleman whose persevering zeal affected so much in the way of the correction of abuses, or whose exertions were productive of such great and important reforms in the racing community.'

Three weeks later, Lord George wrote the last of his racing letters to Richmond:

'I have been so busy and overworked of late, the House of Commons sitting in the morning and continuing sitting till ten or twelve o'clock at night, I have not even had time to write to tell you that Mostyn has bought my entire stud, vans, carts, cart-horses, etc. I imagine he will reduce them to a very low ebb, but from what Lloyd tells me he seems not unlikely to wish as regards a considerable portion of his stud, to wish to be your confederate in my stead; if he should, I trust in God for the sake of the Kents and all the people, but more especially for the sake of Goodwood races that you will encourage such an arrangement as soon as possible.

'I cannot help thinking Mostyn is a man after your own heart – a plain frank honest goodhumoured country gentleman, a sportsman and a farmer, and though not a Protectionist from Party, not much otherwise in opinion.'

Edward Lloyd Mostyn, who later inherited a barony, had bought lock, stock and barrel what was incomparably the finest racing stable and stud in England. It was a transaction without precedent in the history of racing, and should there have been any doubt that Bentinck was more nearly giving away than selling his 208 thoroughbreds, it was soon removed. The running costs of the stable had been £11,000 a year, and Mostyn was not in a position to stand that. He wanted to put the whole lot up for sale at a gigantic auction at Goodwood, and buy in those horses that he intended to keep. Knowing how the Duke would object to that happening on the estate, Kent dissuaded Mostyn from both that action, and his first alternative – to walk the whole lot up to Tattersalls for the sale. Instead he disposed of 30 of the least valuable of the lot at Hyde Park Corner for 3,195 guineas, got £7,000 for another bunch at Tattersalls, and refused £12,000 for five others.

It is impossible, said Kent, that anyone could ever have cared less for money than Lord George did. As Disraeli wrote of Bentinck in his political biography : 'Lord George valued the acquisition of money on the Turf because there it was the test of success. He counted his thousands after a great race as a victorious general counts his cannon and his prisoners.' The £10,000 was neither here nor there; like a man selling his pet dog, he was looking for a good home for 40 yearlings, 45 foals, 70 brood mares, three sires and 50 racehorses in training.

In fact Mostyn did not keep any of them for long. In 1847 he sold what there was left to Lord Clifden, and this included what Kent always regarded as one of the most sensational horses of the century, Surplice. It was the greatest, and perhaps the only real, disappointment of Bentinck's illustrious racing life that he never won the Derby; it was no consolation at all that in 1848 this beautiful mount should win both the Derby and the St Leger – nor even that it was trained to the end by John Kent, and should rest before the Derby in Bentinck's own stables at Headley, on Epsom Downs.

It was while consoling Bentinck over Surplice's Derby win that Disraeli coined the immortal phrase 'the blue riband of the turf'. Perhaps it was not altogether irrelevant that it was a week after the Leger triumph that, while he was walking near his country home at Welbeck, Lord George's heart should fail. He dropped dead alone in the fields, where his body was found by a servant searching for him in the middle of the night.

With Bentinck's retirement, the magic mysteriously departed from Goodwood. Coinciding as it did with the slow decline of Richmond's health and energy, it was more than the course could bear. The interest of the Press fell away appreciably, the annual eulogies ceased to appear, and the same man who in 1845 had written of 'the perfection and paradise of racegrounds' was four years later remarking somewhat patronizingly that 'Goodwood has lost little of its attraction', though at the same time reporting late running of races and a below average attendance despite excellent weather and the improved railway service.

'The effect of Lord George Bentinck's retirement on future meetings here', wrote the man from *The Times* in 1846, 'must be great, for, independent of the immense number of nominations taken by him for every stake, it must be admitted on all hands that the unequalled character of the sport, and the perfection of arrangement attained in every department, to say nothing of the many admirable regulations that have been established and are now become "the law of the land", must be attributed to his Lordship's almost unassisted exertions'.

10

GONE TO THE DOGS

Admiral the Hon. Henry Rous, later to become senior steward of the Jockey Club, once scribbled a line across the top of a letter to the Duke of Richmond. Referring to one of the Admiral's well-known horses, it read: 'Oxygen is lame, but you don't care a —— about racing.' That was not at any time true, but the Duke probably did not care quite enough about racing to keep the business going at the standard that Lord George had set for it. Nothing more conclusively illustrates what Lord George Bentinck meant to Goodwood than the way the value of the stakes rose during the period of his influence, and dropped after his death. In approximate terms, the total stake money was £4,000 in 1832, £10,000 in 1839, £18,000 in 1841, and £24,000 in 1844. By the end of the decade they were back to £13,000. With his going, Goodwood by no means collapsed, but for some time to come it ran on only three legs.

The mechanics of the business were by then well enough organized to turn on without disruption. The grandstand income nudged up and up, from £1,647 in 1845 to £2,132 in 1849 and John Rusbridger, who acted as the Duke's racecourse manager, kept careful note of everything in his leather bound memo book, heavily marked 'Private'. Payments to the local police, for instance: in 1848, one superintendent was hired at £1.1s. a day, two inspectors at 15s., one sergeant at 10s., and 11 constables for

£10.15s. the meeting. Also an extra payment of £1.3s. for 'Conveyance for prisoners and constables and the young man that was knocked down by order of His Grace the Duke of Richmond'. The previous year, he noted with exemplary attention to detail, 'there was 10s. per day paid for watering the roads and which was not the case this year'.

In his little book Rusbridger also wrote down the complex details of where each race was run, which with Goodwood's straights and bends and intersecting loops was even more difficult to remember than it is now. The King's Plate course: 'The horses start on the Charlton Down to the north west of the stand, run over the east of the clump, go to the outside circle of the hill, and return to the east of the clump, about 3 miles and 5 furlongs.' For the Cup Course, 'horses run out to the west of the clump and return to the east, 2 miles and three-quarters', but to achieve the $2\frac{1}{4}$ miles for the Drawing Room Stakes, it was just 'once round to the west of the clump'. Also in his book, the letting of the booths, which were given a surprising amount of space considering they brought in less than £100 a year – a 240-yard frontage, with a depth of 55 feet. But no doubt they contributed considerably to the 'accommodation and pleasures of the humbler classes'.

In March 1854, after nearly forty years as an owner, Richmond dissolved the Goodwood stable. He sold his horses in training at Tattersalls, and all the brood mares to the French breeder, M. Lupin. This gesture was received with less than delight by the English breeding fraternity, but the Duke's friendly intentions towards a country with which Britain had recently been at war was foreshadowed as far back as 1840, when his most distinguished guests at the meeting had been the Duke and Duchess of Nemours. *The Times* approved of their presence: 'Among the British people but one feeling prevails, that of a generous and honest friendship. Glad shall we be to find that the portal thus opened will not again be closed, but that a friendly competition between the two nations will be encouraged by an allowance of weight for French bred horses.'

In his 70th year, 1860, Richmond was so afflicted with gout that he could not greet his racing guests on their arrival at Goodwood House, but was wheeled out on to the lawn to receive them when they returned after the day's racing. Immediately after the meeting he was taken on the long journey to Gordon Castle, where it was thought the air would ease his suffering. Soon after his return to London in the autumn, the Duke died – not in fact from gout, according to the *Dictionary of National Biography*, but from dropsy.

John Kent had been promised that as long as the Duke lived, he would keep horses and Kent would be in work, and there is no reason to suppose that word was broken. Though Kent does not refer to it in his book, he was no doubt kept on the Goodwood staff during the six years between the Duke's abandonment of the racing stables and his death. But even when that sad day came, Kent was only 42 and should have been in his prime as a trainer. It is tragic that so talented a man should have been lost to racing so early, and he himself must surely have regretted the day he turned down the offer (for £500 a year more than he was paid at Goodwood) to go to George Payne with Bentinck's former string. At the time, all he needed to decline the job was the reassurance of the Richmonds that they wanted him to stay, and it is interesting to note that the job was given to the Duchess:

'Immediately upon leaving Mr Payne, to whom I respectfully refused to bind myself, one way or the other, until the evening of the next day, I was ushered into the Duchess's boudoir, where I found her Grace, accompanied by two or three younger members of her family. I shall never forget the scene. Her Grace's kindness and sympathetic nature were well known to all her friends and dependants, and of these inestimable qualities I had already received from her a thousand proofs. When, therefore, she enquired with unrepressed emotion, "John, is it true that you are about to leave us and to train for Mr Payne?", I felt as if I was going to break down completely, and it was with no little difficulty that I could find voice to reply, "Your Grace, it appears that Lord George has offered Mr Payne his stud at a ridiculously low figure, and has recommended me to Mr Payne as better able to train and manage them than anyone else. I have already told Mr Payne, however, that I can enter into no arrangement with him until I have ascertained the pleasure of his Grace."

' "John", rejoined her Grace, "if you leave Goodwood, there will be an end to the delight and pride which we have all taken in the horses. As long as his Grace lives, he will always keep horses, and so long there will be a comfortable home for you." Without a moment's hesitation I answered, "If it be his Grace's wish and your own that I should continue at Goodwood, I will not leave it until you wish me to do so".'

Kent the elder outlived the fifth Duke by nine years (though he was born long before the third Duke built the racecourse), but at the Duke's death he was 78 and off the payroll. Since they first came to Goodwood, the Kents had been living in a cottage that was part of the old kennels, and now John had to find both a job and a home. The Richmonds allowed him a life pension of £1 a week, which in all the circumstances does not seem over-generous, but he remained embarrassingly grateful for the rest of his days.

He decided to try farming, a rash move for a man with no experience of practical agriculture. It was not a great success. He took first a 500-acre farm nearby, Outerwhyke, and later Hoe Farm, in the pretty hamlet of Flansham. Both were more than he could cope with, and in 1889 the Portland family heard of the dreadfully neglected state into which, through sickness and poverty, John Kent had fallen – he was then 71. There is no doubt that Lord George Bentinck would have made ample provision for Kent's retirement had he not himself been cut off in the prime of his life, before he had given much thought to such gloomy matters. It is to the credit of the then Duke of Portland that, more than 40 years after Kent stopped training for Bentinck, he should have felt it his duty to look after the old man.

Portland settled on him a more substantial pension, and provided for him the house in Felpham in which he lived for the rest of his life. Viscountess Ossington, sister of Lord George, was particularly generous and concerned, and it was she who erected a memorial stone in the local churchyard to Kent's only son, who had died two years earlier.

Secure and fit again, Kent played an active part in local life. He worked as Highways Surveyor of Felpham (still not then appended civically to Bognor) until he was 76, sat on the management committee of the Infirmary at Chichester for 21 years, canvassed for Lord Henry Lennox in his election campaign at Chichester, and was a churchwarden at both Whyke and Felpham. He was nearly 80 when his book was published, a painstaking if pedantic record of all he had learned about the Richmonds at Goodwood, on every page of which his respect and affectionate admiration was printed. As the *Daily Telegraph* put it in his obituary (the length of which confirmed the prestige he had won in the racing world), 'he talked and wrote after the manner of a medieval retainer'.

In the closing years of his life, still a marvellous-looking old Victorian, with magnificent mutton-chop sideboards and a bowler hat, he wrote a succession of letters to the Hon. W. F. J. Dundas, the Duke of Richmond's manager at Goodwood, which are almost tearful in their gratitude for the favours the family continued to show him. The handwriting, shaky at the best of times, grows more and more uncontrolled, until, at the end, the most dedicated examination can now produce only the vaguest idea of his intentions. His £1 allowance was paid direct to his bank at Bognor by the Duke's solicitors (Raper, Freeland and Tyacke, whose successors still occupy the same offices in West Street, Chichester), and in May 1901 Kent learned of the illness of the principal:

'I am sorry Sir Robert Raper's health and strength fails him so much, like myself. I fear it is the effects of over-agitation in earlier days. I am sorry to say I have been confined to my room, almost to my chair, for more than two years after a severe attack of apoplexy. I cannot say how grateful I feel for His Grace's thought and kindness to me. I hope and trust His Grace is tolerably well ...

'I am sir, with much respect and humble gratitude, I am your most obedient and humble servant,

John Kent.'

Kent's wife died in September 1903, only a few days before the death of the sixth Duke. On 10th October he wrote again to Dundas:

'I have no doubt but that I received a ticket for admission to the cathedral for the funeral service of the late Duke of Richmond and Gordon, for which I am obliged and so regret I was unable to attend. I do so regret I did not send a wreath as the last respectful duty of an old and trusty faithful servant ...'

A week later there is a marked deterioration in the handwriting, and there appears to be no purpose in the letter but to release his feelings about the family in their loss:

'I fear I have intruded upon you with my letters at this unfortunate time as you must be fully occupied. I do feel so much for poor Lady Caroline. Her Ladyship must feel the loss of the noble Duke so much. I feel it most acutely, few persons more so, I can hardly realize it.

'I saw the present Duke when he was only four days old, in bed with his mother. The late Duke sent me to see him. I sent him a birthday present for many years after. I was at all times treated as one of the family. I do hope sir you will pardon me thus addressing you, but I feel so attached to that noble family.

'I am sir with every respect your obedient and humble servant.'

Another fortnight, another letter, and now even where the words are legible they do not always hang sensibly together:

'I find you sir and His Grace have renewed the annuity the late Duke granted me. I cannot say, sir, how deeply thankful and grateful for so kind and consideration of an old and I trust faithful servant. I really sir cannot find words to express my humble gratitude for all the kindness I have received from the same quarter, which I can never forget, the noble family is most dear to me . . .'

There was one more, in which few words can be read. Written on 28th December, 1903, it is a letter of thanks for a brace of pheasants sent to the old man for Christmas. The following July he died at what the *Daily Telegraph* called 'his little cottage home' at Felpham, and if he was still living at Bentinck House, that is a diminutive way of describing it. He was 85, and his death came, reasonably enough, on the eve of the birth of the new Goodwood, the opening of the present grandstand that took the meeting into the 20th century. Only the previous week, he had offered to contribute to the *Daily Telegraph* a series of articles of his recollections of the racecourse, and in its obituary the paper noted that his mental activity was undiminished.

'It is difficult for modern folk to realize the tenderness and sentimental earnestness of the Turf patriarch whose life has peacefully ebbed away . . . An ancient man, curiously full of modern sympathies, he seemed to be a relic of a far off and almost incomprehensible age.' He was indeed. He had come to Goodwood before the Industrial Revolution, before railways, bicycles and electric light. He even came before Queen Victoria, and outlived her.

The Lady Caroline in John Kent's letter was not the sixth Duke's widow, but his mother, whom Kent knew far better. 'The present Duke', whom he had seen in bed at four days, was the eldest son of the six children of the sixth Duke and Lady Frances, niece of Charles Greville. (The feud between Greville and Bentinck was pursued an unconscionable time. At the Goodwood meeting of 1842, seven years after its origin, the Jockey Club steward Colonel Anson tried to bring the two men together, but at the last moment Bentinck walked away.)

The sixth Duke was born in 1818, the same year as Kent, and seems to have been the first of the Richmonds to complete a formal education: Westminster (like the third Duke), Oxford, and the Army. At 21 he joined the Royal Horse Guards Blue, and

was a lieutenant when he was elected Member of Parliament two
years later. He was a serious politician, like his father, and held
the seat until succeeding to the dukedom in 1860. Subsequently
he held Cabinet posts under Disraeli and Lord Salisbury, leading
the Tories in the House of Lords. The Gordon-Lennox representation in the House of Commons in the second half of the 19th
century was phenomenal, possibly unique. All four of the surviv-
ing sons of the fifth Duke (who had himself sat for Chichester)
were Members: the first son for West Sussex, the third for
Chichester (he too became a Cabinet Minister), the fourth for
Shoreham, and the fifth for Lymington – and all at the same time.
(The second son was lost at sea at the age of 21.) The Parliamentary habit died out after that, and the only other MP in the Richmond family was Walter, fourth son of the sixth Duke, who sat
for Chichester for six years. Another of the fifth Duke's grandsons,
Cosmo Gordon-Lennox, achieved in 1898 greater public fame than
many of his political kin by becoming the first husband of the
celebrated actress, Marie Tempest.

In the way that did not seem at all odd at the time, the sixth
Duke combined a quite extraordinary number of jobs and posts.
Aide-de-camp to Field Marshal the Duke of Wellington, and later
to Viscount Hardinge, he became a county magistrate, chairman
of the West Sussex County Council and of the Westhampnett
Board of Guardians; as well as being for some time Secretary of
State for Scotland, he was Lord Lieutenant of Banffshire, Chancel-
lor of the University of Aberdeen, Vice-President of the Committee of the Council of Education, and for ten years President of
the Poor Law Board. His grandmother had inherited the vast
Gordon estates in Scotland in 1836, and his public positions show
the great interest this Duke had in that country, where in 40 years
he spent £200,000 on farm buildings. His father, on inheriting the
Gordon estates on the death of the Dowager Duchess, had changed
the family name from Lennox to Gordon-Lennox, and in 1876 the
extinct dukedom of Gordon was revived by Queen Victoria in
favour of the Richmond family. The Dukes have since been
known as 'of Richmond and Gordon', though the other original
dukedom, of Lennox, is seldom mentioned.

His Scottish interest did not detract the sixth Duke from
developing the Goodwood estate. Indeed he improved his home to
a greater extent than any Richmond since the third, building more
than 400 cottages for his labourers, most of which are still
occupied today. Such an action must have been regarded by most

mighty landowners as philanthropic madness, coming at a time when more care was customarily taken of the pigs on the farm than of the swineherds, the four-legged animals being of greater commercial value. This was exactly the time when the staple dish of the agricultural labourer was tea-kettle broth (hot water poured over bread and dripping), and meat was only eaten once a week; when the sort of home provided by most farmers for their workers was a two-roomed hovel with neither floor nor ceiling; and when the lowest social class was as far removed from the highest as a pea from a pyramid. Goodwood's life and reputation still depended on a comfortable gulf being maintained through which the peasant could not pass, but in matters of human relationships as well as of racecourse management, the Richmonds seem to have set an admirable standard.

This Duke also added here and there to Goodwood House, though it would seem that his taste was outstripped by his ambition, as his extensions were not subsequently thought worthy of survival. Most surprising of all was his determination to keep pace with technological advance: he built a reservoir behind Carné's Seat, a water-pumping station by the old kennels, and a private gasworks to heat and light Goodwood House. Though he was not responsible for any significant advance in the glories of Goodwood racecourse, there was no doubt that the sixth Duke had inherited the family equestrian skills and its deep interest in the Turf. At 21 he owned a filly called Guava, with interesting parentage: sired by The Colonel, George IV's Derby dead-heater, out of Gulnare, who won the Oaks for the fifth Duke. The Young Earl rode her to win the March Stakes at Goodwood in 1839, and at the 1842 meeting rode five winners, four of them on the final day which amateur jockeys for so long had almost to themselves.

Kent notes firmly that 'he disapproved, as his father did, of excessive betting', but he became a member of the Jockey Club in 1838, at the age of 20, and in due course was elected a steward. One of the most memorable days of all the Goodwood meetings of his time was the first day in 1870. The Stewards Cup was run in the usual Goodwood conditions of the time, hot and dusty, but almost immediately it was over there was a sensational change in the weather. 'A most violent thunderstorm followed,' recalled Thomas Willis in *Records of Chichester*, 'the violence of which appeared to be of serious aspect. Peal after peal of thunder shook the earth, and the lightning in vivid forked flashes succeeded each other, lighting up the surrounding country in awful sublimity.

The beauty of the scenery around Goodwood could never, we imagine, have been better seen than at this moment, when the war of the elements added grandeur to its usual loveliness.' A deluge of rain then fell, through which the remaining races of the day were run, and the return home from the course was accomplished in the midst of what a printing error rather charmingly calls 'drenchin grain'.

Though this part of Sussex is blessed with extraordinarily fair weather, there have throughout the ages been occasional storms of quite frightening severity. The spire of Chichester cathedral was struck by lightning in 1720, and the top forty feet destroyed. The next spire collapsed in a fearful gale in 1861. This must have been a tragic but magnificently dramatic incident, as the spire simply disappeared, falling perpendicularly into the body of the building.

'We could see the spire from our dining room window,' recalled Mr O. N. Wyatt in 1914, 'and one of us looking up from dinner said, "Where is the spire?" It was nowhere to be seen, we only heard a rumble like a cartload of bricks being shot down in the street.' George Tippen, a tinsmith, didn't see it go despite all his watching: 'While the work of strengthening the old spire was being carried out, it was reported to be positively dangerous and likely to fall. On the 21st February, 1861, as a terrific gale sprang up, I sat at my shop door for an hour and a half watching. I left my seat for two minutes only, when a man came rushing by, calling out, "It's down". I ran to the front and looked, and the spire was no longer to be seen. Fortunately there were no accidents, as the men had gone to their dinner.'

The Duke of Richmond laid the foundation stone of the new spire in 1865, and the weathercock was installed in 1868. Shortly after completion, the architect (Gilbert Scott) added one of the new-fangled American lightning conductors, a large part of which was destroyed when lightning struck again in 1883. But we must go back up the hill: this Duke's son played a more vital part in the racecourse development than his father, for although the new stand was certainly conceived in the sixth Duke's time, he was by then a very old man and is unlikely to have taken much responsibility for it. He died in Gordon Castle at the age of 87 (most ancient, so far, of all the Richmonds), shortly before the great works at the racecourse began.

There is no question for what the sixth Duke is remembered in terms of outdoor activity: it was he who revived the Goodwood pack and replaced the Charlton Hunt, which had been given up by the fourth Duke at the beginning of the century, with the Goodwood Hunt – though, even in this, a more prominent part seems to have been taken by the Earl of March, who became Master of the new pack. New kennels were built in the winter of 1882–3 by 130 workmen engaged by a firm of builders from Belgravia : the superb establishment built by the third Duke in 1787 for his pack having since been put to other uses. It became the home of the Kents during the fifth Duke's time, and as the race meeting expanded and more and more police were needed, the roof was raised on jacks to provide sufficient space for two attic dormitories where 70 or 80 members of the Metropolitan Police were laid like pilchards. The building was now enlarged and adapted to provide homes for the four senior members of the hunt staff – the huntsman, first whip, stud groom and kennelman. The new kennels (now a house) were modelled on those built by Lord Leconfield at Petworth : 'While there has been no attempt at architectural display,' reported the *West Sussex Gazette*, 'there has evidently been no expense spared to perfect the arrangements.'

A bundle of old expense vouchers gives us some idea of the range of that expense. There are receipts from Waller, the London builder, for £5,250; one from John Earwicker, a local builder, for work at the stables, £395; bricks bought from Alfred Cheeseman of Bosham, 1,600 white ones for £5.4s. and 50,000 hard faced bricks for £112.10s. Hounds came from all over the place : 25 couple from Frank Gillard at Grantham, £131.5s. Twenty-seven dogs were carried by the Great Northern Railway from Richmond (Yorkshire) to London for £6.15s. and on from Victoria to Chichester for £3.16s.8d. by the London, Brighton and South Coast Railway. 'A pack of hounds in four horse boxes' came by London and South Western Railway from Salisbury to Chichester at £6.14s.

Since the end of the Charlton Hunt, the stables had been devoted to racing. Now a collection of hunters had to be gathered again : Chorister from Lewes for £150, one hunter from Reading, £89.5s.; six horses for £788; seven horses for 770 guineas. There were chests of drawers to buy, 16 chairs, ten mattresses, four yards of cocoa matting, two dozen towels, three pairs of blankets. And of course, from Kohler and Son of Westminster (Martial Musical Instrument Makers to the Army), four copper hunting horns and cases, £3.14s.

They were first blown at 11.30 on the morning of Monday, 5th

November, 1883, and according to the local reporter, 'all the countryside seemed to have turned out for the occasion, noble and simple, pedestrians and equestrians, ladies and gentlemen, the old the young.' During the summer the *West Sussex Gazette* had informed its readers : 'The gentlemen of the hunt will be expected to appear in blue coats, as was customary when the hounds were formerly located at Goodwood. The huntsman and whips will be attired in the old Lennox hunting livery, consisting of yellow coat, with scarlet collar and cuffs, and they will be seen out in this uniform on the Race Course next week, replacing Lord Leconfield's huntsmen, who have for so many years assisted to clear the course at Goodwood.'

When it came to it, the colour of the occasion was enhanced by the scarlet habit of the followers of the Petworth hounds. 'What Derby Day is to the Londoner,' wrote the reporter, 'the first meet of the Goodwood fox-hounds upon this occasion was to the folk of Western Sussex.' The Duke had assembled 34 horses and 55 couple of hounds under George Champion, renowned huntsman of the Southdown Hounds, who had been acquired for Goodwood. But they were by no means the extent of those present; 'Every animal that could go on four legs was in requisition.' The attendance was so vast that Valdoe Coppice, where they met, was almost engulfed. The first fox could find no way through and was immediately trapped by the pack, and the second could offer no better a chase, being cornered in the timber yard behind the house. A local historian takes up the story :

'Although these two short runs did not afford much sport for the old fox hunters who were well mounted, it was a most enjoyable day for the novices, and enabled many to proclaim they were "in at the death", which proud position they never enjoyed before nor have probably since.

'The noble master, having offered so much sport for the general public, trotted off with the pack to Boxgrove Common to try and afford good sport for the habitual sportsman. Unfortunately this effort failed for some little time, as not only was Boxgrove Common a blank, but Bines Furze and Slindon Common also. At last Dale Park contained the object sought for, and after a tolerably good run, another fox was run into upon the lawn in front of Dale Park House, only about 25 sportsmen being in at the death. Thus terminated the ever-memorable day of the re-establishment of the Goodwood or, as it was anciently written, the Charlton Hunt.'

It had taken the Earl of March almost a year to complete the groundwork for the re-establishment of hunting at Goodwood. Before any arrangements were made to build new kennels or buy hounds, every major landowner in West Sussex was told by letter of the Duke's intentions, and permission sought to take the Hunt on to their property. The replies amply confirmed the local paper's summary that the news was received with 'general expressions of delight in the district'. There were dozens of them, from Sir G. Hornby at Portsmouth and Miss Featherstonhaugh at Up Park to Lady Lamerton at Woolbeding, J. Haywood Johnstone at Bignor and Sir Periston Milbanke at Eartham. Though there were one or two responses of neutral acceptance, most of them appeared ecstatically pleased to think that the Goodwood colours would once more be roaring over their land. Since the dissolution of the Charlton Hunt, the Goodwood territory had been hunted by Lord Leconfield from Petworth, who had no option but to agree to give up his rights there. But there was one area of dispute, and it took the arbitration and adjudication of the Masters of Fox Hounds Association to settle it, more than a year later.

A clue appears in the correspondence. Amid the welcomes, one writer notes that he understands the Duke's intention: it comes from Walter Long, Master of the Hambledon Fox Hounds. Hambledon, the 'cradle of cricket' (with apologies to Slindon), lies about six miles over the Hampshire border, midway between Fareham and Petersfield. Well within West Sussex, but exactly halfway between Hambledon and Goodwood, is the fine estate of Stansted Park, whose owner had already said he would welcome the return of the Goodwood hunters to his land. March maintained strongly that Stansted was traditional Goodwood country, but Long said that since Hambledon had hunted it for the past 80 years, it must be regarded as neutral. In all that time, during which Lord Leconfield had had the run of West Sussex, he had let Hambledon hunt two large coverts at Stansted, Lordington Wood and Watergate Hanger, which in his letter March told Long he wished to take back.

The two Masters could not agree on where the boundary should lie between their territories, and neither was disposed to give way. The obvious suggestion that the county boundary should be theirs was not acceptable, as that boundary passed through several coverts and would therefore have made them neutral – an unsatisfactory arrangement, since neither Hunt could plan its action, not knowing where the other might be. On and on the arguing went, both sides intransigent, and settlement was not in sight when the hunting season opened in November.

In July 1884 their cases were heard by the Association, and it was as good as a High Court trial. Counsel were briefed, the evidence and history printed in fullest detail. It seemed to the adjudicators that the dispute hinged on the nature of the permission given by Lord Leconfield to the Hambledon Hunt in regard to the area in question: had Leconfield abdicated his rights at Stansted, in which case Hambledon could after all that time reasonably feel the country was theirs, or had he only said they could hunt there for the time being? Whichever it was – and Leconfield had apparently volunteered in 1871 to call Stansted neutral – March said he had no right to do so, since Leconfield himself was only there by permission of the Duke of Richmond.

The fact that all the parties involved in that permission were long since dead did not ease the resolution of the matter. Long was producing old men who distinctly remembered their fathers telling them this, and March was quite sure that his great-great-grandfather had said that. Leconfield was summoned to Tattersalls for the grand inquisition, and though again it was a question of what his grandfather had done, the Masters decided that the Goodwood Hunt could no longer regard Stansted as their exclusive province. When it was all over, reason returned to banish the obstinacy of the participants, and Long offered several coverts to March for the next season, making the boundary between them not the county mark, but the railway line from Rowlands Castle to Petersfield – which is what March had suggested 18 months earlier. Goodwood were now settled on their country: they were bounded on the east by the River Arun, from Littlehampton to Pulborough, and on the north by its tributary, the Rother, which runs close by the road from Pulborough through Midhurst to Petersfield. On the west came that convenient railway line, and on the south, the sea. It was an area of at least 300 square miles – in most corners of which a piece of the Goodwood estate could be found.

Even with such space, the details had to be right. Hunting gentlemen seldom view with sympathy those who do not co-operate with them, and on the Earl of Egmont's Cowdray estate at Midhurst there was a tenant who was traditionally unhelpful: he preferred to shoot the foxes rather than let them be hunted down by dogs. Leconfield had written about it to Egmont in past years: 'These woodlands supply with foxes the only good bit of grass below the hill that exist in my country, and very good sport we used to have in it, but since your shooting tenant has been there the foxes have almost disappeared from it.'

Egmont, who was a game-shooting rather than a hunting man, replied guardedly. The presence of foxes was obviously not conducive to the breeding of birds, and this was a diplomatic battle between noble gentlemen who were anxious that the wild creatures of the countryside should be allowed to grow up long enough for them to provide some element of sporting competition while they were being killed.

'I can assure your Lordship,' Egmont had replied, 'I will do what I can to show sport to hunting men, but I do not think it sport to find nine foxes in our woods in one day . . .

'Some time back I asked [the former] Lord Leconfield to let me the shooting of a fir plantation of about six acres adjoining your Lordship's woods, as our birds would draw there as we have so few trees. We could not have it as it was let to the Duke of Richmond. In my application, I said if we had that we could preserve both foxes and pheasants. In consequence of the ifs, I am afraid we have the credit of killing all the foxes.'

A year later, in 1880, the correspondence was on again. Leconfield asked Egmont to allow him, or one of his friends, to become the tenant of that land: 'As Mr Hollis only preserves pheasants, poultry and rabbits for the market, he is never likely to allow a fox to live, in fact my best country is destroyed by him. My reason for asking is that if the same destruction is to continue, I must reduce the number of my hunting dogs and dispose of some of my horses and hounds.'

Though Egmont undertook not to let that property again without mentioning it to Leconfield, the lease did not expire until 1883. By then it was March who was interested, and he took up the battle: 'You have a tenant of the name of Hollis who has the shooting of the Maloes etc. I believe he is a yearly tenant and I am sorry to say that foxes do not thrive under his keeper. The worst of it is that not only are the foxes on that particular beat affected, but a strange fox wandering there suffers equally, and consequently a large portion of the woodlands on the downs, as well as those below the hill, are denuded of foxes. Am I asking too much of you if I ask you to let me have the refusal of the lease before it is renewed to your present tenant? . . . My father having given me the management of the hunting I am writing in the interests of a good many besides myself.'

By the final decade of the century, landowners of Richmond's size were feeling a hefty pinch, and towards the close of the 1895 season, Richmond and March announced that the Goodwood Hunt was closing down. Among the many letters of regret they received was this one from the Duke of Norfolk at Arundel Castle:

'I was very sorry to get your letter telling me you did not see your way to keeping on the hounds. I cannot pretend I am surprised. When I got your letter I had just had my lawyer urging upon me the necessity of "drastic reductions" in my expenditure, and I almost wished I had a pack of hounds to cut adrift . . . I seem to have dropped out of hunting altogether, but I am none the less grieved you are going to give up. What is to be the end of it all for all of us is a depressing consideration.'

The most explicit explanation of Richmond's troubles at Goodwood came in the *Banffshire Journal*, which circulated in the area of his Gordon estates:

'From the time of its establishment, the Duke has maintained the pack at his own expense. He cannot do so any longer, not from any want of will, but simply because of the enormous shrinkage in the value of his estate, in common with other landed property all over the country. An effort to keep up the kennels by subscription fell through, simply because many of those who enjoy the benefits and privileges of hunting want to get their sport for nothing. The dissolution of the Goodwood pack is not a good sign of the times . . . It is sad to think that the ancient traditions and customs of the country should be sacrificed, but so long as we continue to pander to votes and refuse to make our interests and our trade our first consideration, we shall never regain our lost position or make any headway.'

On 10th May, 1895 the Goodwood pack was sold at Tattersalls, the bitches for £630 and the dogs for £279.6s. Much of the stable also became redundant, and 25 hunters fetched £1,500, and their saddlery another £250. Three weeks earlier, on 13th April, the last meet had been held, widely covered by the national Press. *The Field* recalled the gay cavalcade of 200 horsemen who had attended the opening meet 12 years earlier: 'What changes! What a different England we now exist with! Was this event portentous? Was it the precursor of that universal bankruptcy which appears to overshadow agriculturists and all who obtain their living from the land? Alas! we fear it may be so.'

There was a strong east wind under a clear sky as the 70 horsemen assembled at Goodwood. Under those conditions, March did not expect much scent raised until the late afternoon, and the Hunt did not move away until after midday. One fox was killed almost immediately, before they raised one which led them a memorable dance. It ran to Boxgrove Priory, Woodcote, Aldingbourne, Boxgrove and Tangmere (about seven miles), 'where the quick eye of the noble Master discerned the sleek coat of Master Reynard glistening in the afternoon sun as he reclined at his ease in a furrow. I shall never forget the angelic smile on the face of Fred White, the excellent first whip. He evidently thought it most amiable of the fox to have located himself just where he did.

'Such a scurry ensued as has seldom been seen in that locality, for reynard betook himself to the road, where the going was easy, and was followed by the whole hunt pell mell. We have heard of a fox having a dusting, but we doubt whether one was seen so completely dusted before.'

The West Sussex roads were evidently not yet blessed with Macadam's attention. Just the same, the fox was too good for them, and went to ground in an Aldingbourne farm. They then pursued another one around what later became Tangmere airfield and on to Oldbury Farm at East Hampnett. There they found a 'yawning ditch, full of water and big enough to engulf a waggon and horses'. In the high back of this ditch reynard had ensconced himself as a last resort, but he was ultimately extracted and broken up. Thus ended the last run of the famous Goodwood Hounds.

'Then there was a long pause,' concluded Scrutator's account in *The Field*, 'and someone said, in a hushed voice, "This is the funeral". Everyone seemed reluctant to move from the spot; but five was the hour, and at length, slowly and sadly, by twos and by threes, the members of the Hunt melted from the sad field.'

11

A COMMODIOUS STAND

The man who took Goodwood into the 20th century, in every sense except the actual, was the seventh Duke. The qualification is only necessary because the title was not his until 1903, by which time his father was 85 and he 58. The 25 years that he spent at the head of the family took Goodwood through the First World War and into the age of the motor car, and he seems to have been exactly the right man for the job. He certainly began rather well, with that extraordinarily attractive new grandstand, the contract for which was signed in December 1903, shortly after the sixth Duke's death. 'A jolly Edwardian building', wrote Nairn and Pevsner, 'like an enlarged Oxford college barge.'

We have already seen that the new Duke had been an amateur rider of some talent, and he served three three-year terms as a steward of the Jockey Club. When he was elected for the third time, succeeding the renowned Prince Soltykoff, the *Racing World* celebrated the occasion by recalling Lord March's record of service to the Turf. Included was one of the most mysterious paragraphs ever to be set in print: 'The prominent part which his Lordship took in that which, though now belonging to past history, will not readily be forgotten, is too well known to require more pointed allusion.' At the time, no doubt, somebody knew what that was all about. This was in 1892, and rather surprisingly in view of later events, the paper also had this to say about March:

'Although the race course in itself does not seem to appeal to his sympathies greatly in a proprietary sense, yet his interest in the Turf as an institution and in its maintenance as far as is possible as a model one, is sufficient proof of his breadth of view.'

The writer believed that his lordship drew the line at pigeon shooting and stag hunting, but was adept at most other branches of sport. 'The grouse, the salmon and the deer know him well', and he once spent ten months in a log cabin on the North American prairies shooting grizzly bear, bison and other fearsome beasts. He was the first of the Richmonds to go to Eton, after which he had a private tutor and joined the army (every Richmond did until the ninth). This one was a Grenadier Guard, but he sold his commission when he was a captain and moved into a lieutenant-colonelcy in the part-time army, the Sussex militia, which he commanded for a quarter of a century, serving with them in the Boer War.

He was married twice, to Amy Ricardo and to Isabel Craven, one of the Earl of Craven's family, but both died young and the Duke was a widower for 40 years. He also lost one son in the 1914–18 war, and a grandson in 1919 from wounds received in Russia. As Earl of March he was a Conservative MP for West Sussex from 1869 to 1885, and for South-West Sussex for three years after that. He was perhaps the only Richmond so far to have been an expert farmer, earning by his notable care in breeding Southdown sheep the position of president of the Royal Agricultural Society in 1916. (His father had been proud of the flock too, and used to parade them in front of Goodwood House every morning before the races.)

A small hint of the changing nature of his age comes from the incidental items in the family account books of the 20 years that spanned the two centuries – a mixture of Victorian charm and Edwardian activity. But for those of us with an inquisitive and fanciful nature, there is always something extraordinarily intriguing about other people's expenses. Even when there are no mysteries concealed in their careful columns (and why, would you not like to know, did the Richmonds at Goodwood have so often to repair the post office bicycle?), even then the humdrum entries of such a family have an enchanting ring. The harness maker at Fochabers, the portmanteau maker, the bicycle engineer at Chichester, the repairer of the tricycle; 5s.0d. for the bird stuffer, £1.4s.9d. for Debrett's works, 4s.0d. for the beef tea man – there is something about such debts that would make them a pleasure to pay.

Gordon Castle is just outside Fochabers, way up in the north of Scotland. A journey there was some project: Robertson and Jessie, fare to Fochabers, £5.12s.8d; travelling expenses of household, Goodwood to Gordon Castle, £90.8s.9d. That was when the Goodwood season was over. Then there was carpet beating at Gordon Castle and £4.4s.od. for sleeping there during the absence of the family.

There were huge and ceaseless amounts paid to two fly proprietors at Chichester, Morgan and Hutchings, but never an entry after 1896; McCarthy, the carter of Halnaker, was kept busy too, and Enticknapp the chimney sweep. The Richmonds were regular patrons of a London cheesemonger, and of dressmakers in all parts, and as you would expect from a family who built their own gasworks, they were soon in touch with the marvels of modern science: a photographer was hired in 1887, and in 1906 they paid 3s.7d. for the telephone service.

Golf got a grip on the sixth Duke's offspring: as well as repair of golf clubs for Lady Helen, there was £1.6s.od. for golf tools from London, and £1.2s.6d. for the Tooting golf club maker (Tooting?). Very soon after those entries, in 1900, golf came to Goodwood in a big way. The Chichester Golf Club, which had existed for some time with nothing more elaborate than a nine-hole course at North Mundham, moved up to Goodwood Park at the invitation of the Duke (perhaps his family were bored with the four-mile journey to Mundham), where a short 18-hole course was laid and maintained by estate employees.

By 1911 the club members (whose captain was then Lord Bernard Gordon-Lennox, a brother of the seventh Duke) was ready for something more elaborate, and James Braid was called in to reconstruct the course. It cost the club, which was by then the Goodwood Golf Club, £1,500 and the work was not completed until Spring 1914. By the end of the year the War Agricultural Committee required the local farmer to cultivate two of the holes, which were replaced. Since then there has been a certain amount of alteration and adaptation, but basically it remains the course that Braid laid – 6,033 yards in 1900, 6,110 in 1975.

Like the racecourse, it is rare and beautiful. Not a championship course in terms of professional craft and cunning, but a prize-winner for the startling variety of its terrain and the sheer romance of the situation. Some holes are superbly sliced out of

the forest in Target Bottom, some climb up the open acres of
Lavant Down and even through the ancient escarpments of The
Trundle. From the seventh tee you get that shattering view, from
the Isle of Wight nigh to Littlehampton; three of the greens
cluster maddeningly together on a ridge; and one short hole, the
fifteenth, is as testing and twice as enchanting as any of its length
that you might meet.

There are some among the ageing members who are not too
keen on the hills – either on tramping the four miles from hole to
hole, or on the uncomfortable, tip-tilted lies with which they are
often presented. They may find comfort at the clubhouse, Wyatt's
stunning flint kennels, from the windows of which, over the
eighteenth green, you see the gentle switchbacks of Goodwood
zipping on and up, through a gap in the trees, to the back of the
big house. The same outlook that the hounds had in 1787, and the
Kents 50 years later.

But forget golf, and come back up the hill where we were.
Edward Moorhouse visited Goodwood while he was preparing his
book, *The Racing Year 1903*. It is quite clear from his comments,
if there were any doubt from anybody else's, that Goodwood's
racing prestige had by then lost a great deal of its gloss : some of
the paltry races, he wrote with undisguised contempt, were not
worthy of the magnificent frame in which they were set.

'Goodwood is nowadays mainly dependent on the importance
which attaches to it as an event in the social calendar. The programme of sport it has to offer cannot, regarded as a whole,
advantageously be compared with that associated with Ascot,
though in other respects the two meetings have a good deal in
common. It may be that before very long a reformer will appear,
one who, possessed of a proper appreciation of the change that
has come over racing in recent years, will remodel the famous
Sussex fixture, repel much of the dross that now cumbers the
ground, and replace it by material of a more "toney" character.
The spirit of improvement is already hovering over the place. The
old grand stand has disappeared; in its stead a modern and vastly
more convenient structure is rising, and will be ready for the next
meeting. The zeal for effecting improvements will not, we may
be sure, exhaust itself in this effort.'

Moorhouse was prepared to concede that, despite its short-
comings, Goodwood was Goodwood. 'It has no rival, and is never
likely to have one . . . There is an atmosphere of gaiety and
irresponsibility which one does not associate with any other

meeting to quite the same extent.' But that faint praise must have been small compensation to the new Duke, as he contemplated the problem of restoring the pride of the Goodwood race meeting.

It was of course a great help that he was starting with a new grandstand. Such a huge and impressive innovation always draws the customers – and if it did not, Richmond was in trouble. The estimated cost was £27,900 (plus £346.10s. for pulling down the old one), but in the end he had to spend nearly £37,000. The builder was more or less local: Walter Wallis of Balham (telephone number, 56, Balham), who had a branch in Littlehampton. The architect was Arthur Henderson of Esher, who had designed the grandstand at Sandown Park (demolished in 1972), that the old Duke greatly admired. He was on five per cent of the total cost, plus the expenses of his 51 visits to the site, which cost him £2,130. The hammers began swinging on 7th December, 1903, with the daunting penalty clause for Mr Wallis that if he did not complete by 31st May, he would lose £250 a week.

Presumably he had to pay up. On 4th May the *Chichester Observer and West Sussex Recorder* noted that in order to get the stand absolutely finished in time for the next meeting, 'unusual energy will have to be displayed by the builder'. At the end of May the best the paper could say of progress was that the stand 'is beginning to assume something of a business-like aspect, and the vast strides which have been made by the builders during the past week or two lead one to suppose that, after all, the operations will be completed in good time for the July meeting.

'So far advanced are the operations that it is now possible to form some idea of what the gigantic structure will be like when completed. More than four times the length of the old stand, and stretching from the lawn to the boundary of the paddock, the new stand will have many advantages in addition to the enormous increase in accommodation which will be afforded.'

As well as the main stand, a Press stand was built at its west end, and a subway that ran under the whole of the front of the stand, 'which will enable those ladies on the lawn to reach the paddock, and at the same time avoid the crowd which is always to be seen in front of the stand'. There was also, of course, a royal pavilion attached – we are now with the redoubtable Edward VII, the most determined of racegoers, who as an owner had already twice won the Derby – and here all did not prove absolutely well.

It was good enough for the King, but alas! not for the Queen, that lovely lady of fastidious determination.

With the Prince of Wales (later George V) and his wife, then known as Princess Victoria, the King and Queen arrived on the evening before the meeting opened. They were staying at Goodwood House where the hospitality was not exactly spartan, but nevertheless 'numerous dainties for the table' were sent down from Windsor, and also 'a few articles of furniture from Buckingham Palace, as being necessary for the Queen'. The standard of attention to the royal needs in the stand can be judged by the very fancy work in the toilet division of the King's Pavilion. The King had a lavatory in statuary marble with his monogram, a double-thickness mahogany seat, and a marble frieze and skirting. All the metal work was silver-plated, including the door hinges and the flushing handle. Goodwood might be going popular, but it did not intend to ignore the niceties of life.

There was a 'Hers' too, but it only appears on the work sheet as 'extra lavatory for Her Majesty', and there may lie the rub. The following March architect Henderson was back again to superintend 'the erection of a new pavilion by the lawn at the Grand Stand, Goodwood Park', and another firm of London builders was engaged to make 'sundry alterations and additions to the race stands'. The local paper noted the following year that 'The royal box at Goodwood has been moved to meet the wishes of the Queen, and it now overlooks the wood, where the picnics under the trees make a pretty sight'. The rebuilding of the royal quarters on the east end of the stand cost another £4,500, and even then Queen Alexandra was not quite satisfied. In March 1906 the builders were back again to attend to a few details, the area of which is made quite clear on their specification – which this time is headed 'Queen's Pavilion':

'Enclose forecourt and steps to subway; ventilate Queen's WC, drain etc.; enlarge window at end of Queen's private room; electro plated towel rail; mahogany moulded shelf and mirror; No. 1 French polished paper box. All, £275.'

By the time everything was done and Henderson had taken his fee, another £6,400 had been added to the original cost. The detailed costing which Wallis supplied at the end of his part of the job included payment for 33,541 hours of labouring at 7½d. an hour (£1,048), 118 fares from London, 468 weeks' lodging at 4s. a week, and 15 fares from Littlehampton. He also bought two dozen shovels and two dozen pecks (not synonymous with pick, but a tool shaped like a hoe), and paid £6.6s.9d. for sharpening them. The construction of the subway cost £1,182, and there was £1,603 for remetalling the roads that had been broken up by the heavy transport in the area, for which there were 'A large number of navvies specially engaged, entailing their railway fares, return travelling and lodging money'.

It had been a bonanza year for anybody in the neighbourhood who owned large carts and horses, or even more advanced forms of transport, as material for the stand and for a new road was brought up from the gravel and flint pits. As is still so often and charmingly the case in rural areas, specialists were thin on the ground but jacks of all trades abounded. James Earwicker of Boxgrove, whose father had enlarged the stables when the Goodwood Hunt was formed 20 years earlier, was hired to build stables at the stand, for £120. His account headed 'James Earwicker, Builder, Wheelwright and Undertaker; Painter, Paperhanger and Wood Turner', showed that he also supplied 114 'pannels of fencing' for £18.10s.6d., cleared and fenced the new selling ring, and repaired 'the old stables in the trees' for £85.10s.; and that he supplied 1,542 tons of broken flints for £188.14s.

From East Dean Farm, James Mackenzie brought 125 tons of flints for the racecourse roads (£369); 1,650 tons of gravel were carried to the course from the Summersdale Pits (£336) by J. D. Foster of Emsworth, 'Shell-fish merchant, ship builder-owner (sailing and steam), sailmaker, timber merchant, steam saw mills, general engineer and smith'. A large part of the haulage work seems to have been done by Mrs John Sparks of Yapton (Proprietress of Steam Thrashing and Ploughing Machines), who charged £635 for 'digging and hauling stones from the estate pit to Goodwood' through June and July 1904, and a further £93.12s. for hire of four steamrollers in July.

James Penfold, of the Tortington Iron Works, near Arundel, was also in that line of business, as well as being an iron and brass founder and an agricultural implement maker. He charged £96.4s. for the hire of three steamrollers and for carting gravel. Thomas Field, of Pound Farm, Chichester ('dealer in horses, job master, hire carter') was also on the gravel run through July and was used 'to cart ambulance from paddock to station'. The Duke had obviously decided to provide a new ambulance with his grandstand, as Henry Farr ('agent for Globe Parcels Express Co. for delivering of parcels and luggage to all parts of the kingdom') brought another ambulance up to the course. The fire engine was brought up to scratch with spare parts from Merryweather & Son, of Greenwich; Stevens and Sons of Southwark supplied the new number board and stand (£239).

There had been a good deal of bother about the new road behind the grandstand. You may recall that racing had originally taken place on the level turf beside the Harroways, and that when the third Duke had actually formed the racecourse and built the stand in 1802 he had moved the road back a bit to give himself room. With the very much larger stand and ancillary buildings that the seventh Duke was building, the road needed moving again: but by then the local authorities were rather more concerned with what went on up the hill at Goodwood than they had been in the old days.

The Duke believed that Harroways was a private road – it was gated at one end, and he repaired it – but his solicitor was not so sure. On the Tithe map, said Sir Robert Raper to Dundas, it was marked as a public highway: 'That is, one to which the public have access without let or hindrance whether it is repaired by a private owner or not.'

'I have no doubt,' he went on, 'it was originally a public road and went straight up the course, and I think the probability is that when it was diverted in order to make the course and build the race stand, the then Duke of Richmond from that date agreed to keep it in repair from The Trundle to Counter's Gate, but this is mere conjecture.

'I should not like to advise His Grace that he could safely carry out the proposed alterations to the extent shown to me on the plan which you produced – I think it quite possible that someone or other may raise an objection.'

It was therefore necessary, he advised, to apply to the local magistrates to have the highway diverted at Richmond's expense, and the result of such an application could not be anticipated:

'We must always remember that there are one or two Puritans on the Bench who would possibly like to abolish the Races altogether, if they could; this is rather a treasonable remark, so I hope you will not let anyone see it, except His Grace. Unfortunately it is purely a matter of chance as to what Magistrate may be on the bench when the application is made.'

In the end, all was resolved satisfactorily in time for the 1904 meeting, which with the new stand and the royal family was much the most spectacular ever seen. Unfortunately the required period of mourning for the sixth Duke was not yet over, so

Richmond could not entertain as lavishly as usual at Goodwood House. However, with the stand there was a new caterer's kitchen and the Duke made sure that the new caterer used it properly. His agreement with V. Benoist Ltd, for the meeting gave the firm, for the consideration of £250, the exclusive right 'to sell all things eatable drinkable and smokable (hereinafter called "Refreshments") at the Grandstand Paddock and Private Inclosures'. The provisions were to include 'fish poultry meat vegetables salads sweets pastry cakes cheese wines and spirituous liquors beer ale porter water aerated water coffee cocoa and tea with such accompaniments as are usually served therewith'.

They were to be provided 'in such quantities as shall be amply sufficient for the requirement of those persons who shall attend', and must be 'of the finest qualities and brands only of their several and respective kinds'. The caterer was also to provide two marquees, which the Duke would erect and furnish, and 'a good and sufficient supply of competent waiters so as to afford a proper attendance on the persons requiring refreshments'.

Even the prices were agreed in the contract, and revealed a strange differential in the cost of lunch to the plebs outside and the patricians within the sacred enclosures. Luncheon in the paddock was to be 2s.6d., in the private members' tent 7s.6d., in the large public tent 10s.6d., and in the open under the trees 12s.6d. Champagne was between 12s. and 14s. a bottle, or 1s. a glass. Chablis was 4s. a bottle, sherry 6s., and 6d. would bring a glass of sherry, brandy, gin or whisky. Bass was 9d. a bottle, cigars from 6d. to 2s.6d. and cigarettes 9d. or 1s. a box.

After the meeting Dundas had a letter from Lord Manners at Belvoir Castle, Grantham. 'I noticed you had Benoist to do the catering at Goodwood,' he said. 'May I say that I do not think he can do that sort of work as well as Gunters, of which I have the pleasure of being chairman. He is all right as a cook – but as a caterer I venture to suggest he leaves a good deal to be desired.' Nevertheless Benoist held the contract for four years, after which it was awarded not to the somewhat impertinent Lord Manners, but to Bertram and Company – for £400 a year. The letter from Benoist acknowledging their rejection was in the circumstances a miracle of respect:

'We beg to thank you for your honoured favour of the 13th instant and deeply regret that His Grace should have arrived at the decision which you have kindly intimated to us. We beg to thank you for the many courtesies we have received at your hands during the three years we had the honour of catering for the Goodwood meetings.'

The city, as well as the racecourse, was honoured by the royal presence in that summer of 1904. The King agreed to pass through the centre of Chichester when he left Goodwood after the meeting, and catch the train there instead of at the nearer station of Drayton. The preparations in the city for this phenomenal occurrence were almost unbelievable, and despite the fact that the royal carriage stopped at the Market Cross for only three minutes, to receive a loyal address, the *Chichester Observer* managed to make no less than six and a half columns of the occasion.

'It is over', the writer opened, still shaking with emotion. 'The King and Queen have passed through our city . . . We are so happy, so proud.' The mayor handed over his address, and though the King's reply was as short as conscience could possibly allow it, he handed that over too (to be read after his departure by the Town Clerk), and uttered what would now be considered the most perfunctory civilities before moving down South Street to the station, where the Duke of Richmond was waiting to see him off. It was a gesture and no more, but it sent the citizens of Chichester into ecstasies and guaranteed their devotion to the throne for life.

In 1905 the King and Queen came again to Goodwood, but not to Chichester, and the local *Observer* clearly had its fashion correspondent at Drayton Station to record the arrival. 'King Edward, attired in a grey lounge suit with a light grey bowler hat, looked remarkably well, and, as usual, was very genial. Queen Alexandra, too, wearing a lovely dove coloured coat, a toque trimmed in white and grey ostrich feathers, and a white stole, looked radiantly beautiful.'

There were some more changes on the course that summer. 'While fully recognizing the advantages of the increased accommodation,' said the *Chichester Observer*, 'many growls are expressed at the increased charges for the same.' The lawn and paddock, for which the charge used to be 35s. for the four days, was up to £5; the correspondent noted, what was more, that only one race started to time on the first day, and there were many long delays; also that there were more roughs, toughs and cardsharpers than he had ever seen before.

Though he does not mention it, there must too have been more cars than had been driven to a meeting before – and every year more and more and more. There were certainly enough, even if they could be counted in dozens, to make it worth while for a man from Twickenham to bid £105 for the use of a two-acre site at the top of the hill, on which he had the right to charge for horse, carriage and motor parking, and to supply petrol and carry out repairs. This was the first time such ground had been auctioned, rather than leased at a fixed rent (the ground for booths by the course was dealt with the same way), and the success of the operation convinced the management they had been too generous in the past.

Despite the doubts expressed by Edward Moorhouse two years earlier, it seemed that the popularity as well as the economic potential of Goodwood was rising again. Things may not have been quite what they used to be for the topmost classes, but there would continue to be a good turnout even in that department as long as there was a chance of getting close to the King on the members' lawn. The Duke of Richmond was back to one of his top level house parties, including this time Count Albert Mensdorff-Pouilly-Dietrichstein, which was bad news for the major domo. The *Daily Mail* reported that year:

'There were not wanting prophets of evil who predicted a financial disaster for the Duke of Richmond when he set up with lavish expenditure the great, barren new stand on the breezy heights of the South Downs, but events have justified the enterprise, and Goodwood has established itself more firmly than ever in the graces of the racing public.' It was certainly taking enough money on the course for Dundas to request an armed police guard when they took the cash down to the bank at Chichester. He was given two policemen, unarmed, but the superintendent at Chichester said he would have no objection if Goodwood's own man were to be armed!

As the century turned another of the joys of contemporary life was becoming more active: the Press. Not just the old faithfuls like *The Times* and the *Sporting Magazine*, but newspapers from all parts, and some of them strange ones, were applying for passes to the Goodwood meeting, and it was up to Mr Dundas to decide which applications to reject. In 1898 (the year that the only gentlemen allowed to park in the private drive, other than the family, were the Duke of Westminster and Leopold de Rothschild) Dundas issued passes to *The American Register*, *The Globe*, *Land and Water*, *Paris Sport*, and the *Licensed Victuallers Gazette*, but he turned down *Little London's Pleasure Guide*. There were also complimentary tickets for the Inland Revenue officer and the Surveyor of Taxes, but perhaps he had no option there.

9 Perhaps the most extraordinary pictorial record of a race meeting ever painted: the Lawn at Goodwood, 1896, with 66 of Britain's élite positively identifiable. The focal group shows the Prince of Wales and his eldest son, Prince Albert Victor, Duke of Clarence (who died before his father), with the Countess of Kildare and the Duchess of Montrose. On their right, the seventh Duke of Richmond helps Lady Leveson Gower up a bank. Below the Prince's left elbow, stage celebrities include Adelina Patti, Gilbert and Sullivan, and (around the 'In' sign) Forbes Robertson, Squire Bancroft, Madge and William Kendal.

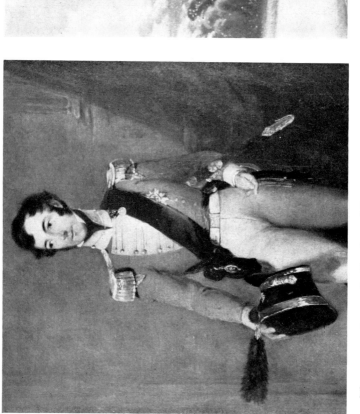

10 The man who made Goodwood Racecourse glorious, the fifth Duke: 'The perfection of honour, honesty and integrity'.

11 The ninth Duke, who as Freddie March raced cars rather than horses, later established the Goodwood motor circuit.

The next year both the *Leeds Express* and the *Leeds Daily News* got in, but *The Topical Times* and, strangely, *The Stable* did not. In 1900 the local papers were swelling: in came the *Birmingham Post, Sheffield Telegraph, Chichester Observer, Northampton Herald* and the *Irish Field*; the *Catholic Herald* and the *Railway Magazine* stayed out. The *Daily Express* first appeared on the list in 1901, with *The Queen, Madame,* and *Sportwelt*; a year later, the *Daily Mail, Yorkshire Post, Westminster Gazette* and *Daily Sport,* one of the early casualties in Fleet Street. *The People* was on the scene in 1903 and the *Daily Mirror* in 1904, but among the rejections in 1906 were the *Estates Gazette* and *The Jockey*, which looks like a case of the old Goodwood snob system raising its ugly head again. That, finally, was the year in which a man arrived at the gate with some bulky equipment and a note addressed to the managing director. It came from the Palace Theatre, Shaftesbury Avenue, and read simply: 'His Grace the Duke of Richmond has very kindly given us permission to take Bioscope pictures of the Goodwood Races, and the bearer of this is our operator.'

It was unfortunate for the Bioscope operator that the Queen was not at Goodwood that year, so most of the gentlemen in the stand rather daringly sported straw hats. The Duke himself kept formally to what was then known as a grey billycock, which later came to be called a bowler (the style was said to have been designed by a hatter called Bowler for a client called William Coke). Worn with a lounge suit, even *The Times* agreed that it was probably the most suitable garb for a racecourse. King Edward remained adamant that there should be no lowering of sartorial standards when the royal flush was in hand, though when the whole family turned out for the 1909 meeting (the King's last), they were greeted by a downpour and all the top hats sheltered under umbrellas.

The Times nevertheless managed its statutory one column a day on the clothes at Goodwood, devoting itself in times of rain to a detailed dissertation on the waterproof capes to be seen. Unfortunately there was not at that time much distinction about the costumes men wore, otherwise the fashion correspondent would surely have found something to say about the incredible Lord Lonsdale. Regardless of the trend for smelly motor cars, he continued to arrive at the course in a superb carriage and four, with his postilions dressed, as ever, in bright yellow livery.

This was the year that Raufe Hussey-Freke, who had taken over from Dundas, discovered (after the meeting) that the course

F

for the Stewards Cup measured 25 feet too long on the outside berth, due to the simple fact that the start and finish lines were at right angles to the inside curve of the course. By the time they reached the far side of the track, they were well behind at the start and well ahead at the finish. Goodwood Cup day somewhat unaccountably remained the high spot of the festivities, though the race itself no longer attracted much talent. 'The race for the trophy is supposed to be a special event, as on occasions it has been', remarked *The Times* rather grumpily; 'this year it seems likely that four or five horses at most will run, and they are such indifferent animals that it is impossible to feel interested in them.'

The racing world had changed: a long race was by then something like the Derby, a mile and a half. Few trainers were interested in nags that plodded more than two and a half miles, when most of the prize money lay in breeding good sprinters. That was an early sign of the 20th century sporting malaise, expressed in the dense and relentless cry, 'Get on with it!'

Edward VII's share of life ended early the next year, and hardly a soul on the course regretted his winning the Sussex Stakes – which had become and have remained the chief prize of the meeting – with Minoru, which had earlier that year narrowly won the Derby. The jockey on both occasions was the royal favourite, Herbert Jones, who in 1913 was riding George V's Anmer when it was pulled down by a suffragette at Tattenham Corner. Throughout his adult life, the King had supported racing with considerable enthusiasm, and by that example had caused many other wealthy men to do the same at a time when the prevailing puritanism of Victorian life threatened to turn society against the sport. At his death, one racing journalist wrote of 'the Herculean pillar lost to our manly pastime, against which, if I am not mistaken, the irons will be heated again to burn holes in its structure and existence'.

12

TWO WARS

There used to be two racecourses in this country where attendance was positively obligatory to those whose lives were geared to being seen in the right place at the right time, and when Goodwood began to slip from the pinnacle of its 19th century supremacy, it was probably most accurately reflected in the Duchess of Doomsday's decision that it was safe to give it a miss that year. Ascot it was never safe to miss, but it is remarkable, in view of the ease of access to the Berkshire course for the London set, that Goodwood not only challenged but for many years eclipsed it. When you think that Ascot was established for nearly a century before there was a meeting at Goodwood at all, it is almost unbelievable that within thirty years the quality of racing on this rural patch had by so far outstripped that at any other course in the country. But if Goodwood was a professional masterpiece, it was a social miracle. It was, after all, about as accessible to London in 1830 as the Isle of Skye is today. A trip to Goodwood meant packing a trunk and suffering a most diabolical journey on filthy roads. And yet they came, and came again.

Indeed, if Edward Moorhouse is to be believed, they went on coming despite the paltry quality of some of the racing (perhaps because to them it was irrelevant). If you remember, he stressed in 1903 that Goodwood was then dependent on its social rather than its equine attraction. The sport, he said, 'cannot advantageously be compared with that associated with Ascot' – and at that time, that was the regular and frequent tenor of comparison. Racing at Goodwood, somebody else wrote, 'in no small measure corresponds with that at Ascot, though the latter is on a higher level'. Socially and aesthetically, comparison between the two was drawn just as frequently, though one would have thought that it did not require a particularly sensitive acumen to discover a basic difference between them : Ascot is a society parade, and Goodwood a society picnic. Or as, with another emphasis, *The Times* put it, one might as well try to compare a delicate etching with a massive piece of sculpture. The men from *The Times* are in touch with the scene, and their explanation of it sixty years ago is almost as relevant today :

'The great whirlpool of the city, which three months ago sucked everything and everybody to itself, and has kept them whizzing round and round in its vortex, has somehow lost its velocity. Now it is as if the coils had begun to unwind; the springs work with a reverse motion; the thrust of the current has become centrifugal and out we go, mere jetsam, flung first to Goodwood, then Cowes, then out into the far still waters of the Scottish moors . . . To all the gaiety of town, Goodwood puts a fitting close, a fashionable event with a dash of rusticity; a sort of trial flight into the country, such as the swallows practise before embarking on the great migration; a trip as it were to a half-way house preparatory to the final plunge into rurality.'

By 1910 the trip could be made with comparative ease – in some ways more easily than it can be today. There were two railway companies competing for custom : the old London, Brighton and South Coast not only operated to Drayton and Chichester from London Bridge, as it had done for 65 years, but now had a line from Victoria to Singleton, Lavant and Chichester, on which they ran 'at greatly reduced fares' two specials a day in each direction throughout the Goodwood meeting. And the London and South Western Railway Company, which in the old days could get no nearer than Fareham via Southampton, now operated from Waterloo to Midhurst, change for Singleton, 3 hours 5 minutes the whole journey. Midhurst, Singleton, Lavant, Drayton – ghost stations, these, today.

The King's death cast an inevitable blight on the 1910 meeting. The court was still in mourning and Goodwood was short of a good deal of its customary glitter; it was also dreadfully cold on the first two days, with overcoats essential in all enclosures and the corn not yet ripe in the fields. George V had promised to come in 1911, though he had no runners at the meeting, but at the last moment was embroiled in a political crisis (it was a year of much industrial unrest) and had to disappoint the Duke. In compensation, it was stupendously hot and gentlemen on their way down to one of those elfin stations were able to contemplate, in their morning papers, the wisdom of this advice: 'Make up your mind to shave yourself this holiday. There's nothing to learn before you can use a Gillette.'

After that meeting there was a delightful bit of nonsense of the kind that so often seems to crop up among racing gentlemen. According to the records of the Corporation of St Pancras (the same Chichester society to which the first Duke presented a buck in 1689), Mr D. Kimbell bet Mr W. P. Breach 20s. to 2s. that Mr Breach would not ride a tricycle from Mr Curry's house at Goodwood up the hill to the grandstand in fifteen minutes. This event duly came off on the following Monday, and Mr Breach rode up the hill in ten minutes.

The upper classes were faintly astonished the next year to learn that shop assistants were to be given half a day a week off as well as Sunday, a fact that helped to swell the local mid-week attendance. 'Goodwood evidently retains its popularity with all classes,' said *The Times* some what sniffily on the first day, when for the first time tents were seen under the beeches, replacing the more picturesque idyll of tablecloths and picnic baskets. Despite the King's presence, one of the Duke's house-party, a distinguished diplomat, took Goodwood further from the Victorian era by appearing 'comfortably and becomingly attired' in white ducks and a Panama hat. He probably changed for the second day: it was one of the wettest in history, and the road behind the stand turned into a muddy brook.

Goodwood was in many ways becoming less delightfully rustic, despite the white ducks. For most of that deprivation, you can blame the motor car, which was, at least with the moneyed classes, emerging from the cocoon of rarity and threatening to become a nuisance. The coaches and carriages, which had been a more conspicuous feature of Goodwood than of any other meeting, were disappearing so fast that one commentator bitterly foresaw the day when the only horses to be seen would be on the course. But despite the growing mechanization and sophistication of the meeting, Cup Day remained by tradition almost a recognized holiday in the farms and villages of West Sussex. At least until the war, a distinctive feature of that day each year was the immense number of farm workers and country people of all kinds who managed to get to Goodwood: 'On foot and in every kind of conveyance they pour in a continuous stream throughout the morning, by every country road and by short cuts across the familiar fields towards the Park. Nowadays, in dry weather motors make the roads dreadfully dusty, and constant hootings send the countryman who trudges to the course on foot hustling off into the turf and tangle of the roadside. But the excitement and dissipation of the crowd upon the course, the joy of watching the great race from Trundle Hill, and above all, the chance of seeing the King, are worth some inconvenience.'

The flat racing season of 1913 was one which George V must have remembered all his life – the year of Emily Davidson, the Derby suffragette ('A most regrettable, scandalous proceeding,' he wrote in his diary that night). A few weeks later he came down for the Goodwood meeting, leaving Victoria on the day before the meeting at 5 p.m. and reaching Chichester at 6.30. In the station yard he inspected members of the local division of the National Reserve, who were to be front line men a year later. He had just come to the end of the line when a woman in nurse's uniform dashed across from a waiting-room and attempted to thrust a written petition at the King. She reached him just before a police inspector caught up with her and hurried her out of sight.

The Chief Constable of the county and the King's private detective questioned both the offender, Nurse Gifford, and her companion, a young Argentinian woman. According to the official statement, they confessed to being followers of Mrs Pankhurst, though boasted would more likely have been the right word. 'At the end of the examination they were informed that as a result of the King's clemency, no charge would be preferred against them, and they subsequently left by train for Bexhill.'

That diplomat's white ducks had obviously had an effect, for many of the men at Goodwood that year wore light summer suits, with straw or soft hats. The King, who again was not accompanied by Queen Mary, wore a brown suit, and there was hardly a silk hat in sight. Cup Day saw the greatest crowd Goodwood had ever known. Seats in the Pullman train from Victoria were unobtainable nearly an hour before the train left, hundreds of cars packed the enclosures, and long files of men and women could be seen trekking over the Downs as though along a new Pilgrims' Way. King George's horse Brakespear obliged the multitude by winning the first race, 'whereupon every man in that great assembly cheered or waved his hat, and the enthusiasm could not have been greater if the royal colours had been on a Derby winner'.

It was altogether a lively day. There was a fire in a luncheon tent under the trees, pickpockets in the grandstand lifted £55, and there was one splendid commotion during the lunch interval (it was the practice at that time, when royalty were present, to have an hour's break after the second race). It brought home forcibly to those in the privileged parts, wrote one reporter, that even Goodwood has its seamy side. A man, dishevelled and bearing the marks of violent handling, was seen to run on to the course from behind the railings on the popular side, with a shouting and excited mob in pursuit. He made straight for the grandstand enclosure, 'and to the astonishment of the well-dressed crowd, who were quietly taking their afternoon promenade, the hunted one scaled the high railings and tumbled over into their midst' – but not before the first of the enraged pursuers had cracked him over the head with his umbrella.

There is no more detested villain on a racecourse, where a good deal of malpractice is taken for granted, than a welsher – a book-maker who absconds with the money he owes successful punters, usually because he has too little of it to meet his commitments. And that was the cry on this occasion : 'A welsher !' It was almost enough to make the elegant promenaders put the boot in, but in the nick of time the man was rescued – and identified – by two policemen. He was himself a plain clothes police officer who had been in the act of arresting a pair of card sharpers whose three-card trick had been successfully conning the simpler of the souls massed on the grass. When the two realized they had been rumbled by the law, an accomplice in the crowd shouted 'A welsher – get him !' and began to assault the detective. He found no lack of support, and soon the righteous policeman was getting so thoroughly beaten that to run for cover was his only salvation.

On the Saturday after the meeting was over, the King stopped in Chichester, but not with the impatience his father had shown. He spent an hour there, opening the reconstructed Infirmary and Dispensary, which was by then the West Sussex Hospital. The King did as he was expected, tacking the 'Royal' on to it that the hospital still proudly carries. By the time Goodwood came round in 1914, the Archduke Franz-Ferdinand had been assassinated at Sarajevo, the Austrians had attacked Serbia, and a racecourse was no place for the King of England. Naval officers had been recalled to their ships, and Britain was within three weeks of war. In May 1915 all race meetings except Newmarket were suspended by the Jockey Club, and Goodwood was deserted until 1919.

'Once again, after a break of four years caused by the Kaiser and his minions,' wrote the *Chichester Observer* columnist with admirable disdain, 'we are welcoming the invasion of Sussex by society.' It was, he noted, 'entirely a motor meeting, and the dust was trying'. The Goodwood management was not unprepared for the advance of the internal combustion engine, and in May, Raufe Hussey-Freke, the Duke's manager, had concluded an arrangement with the Royal Automobile Club to manage all the vehicle enclosures there for five years, for half the money received – 'the term "vehicle" to include all motor vehicles, horse-drawn vehicles aeroplanes and airships'. It didn't all work too well that first year, to the annoyance of the correspondent of *The Times*: 'An innovation which is hardly to be commended awaited visitors by road, for each car was charged a toll of half-a-crown on arrival on the course. The delay in collecting this trivial amount was most vexatious and caused unnecessary congestion of traffic.' The congestion was in fact so dense that he might have been writing of a day fifty years later: 'A long procession of vehicles, horse-drawn and petrol-driven, moved a few yards and halted, moved and halted again. When still at a considerable distance from the course, all hope of seeing the first race must have been dissipated.' At the height of the chaos, the Duke discovered that 'an official' had closed a road that should have been open, an error for which the police and the RAC enthusiastically blamed each other. The police were out in some force that year – 122 from London, with ten horses, as well as the local contingent.

The Duke's decision to tidy up the stalls that were beginning to proliferate along the course was not universally popular, particularly with those who owned them. During the weeks that preceded the 1919 meeting he received this letter twice, in differing hands, from Mr W. Witchalls of Hackney: 'I was surprised to read in the sporting papers it is proposed to do away with the Stalls for the Sale of Refreshments in the usual places. May I Respectfully point out to your Grace that I have personally attended the Races for 30 years selling Salmon and Eels and my father before me for 20 without any complaint. Whilst pointing out the possible inconvenience to my many old Patrons, might I venture to ask the favour of your permission to be allowed to take my old or similar position and Carry on. I might add that I have had 33 children and Relations Serving overseas doing their bit and I am anxious to continue to do mine.' The plea must have had an effect; on the back is pencilled 'excepting in silver ring and by the road immediately behind it.'

For four years the shortage of manpower on the estate had

caused considerable deterioration in the condition of the race-course buildings. The bricks of the grandstand are particularly porous and are always subject to erosion, but there was more than that to worry about. In 1910 two new, less imposing stands had been built down the course by Hill and Smith, of the Brierly Hill Iron Works in Staffordshire. One of 200 feet had cost £1,025, and a much smaller job was £540. The ironwork on both of them had suffered alarmingly, and an investigation by the Virgilio Aircraft Company, of Northgate, Chichester, disclosed a great deal of work to be done – too much, in fact, to be completed before the meeting. It cost in the end £2,250, to bring them up to scratch, and it didn't help that Goodwood was £37.5s.10d. short in the turnstiles that year, as well as finding one forged pound note and 11s.9d. in foreign coins.

The war had done more damage to Goodwood than that. Apart from the deaths of the seventh Duke's third son, and of his senior grandson (who would have been the ninth Duke), the Earl of March himself received a dreadful blow in September 1915, a few days before he should have left for Gallipoli in command of the Sussex Yeomanry: he contracted spinal meningitis, and never walked again. The Earl had by then written his two books, *A Duke and His Friends*, and *Records of the Old Charlton Hunt*, and he devoted much of the rest of his life to helping to brighten the lives of disabled soldiers and sailors after the war.

The fact that he was a cripple did not deter him from pursuing the family interest in the Turf. In fact as soon as he succeeded to the title, in 1928, he did something his father had never done: he became a racehorse owner, though unfortunately not a very successful one. The death of the seventh Duke coincided with the departure of Mr Hussey-Freke and the arrival at Goodwood of a name that will never be forgotten: Hubbard. For nearly 50 years now a Hubbard has been immersed heart, soul and elbows in the business of Goodwood and its racecourse, and in any final reckoning there may be, the Hubbards, father and son, cannot be far behind Bentinck and the Kents in the contribution they have made and the affection in which they have been held by the family.

The first one, Captain Gerald Hubbard, had met the Earl of March in the army, and without much delay was set about horse buying. In 1929 they bought at the Newmarket sales True Blue (250 guineas) and Fleur (750), and the next year Scarlet Facings (170) and Fontinalis (420). All of them went to train at Lavant with Charles Chapman, but only Fleur found success. In 1930 it won at Lingfield (the first win in the Richmond colours since 1879) and at Gatwick, but none of the other three was ever placed. They were all auctioned, and fetched a total of only 149 guineas. Gerald Hubbard later bought Successful for 750 guineas, but that wasn't either. The trainer Basil Jarvis bought the Duke a useful runner that he named Grey Carey, after the second Duke's favourite hunter, and this one too had a win at Gatwick. Perhaps the best of all was one of Fleur's foals, Cyclone, which won twice and was sold to Lady Rosebery for 440 guineas. But the Duke died in 1935 without fulfilling his dearest wish – to have a winner at his own meeting.

In 1938 young Ralph Hubbard, who had been working with his father at Goodwood for five years, acted as clerk of the course in his absence. Captain Hubbard, seriously ill with osteomyelitis, was back in a wheelchair the following year for the final meeting of the pre-war era. Just a month later war was declared, and the grandstand and much of the grounds of Goodwood were occupied by the military.

Probably nobody who attended that 1939 Goodwood Week will ever forget the perilous atmosphere that hung over it, the certainty that disaster could not be averted. Looking back on it now, it is almost unbelievable that the racing could go on, and that the reporters could discuss the continuing efforts of the police to handle the traffic, and that they could marvel yet again at the draining capabilities of this most ancient of all racecourse turf, which survived a tremendous storm on the Monday, but provided perfect going on the Tuesday. But discuss them they did, and so too did *The Times* continue, as it had done for nearly 40 years, to devote almost a whole column to the clothes its fashion correspondent noted at the meeting ('Well up to Ascot standard', she said). Since it was the last time it ever happened – the post-war newsprint shortage combined with clothes rationing to squash any possibility of the idea emerging again – we should not pass the occasion by too hurriedly.

Such journalism used to be echoed, or perhaps had its root, in those excessively boring local news-sheets which listed in detail the presents received by the more acceptable of the brides and bridegrooms of the week, or painstakingly and painfully recorded the name of every person who entered the church for a notable funeral. But this was *The Times*, and these were the ladies of London and the ladies of the county, and they were presumably every bit as pleased to see their gew-gaws recorded in those distinguished columns as any Women's Institute marmalade queen is at seeing her name in lesser pages. *The Times* certainly made a fetish of it, taking care to record – factually and without comment – the turn-outs of about fifty ladies of the lawn each day of the meeting. Since they knew, or hoped, it was coming to them, the Goodwood clientele made every effort to see that the clothes were worth describing. Nobody dreamed of repeating an outfit during the four days, as some of the most socially distinguished of the guests automatically qualified for description every day. Just a fragment, then, of the way it was the very last time it happened :

'Baroness Beaumont brightened her black ensemble with magenta gloves, waist belt and pochette, and there were magenta birds on her black hat. The Honourable Mrs Micklethwaite's stone-coloured dress was matched by her fox cap, and her close-fitting cap of brown straw was edged with gold *galon*.'

Life, of course, did go on almost as though nothing was about to happen, however sure we all were that it was. Within a long sight of The Trundle you might have seen the boarding houses of Bognor Regis being cleared out for the London evacuees, and 240 British bombers exercising over France. But on the Wednesday of the meeting Adolf Hitler attended the Wagner Festival at Bayreuth, and Tommy Handley made his first ITMA broadcast. The King, understandably, was not at Goodwood, but he did visit the Oval, where *The Times* photographed him shaking hands with a man they described in their caption as 'a member of the West Indian cricket team'; and at about that moment, the Home Secretary announced there would be a full-scale black-out rehearsal on the night of 9th August.

On the Thursday of that week, Denis Compton hit 214 not out against Derbyshire ('He is, in fact,' said *The Times*, 'a genius'), while 100,000 members of the Territorial Army got under canvas across southern England, and the distribution of gas masks to all adults proceeded as fast as possible. On Friday, John Logie Baird for the first time transmitted a coloured picture through a cathode ray tube (it was a photograph of the King), the barrage balloons went up over London, and at about 4.35 in the afternoon the last horse in the last race to be held at Goodwood for seven years galloped past the winning post.

13

FREDDIE MARCH

There had never been a Richmond quite like the ninth Duke. Being the third son (the second to survive infancy), the required first name of the heirs, Charles, had been tucked behind Frederick; and it was alarmingly clear long before he succeeded to the title in 1935 that he was obsessed with racing not horses, but cars. After his elder brother died and he took the earldom, this lively character was known as Freddie March, and there was nowhere he was better known than behind a steering wheel at Brooklands, that magical concrete track in Surrey from where a whole generation first learned what speed meant.

March seemed to spend a lot of his time driving cars that looked about as big as the Flying Scotsman, but in fact his most celebrated victory was with an MG Midget in 1931, when he won the Double Twelve, a 500-mile race. During the war he served first with Fighter Command, then in Washington with the Ministry of Aircraft Production, and lastly as a staff officer in Britain. He was still a Flight-Lieutenant when in 1946, at the age of 42, he was elected president of what was then called the Junior Car Club. This fatuous misnomer led to both the public and the Press thinking that the Duke was at the head of some sort of organization for teaching schoolboys the Highway Code, but it was not until 1949 that it became the British Automobile Racing Club.

Just down the hill from Goodwood, a couple of miles to the south-east, was one of the RAF's most famous fighter airfields, Tangmere; even nearer was what amounted to an extremely large field which had been used as an annexe to Tangmere – now we call them satellites – and was known locally at the Westhampnett strip. In fact it was between Westerton and Lavant, one mile from Goodwood House, and extremely adjacent to the prosperous Chichester suburb of Summersdale and the enormous psychiatric hospital of Graylingwell. These petty geographical facts were to prove not unimportant.

It did not occur to the Duke of Richmond that right on his doorstep he had a potential motor racing circuit, not until his racing buddy Tommy Wisdom suggested it to him; he had got the idea from a wing-commander whose brother had flown from Westhampnett during the war, which just goes to show that idle chatter can sometimes be significant. Westhampnett was, and still is, a grass airfield, but it did have a winding concrete perimeter track of about 2.4 miles, and it was this that, in August 1947, the Duke invited the Council of the Car Club to consider for an experimental meeting the following year. It was held on 18th September, 1948, without stands, pits, or paddock buildings, and with the safety factor so risky that no more than 12 cars were allowed to start in any race. Despite the hopelessly inadequate accommodation (many of the spectators could not see the track at all) and despite the fact that the meeting had very little advance publicity in the Press, an astonishing turn-out of 15,000 was herded into roped enclosures.

It was astonishing. Not only did motor racing at that time mean little to the public, or so the RAC thought, but the national newspapers were so restricted in size that there were few column inches to spare for a sport that had not proved its drawing power with readers. Reg Parnell was one of the few names that was known among the post-war competitors, and he narrowly won the five-lap Goodwood Trophy in a Maserati. A minor race was won by a young driver of outstanding promise, Stirling Moss. Among the spectators were about 1,000 Club members, 10,478 who paid at the gates, and more than 3,000 who found it was not difficult to disregard such formalities, simply by walking through the hedges. There were 22 coaches in the parks (none of them horse-drawn), 1,419 cars, 294 motor cycles, and 36 bicycles. About £5,300 was taken at the gate, of which £1,000 was profit. A fairer start than had been believed possible even by Tommy Wisdom, who drove a Bentley in the opening cavalcade, immediately behind the former Freddie March in a new Bristol.

Flushed with that success, the Duke and the Club immediately set about making slightly stouter preparations for an international meet on Easter Monday, 1949. The difficulties of erecting even primitive buildings were very much greater then than it is possible to realize now. The country was desperately short of building materials, and particularly of steel. Car manufacturers were threatened with the withholding of supplies by the Government if they failed to comply with an order to export three-quarters of their production, almost an impossibility for the back-yard garage builder, and chromium was so hard to come by that the advice was not to polish it, and so wear it away unnecessarily. In the circumstances, it was a good effort that the Goodwood circuit had four stands on show for that next meeting, three overlooking the finish and one on the Lavant Straight.

But the warnings of that first meeting were not sufficiently heeded, or the organizers had perhaps not yet appreciated how insanely reckless a British crowd can be when thwarted by a piece of barbed wire and a pair of stewards. Nobody had foreseen, or indeed seemed able to estimate, the size of the crowd that overwhelmed that pathetic little course. The hedges had been reinforced with wire, but the boys had brought their wire-cutters with them, and after that, they uprooted the hedges. At some points the track was only a few yards from the public road, and crash barricades had this time been erected to avert the nastier forms of disaster. The crowd scaled the barricades, and sat on the grass verge with their feet on the track. Motor racing was something new, and it was the only sport around that could, briefly, fill the gap left in these men's lives when peace came. They had lived with danger for six years, and a good many of them liked it. Reg Parnell's Maserati won the Chichester Cup (five laps) and the Richmond Trophy (ten laps) and set a lap record of 87.1 m.p.h. Moss won another race, in a Cooper.

The success of that meeting genuinely frightened the organizers. Two days later an emergency meeting of the BARC was convened by the Duke, and the proposed Whitsun meeting at Goodwood was abandoned. Richmond said he foresaw the possibility of a major disaster unless he could greatly strengthen the barriers and enclosures. By September, they had effected a considerable improvement, and though there was a huge crowd, it was reasonably well controlled. Moss and Parnell won again, and the lap record crept up to 89.26.

Something quite extraordinary happened in 1950: the BRM, the most astonishing racing car ever built. The BARC had by then settled on an annual programme for Goodwood, which was to hold international meetings at Easter, Whitsun and in September, and Club meetings in May, June and August. The Easter meet was held in the most violent weather, and Parnell won the Richmond Trophy in a cloudburst that blinded those drivers who were still wearing goggles instead of a visor. On Whit Monday – the first day without petrol rationing – Goodwood staged the first classic race for 500 cc cars, later to become the Formula Three class. And then there was September, and more steady rain.

The very appearance of the BRM, with Parnell at the wheel, was enough to tighten the apprehension of the crowd. When he started it up for the Woodcote Cup, the other drivers on the grid were not sure whether their engines were running or not, and 'its shrieking, wailing exhaust note sent shivers down the spines of enthusiasts', recalled Rodney Walkerly in *Brooklands to Goodwood*. 'When the flag fell, the BRM stood still on the rain-drenched track with its rear wheels a blur; then suddenly, the treads bit the road and Parnell was off, passing car after car almost with contempt.' He won that race by a mere two seconds, but the Goodwood Trophy from Prince Bira's Maserati by 13 seconds, and the crowd were in an ecstasy. All that and, recorded the BARC, 'a member, who should not be named, was suspended *sine die* for being rude to the Stewards'.

The circuit was resurfaced that winter, and at the next Whitsun meeting the *Daily Graphic* sponsored the Festival of Britain Trophy, which attracted a marvellous entry – Farina and Graffenreid in Maseratis, Bira in an Osca, and Parnell, who won in a Vandervell Ferrari. The lap record was broken three times during the race, and rose to 94.54. 'It was the speeds seen at this meeting', said Walkerley, 'that caused the thoughtful expression worn by the Duke of Richmond and started him thinking about applying some sort of brake.' After the autumn meeting, he did. Giuseppe Farina, in an Alfa Romeo, lapped at 97.36 m.p.h. The echo of his engines had hardly died away across the fields when the Duke voiced his grave concern that the speeds now being attained were too great for the safety of both the drivers and the crowd. Various modifications to the course were discussed, and it was eventually decided to hold the drivers back between Woodcote Corner and the finish, where they tended to cut the corner, by building a wall half-way across the course, and to line the inside verge with light wattle fencing.

The wall looked horrifying enough to clip several seconds off the lap time, but in fact a large part of it was on rollers. It was christened Paddock Bend, but became known as the chicane (the cheat). It was used at the Easter meeting of 1952, when Fangio, Mike Hawthorn and José Gonzales competed, and the lap record was down to 90. A touch of Le Mans had before that come to Goodwood, with a nine-hour race for sports cars, from 3 p.m. to midnight. The *News of the World* sponsored it with a first prize of £1,000, but there were not enough motoring enthusiasts in Sussex to make the occasion a fiesta. Even fewer of them turned up the next year, and this was an event that never really broke through. Among the unexpected excitements of the 1953 Nine Hours was that the thirty starters pushed their cars so hard the pits were in danger of running out of tyres. They changed 175, and fresh supplies had to be rushed to the circuit during the night.

Once again Goodwood and the Richmonds had led the way with enterprise and distinction on a race track, but though the public interest in motor racing continued to increase, it was outpaced by the number of circuits and meetings that sprang up across the country. After six years, the surging excitement of the Goodwood circuit had lost its novelty appeal. The sport lacks any aesthetic attraction of a relaxed nature, perhaps because it is an unnatural one, and it was settling down to hold an almost maniacal attraction for a hard core of enthusiasts. Goodwood was still averaging up to 30,000 at the gate, but that was not really enough. Indeed, at a time when the demand for starting money was beginning to rise alarmingly, it was a long way short of the necessary target. There were other problems: though both the brevity of the occasions, and the limit of their appeal, meant that the locality was by no means as disrupted as it annually was for Goodwood Week up the hill, those of the public who do not care for racing of any kind find greater offence in cars than in horses. The noise was a major complaint at Chichester (there were three BRMs at the September meeting of 1952), but beyond that came the harsh matter of television interference, and that is something of which you can never accuse a horse.

At the annual meeting of the BARC early in 1954, members discussed an impassioned plea that the fitting of suppressors to engines should be obligatory, so that patients at Graylingwell Hospital, for instance, should not suffer the virtual obliteration of their TV programmes for the duration of every meeting at Goodwood. Seeing the other man's point of view does not come easily to any of us, and the more devoted you are to a cause, the less you can understand opposition to it. The matter was dropped without a decision.

There was an interesting sensation at the Easter meeting that year. The Richmond Trophy had been renamed the Richmond Formula Libre Race for the Glover Challenge Trophy, which lacks a certain crispness, and the leading contenders were Wharton in a BRM and Salvadori in a Maserati. Wharton won it, but Salvadori (who had also been second to him in the Chichester Cup) immediately complained to the stewards that he had been deliberately and persistently baulked whenever he tried to pass him. Where to overtake is a frequent problem in motor racing, and not an unattractive one, but it was particularly difficult on the winding Goodwood circuit. Only on the Lavant Straight was there time to take the lead through superior speed alone, and Wharton had managed to thwart Salvadori's attempts to do this from beginning to end of the race.

The objection was not upheld by the stewards, and when he received the trophy, Wharton spoke to the crowd: 'If we are always to give way to the chap behind, just because he is behind, it isn't going to be motor racing. I think Roy and I understand that, and I hope we shall always be good friends.'

Only 13,000 attended the September meeting, despite the last appearance of the BRM, and the next year racing in general suffered an understandably severe drop in support after a Mercedes left the track at Le Mans and killed 80 spectators. There were two fatal crashes at Goodwood in 1956, and Moss lifted the lap record to a point less than 2 m.p.h. slower than it had been before the introduction of Paddock Bend. In the winter of 1957, after the smallest crowd the circuit had ever known, big improvements were made in course facilities, including a public enclosure inside the course, approached by a subway under the Lavant Straight. The paddock was redesigned, so that the public could still watch the work being done on the cars when they came into the pits, without actually breathing down the necks of the mechanics. Most significant of all, as it turned out, two grass landing strips for light aircraft were cleared in the centre of the old airfield.

Despite a bitterly cold Easter (there was thick snow in the south of England a day or two before the meeting), 55,000 came through the gates – inspired perhaps by the fact that Mike Hawthorn had won the world championship (less than a year later he was killed in a private car on a public road). Leading the way in the Formula Two race were a couple of newish names, Jack Brabham and Graham Hill. A year later Stirling Moss won the 100-mile Formula One race at an average speed of more than 90 m.p.h., and the next day, in private, lapped the Goodwood circuit in a BRM at over 100 m.p.h.

The RAC had held their Tourist Trophy race at Goodwood for the first time the previous September, and on the second occasion there was an incident at the pits that was nearly a major disaster. The Moss/Salvadori Aston Martin came in for refuelling, and the fuel hose from the pump burst into flames. Fortunately, it happened even before the car's petrol cap was off, but the reservoir tank behind the pit exploded and the fire spread to the next pit. When the team's second car came in, Moss took it over and won the race in it. His original Aston Martin was subsequently found to be scorched, but otherwise quite unharmed.

Stirling Moss, in particular, will for ever remember the Goodwood circuit with pride and pleasure – it seemed always to bring out the best in him. But so too will hundreds of drivers and thousands of spectators. Once again, it was something different; lacking the beauty and the magnificence of the other course on the hill, but an oddly lovable circuit, one for which the habitué felt a genuine warmth. It went on happily enough, though with decreasing financial stability, until 1966. By that time starting money had reached staggering proportions: £2,000 a head was standard, and some demanded £4,000. Goodwood could just no longer cope. The last public meeting was held on Whit Monday that year, and on 2nd July the BARC had a day there to themselves. It was no easier to drive away that evening than it had been for the Goodwood Hunt to leave the scene of their last kill in 1895, just two miles down the road at East Hampnett. As somebody said then, it was a funeral.

Meanwhile, back at the equine end of the business, something like normality was returning to the racecourse. The news came remarkably soon after the end of hostilities, with a letter to the Duke of Richmond from Lord Nathan of Churt, at the War Office, in September 1945: 'I thought you would be glad to hear from me that the whole of the requisitioned portion of the racecourse, with the exception of land occupied by hutted camps, can now be released. I am told that the retention of these camps should not interfere with racing.'

Once the RAF Regiment had vacated the grandstand, in which they had contrived to live throughout the war, nothing was likely to stop Goodwood putting on as good a show as it could for 1946. To be able to 'do Goodwood' again meant so much more than any other meeting; it meant dabbling again in luxury, leisure, beauty – items we had seen little of in the preceding seven years. If Goodwood Week was on the calendar, the war must be over. As *The Times* said on the morning the meeting began, it is the only one in England where great racing can be watched in comfort in the heart of the English countryside in a holiday mood : 'Fashionable metropolitan Ascot and professionally severe Newmarket have not got its charm.'

There was not much room for any paper in Fleet Street to expand on the subject. Before the war *The Times* had used substantial previews of Goodwood on both the Monday and the Tuesday before the meeting, and a column and a half each morning reporting the racing, as well as that survey of bonnets and blouses. Now racing was down to half a column however many meetings there were, and the entire sporting news of the nation had to be confined in half a page.

It was as good a re-start as Goodwood and its customers can possibly have hoped for. If not quite the comfortable, well-appointed Goodwood that they remembered from 1939, it was better than anything they had seen since. The crowds, hungry for their fun, were enormous : on the first day 9,000 people arrived at Chichester by train, 10,000 went to the course by bus, and as many cars as could be coaxed up the hill on the meagre petrol ration packed into the parks. 'A most welcome revival', noted *The Times*. Better still the next year : 'Truly glorious', was the phrase; and so the story went on, year by year record crowds at the course till it seemed the old place would burst. For nearly ten years after the war, the desire for entertainment among the people of Britain, who had for so long bitten on the bullet of austerity, seemed insatiable. It was not just racing : we are talking now of a time when every town of 50,000 inhabitants had its own repertory theatre, and flocks of amateurs as well.

Goodwood's peak came in 1953, when on one day there were 55,000 at the course, and 21,000 of them were massed on the slopes of The Trundle. As Ralph Hubbard said recently, if you got crowds like that now, there would be a riot. Over the past twenty years, people have got used to having room to breathe, and even to move; in those days, any discomfort was gladly suffered for the joy of participation – though a traffic jam that was still a mile long when the first race finished was not among the pleasures of the day. Gently from that gigantic year (the summer of the Queen's coronation), attendances at Goodwood declined, as they did everywhere else. There were other things to do, other ways to watch racing, other ways to spend money; our leisure time increased, but so, vastly, did the demands on it.

Year by year, there were things by which the Week was remembered. Royal visits used to be red letter days, but they became so frequent that one almost overlooked them. No longer was the course in a turmoil because the monarch was coming – indeed Queen Elizabeth would be most upset if it were so. She is likely to come with the least possible notice consistent with courtesy, and in the hope that nobody will put themselves out. Sometimes she may fly in to a local airfield alone, but for her policeman, and the local constabulary will escort her to the course. The informality of the occasion is inevitably matched by a considerable lessening of the homage in which she is received by the average man in the enclosure, and that too seems to be to her liking. She is there, after all, not to hold court, but because she likes racing. The reporters of the event react similarly: fifty years earlier, the King's presence would have dwarfed their accounts of events on course; today, Her Majesty barely warrants a mention in the final paragraph.

On the year before her coronation, the meeting was held during the second week of the Helsinki Olympics, but local memories are more likely to tell you that 1952 was the year of the first broadcast commentaries to the popular enclosures: 'A straightforward account', notes one reporter, 'of the changes in the running without any of the dramatization which has often been the subject of criticism in similar commentaries for the BBC.' It was also the year of Aquino II, and who, among those who saw it, will ever forget that running of the Goodwood Cup?

Aquino II was a useful horse, and started as second favourite at 2–1. But it is a long race, and it was a hot day, and Aquino just did not fancy it. As soon as they were away, the horse tried to turn round and go back to the paddock; frustrated in that, it ran a furlong and then swerved from the rails to the middle of the course and tried to stop. Ordered, urged, beseeched to continue, Aquino obliged until the bend out of the straight (the Cup course, remember, starts at the finish and covers the straight twice). There, from behind its blinkers, the horse's attention was caught by an adjacent field of long grass, plentifully dotted with purple wild flowers. Soon there was a break in the railings, and Aquino ambled out and settled down contentedly to watch its colleagues get on with the other two miles. It was surely one of the most richly funny moments in the history of racing, and though it was extremely disappointing to a lot of punters, it was oddly satisfying to those who like to think that a man cannot make a horse do anything.

No doubt there were some on the course that day who remembered the time 43 years earlier when, in spite of all a jockey's efforts, another horse exercised its will in an entirely different fashion. The Duke of Portland's Roche Abbey ran and won the Singleton Plate in 1909, finishing so full of energy and ecstasy that it could not be stopped. It galloped on up the slopes of St Roche's Hill, for which it perhaps felt some affinity, unseated the jockey and disappeared over the brow of The Trundle. The jockey returned to headquarters somewhat sheepishly and was unable to fulfil the obligatory weighing-in, since the saddle which he was supposed to carry was last seen heading at some speed for the Hampshire border.

The sight of dozens of hats at a time bowling down the course throughout the afternoon was a merry one for some in 1954, though the merriest time of all was had by the bookies on the first day. The gales so upset form that of the six winners not one started shorter than 5–1, and one was 50–1. There was a deluge in 1956, one of the very worst Goodwood days in memory (1912 was a shocker too, but judging by the language used to describe it, the wettest in history was in 1839 : a cloudburst was followed by a 'perfect hurricane'. The horses ran fetlock deep in mud and it was 'one of the most miserable days to which a racegoer may by possibility be exposed even in the darkest recesses of his imagination').

A great improvement in the manipulation of traffic was noted in 1958, by which time prize money had advanced to almost £50,000 (£34,500 from the racecourse), and attendance had continued to retreat. Some may remember the year best for the fact that, for the first time, the availability of Goodwood airfield made their journey that much easier; others for the fact that the lawns of the popular enclosures had become tarmac yards. This was the year, too, that clerk of the course Ralph Hubbard disclosed that a new grandstand would one day come to Goodwood; but it would cost £150,000, and a lot of money must be saved first. Probed on the question in 1960, he said that if the necessary finance could be arranged, and if there was no slump in racing, the stand might be built in the winter of 1962-3. It would either be a more elaborate stand on the same site, or the road behind the stands would be diverted, and the new stand put on or close to the existing road. (It is still a dream, though now a vastly more expensive one : but in the winter of 1974 there was a gleam of reality when that road was diverted.)

The removal from its traditional date of the August Bank Holiday, in 1965, could have considerably affected the pattern of Goodwood racegoing. For much longer than anybody could remember Goodwood Week had begun on the last Tuesday of July, thus ensuring that it was usually followed by the Bank Holiday weekend. The racecourse management chose this moment to disrupt tradition even further : for the first time, there were meetings at Goodwood other than the Week – three brief ones, in fact, later in the year. The details, though not the sound principle of making proper use of the facilities, were subsequently adjusted to provide two-day meetings in mid-May, late August and mid-September, in addition to what had become a principal meeting of five days. That did not appear to suffer unduly from the postponement of Bank Holiday, and *The Times* was pleased to note that 'The high holiday spirit has been preserved and encouraged. Goodwood seems to have been able to fulfil the urge for exciting sport in surroundings that are equally refreshing for the claustrophic town-dweller and the jaded, professional racegoer.' While retaining the most delightful of its traditions, Goodwood was beginning to make sense; yesterday was not forgotten, but its eyes were on tomorrow.

14

ANOTHER DAY

Even the stateliest homes have a struggle to get by on nothing but 30p a head at the front door. Goodwood House is not among the country's most magnificent, though some of the 18th century interiors are as beautiful as anything you can find elsewhere, and there are an extraordinary number of people who have lived in West Sussex all their lives without even bothering to go inside it. So to make the house and the 12,000 acres of the estate that remain into a viable proposition has been a testing job for the family, and one that occupies them fully.

The ninth Duke withdrew from active involvement in estate affairs some years ago, and no longer lives at the house. In theory, Goodwood no longer belongs to him, nor to his heir. It is owned by the Goodwood Estate Company Ltd, the shares in which are held by trustees on behalf of the family. Various independent limited companies operate, autonomously and self-sufficiently, the differing activities of the estate. Each pays a rent to the parent company, by whom they are wholly owned. There has to be a genius behind a plan of that sort, and it is the Earl of March, an experienced accountant and businessman, whose aim it is to make full and efficient use of all the facilities that surround him. He and his family live in one section of the house, and the estate offices occupy much of the first floor; below are the state apartments, often open to the public, and the ballroom, which did duty during the war as a military hospital. Its restoration and re-decoration was not completed until 1970, when it accommodated the coming-of-age ball for Lady Elinor Gordon-Lennox, which the royal family attended.

Among the least expected ventures at Goodwood are those controlled by The Goodwood Terrena Ltd, which took over where motor racing left off. The old Westhampnett fighter strip is now generally rated the best grass airfield in the south, and has assumed greater importance since the closure of the Portsmouth airfield. It is a fully licensed commercial concern, which operates its own flying school and air taxi service. The school is notably successful, and is now being intensively used. In three years the annual movements logged there rose from 12,000 to nearly 60,000.

The motor circuit still exists, though it has not been used for a race meeting since 1966. There is a motor racing school there, and a pre-driver school at which children can learn both private and racing techniques. The circuit is also used by manfacturers for car testing, and by film companies shooting race scenes. All part of the March principle: it's there, make it work.

Most intriguing and potentially exciting of all the recent Good-wood developments is the equestrian centre, still being developed. The William Chambers stable block was there, with its 100 loose boxes, but how often had they been fully used since Lord George Bentinck gave up racing, and the sixth Duke closed the Goodwood Hunt? Lady March (formerly Susan Grenville Grey) is an expert horsewoman, and it was no doubt her enthusiasm that encouraged her husband to take some very bold steps in this direction. In August 1971 the hills and woods and fields of the estate contained their first horse trials, a one-day event that included the full pro-gramme of dressage, cross-country riding and show jumping. It was repeated in the two succeeding years (Princess Anne com-peted in 1972, but in 1973 the event clashed with the European championships in Kiev).

Through that, Goodwood laid its hand on something quite magical: dressage. This is the aspect of horsemanship in which Britain, by and large, lags so far behind much of the rest of Europe that her riders go into a three-day event with a handicap that is only overcome by their inbred brilliance (through hunting) on the cross-country course. Richard Meade, the gold medallist at the Munich Olympics, was 14th in the dressage section; Princess Anne, then the defending European event champion, was 16th after the dressage in Kiev; and even our specialists could do no better than 10th place in the Grand Prix dressage team event in Munich.

It is a pernickety business, and one which until recently has interested spectators in Britain even less than it has the riders. It is that part of horsemanship that demonstrates the degree of discipline by which both horse and rider are bound, the perfect obedience of one to the other, the accuracy and the understanding they have achieved. Until a spectator has become familiar to some extent with the requirements of the exercises, a little watching goes a long way. But perhaps the day of dressage has arrived: we have reached saturation point and beyond in show jumping; cross-country courses are necessarily few and often inaccessible; and just consider the potential perfection of a dressage competition on the lawn in front of Goodwood House. The toppers and tails, the plaited manes, the delicate steps: it is the ballet of the horse world, and one can well see Goodwood becoming its Covent Garden. Such, at least, is the hope of the Marches.

It does not, indeed, take a great deal of imagination to see that with care and enthusiasm Goodwood could one day become an equestrian centre of international renown. Dressage on the lawn, show jumping on the cricket field and cross-country up hill and down dale, providing the agricultural land can be avoided – dairy farmers are not happy to see horses on their pasture. And just beyond the stable block, tucked away in the trees beside Goodwood House, there is now an indoor riding school, completed in 1973. The pieces begin to fall into place. It now seems likely, too, that the golf club will be able to have a new clubhouse more conveniently situated nearer Lavant, where there are plans to enlarge the course, or even lay another one. One might have thought that would free the original kennels to be used as the administrative and social headquarters of an equestrian centre that could one day, and so appropriately, bring as much glory and joy to the area as the Goodwood Hunt once did; but Lord March says firmly that is not to be the destiny of the kennels.

Dreams, but not unreasonable ones. And a little further up the hill from the kennels there are at last signs that a long-living dream is approaching the edge of reality: a new stand. As Nairn and Pevsner said, the new designs will have a job to catch the atmosphere as well as the old. But as Clerk of the Course Hubbard says, you try paying the maintenance bills. In April 1973 the new plans were unveiled, and they received outline planning permission from the County Council. All Goodwood needs to go ahead now is £3,300,000 – the cost to which the project has risen from the £150,000 that Hubbard talked about in 1958. The project, of course, has changed, as well as the price. The new grandstand will be set back where the road is now, and the existing old buildings will be demolished, as well as the much newer stand that faces down the course. The paddock comes away from beside the stand to behind it, which will be a loss to the customers on The Trundle, and is to be very much bigger, with tiered seating all round it forming an arena of which other recreational use might be made.

The finishing straight, which now tapers towards the winning post, will be widened from its present minimum of 76 feet to a uniform 100 feet – enough to allow 'resting' of strips of it by moving the rails. The low Sussex Building, that took the place of Queen Alexandra's beloved beech trees, will remain and be enlarged. Already, since the 1974 meeting, the old Harroways road has been moved again, and now cuts the corner down the hill in a great curve to leave room for the new development.

It won't be the same, nothing will be the same. But what can we do, bring back Bentinck and ban the horseless carriage? The 'new' Dukes of Richmond are this year celebrating the 300th year of their family's existence. Glorious Goodwood is growing up.

APPENDIX

THE HISTORICALL ACCOUNT OF THE RISE AND PROGRESS OF THE CHARLTON CONGRESS

That was the heading written by its anonymous author above the extremely long, but entirely fascinating, epic poem in which the early history of the Charlton Hunt is both encapsulated and embroidered. No trace exists of its origin except a handwritten note on the fly-leaf of the manuscript book in which it is set down: 'This was brought to me by a Porter in the beginning of February 1737. R.'

The author seldom uses one phrase where two can be accommodated, and entwines the whole with so many allusions to matters of history, legend and contemporary activity that there are times when understanding fails me. But it is a unique record of local and social history that richly repays careful reading. The original is peppered with the aggravating habit of referring to persons then living by the first and last letters of the surname only, and where I was sure to whom he was referring, I have completed them. I have also taken the liberty of altering some of the quirkier forms of spelling, and of removing most of those initial capitals for common nouns that were standard practice in the 18th century, but in mass are now rather aggravating. The Diana to whom the writer constantly refers is not a Duchess of Richmond, but the Roman goddess who is often represented as a huntress, and misrepresented as being the goddess of hunting.

The poem is preceded by a letter, unsigned, to the Duke of Richmond:

'My Lord.

The fine Chaces I have seen at Charlton, the Kind and Generous reception I have met with from yr Grace, and the rest of the Agreeable Company there; tho' an Unworthy Stranger, who never can have it in his Power, to make the Grateful Acknowledgement, which nevertheless glows in his Plebean Breast.

As it has been my Nightly Dream, so it has been my Dayly talke, and my Study, to Learn as much as I could of the first rise, and long continuance, of the most agreable Society of the king, that ever was

here it is my Lord, rough, and unhew'n I send it you.

Omissions you'll excuse, the whole you must Despise, but I have eas'd my minde, and have the Satisfaction of taking this Occasion to assure your Grace; with all respect, that no body can be more your Graces

> most Obedient
> and most Humble
> Servt.

Amidst the South Saxonian hills, there runs
a verdant fruitful vale, in which, at once
four small, and pretty villages are seen;
Eastden the one, does first supply the spring,
whence milky Lavant, takes his future course;
Charleton, the next, the beauty of the four,
from twenty chalky rills, fresh vigour adds,
then swiftly on, his force redoubled, he
thro' all the meads, to Singletown does glide;
more strength, he there received, at Westden next,
his last recruit he makes, then boldly runs,
till less confin'd, he wider spreads his fame,
and passing Lavant, there he takes his name.
He then begins, to do what good he can,
during his short liv'd transitory reign :
here mills for corn, demand his present aid,
there farmers beg! his virtue he'll impart,
t' enrich their lands, for greater future crops.
Requests all granted, to the ocean, he
as proudly marches, as the greatest of
all the confed'rate rivers of the land.

In this sweet vale, by hill, and Downs enclos'd,
an age ago, Diana fixed her court.
Her nymphs, in other regions she employs;
in softer chases, and in summer sports.
With little beagles, or her deep mouth'd hounds,
on foot they hunt, on moss, and in the shade,
for pity twere, to hurt, or tan a maid.
The British fierceness, to Diana known,

the inbred goodness, of their coursers too;
like all her sex, She ev'rywhere would be,
ador'd; but how to suit it, with her chastity?
The country's beauty, and the British hounds
tempted the Goddess, here to raise her fame;
at last in private, weighing well her scheme,
She thus resolves! I'll be ador'd by men;
by Britons bold, where nymphs shall ne'er resort,
rough is their nature, and they love all sports;
a new one, I'll invent, to fit their taste,
their hounds, their horses, and their daring youth;
at once I'll suit them and they'll still do good,
the wily fox, their furious chase shall be,
a small but well chose band, I'll then select,
from all the huntsmen, Britain can produce;
and Charleton, is the place, where I will fix
my Temple, where my votaries shall hunt.
Charleton, from whence so called, no record tells,
unless that Charles of Richmond Duke, by fate
long since determined there at last to come,
to grace her beauties, with his palace gates,
and vie Chantilly with her neighbouring woods:

A vast, high mountain, to the south does bear,
the name of one Saint Roke, unknown elsewhere,
a Roman, or a Saxon, camp is trac'd
on his high summit, in the centre there
a post, and stone well quadrate does appear:
a Lodge of ancient Masons here is held,
famous besides, for what did there occur,
the Church was robb'd; what's more, 'twas by a Peer.

Northward, and rising close above the town,
another mountain's known, by Leving Down;
a Pirenean path, is still there seen,
where Devon's Duke, full speed, did drive his well
bred courser down, and flying, leap't five bars;
incredible the act! but still 'twas fact,
but Lo! the next great pointe de vue,
the great conspicuous Bow, his bulk so vast,
his length and height, his head so near the clouds,
from Gallias shore, he's plainly seen, and known;

the boldest land mark, of our British coast,
with yews and black thorn, his great crest is crown'd;
green all the winter long, and white in Spring,
tis here wise nature, scorning all low arts,
her various beauties, on each side imparts,
from Kingly bottom, here the wand'ring eye,
with Southern prospect all the ocean views;
sees all the trade, that passes, to enrich
our British Isle, or please luxurious tastes;
in peace, tis this, the pleasing prospect yields;
in war; the Dunkirk lurking privateer,
hov'ring along the coast, is seen to watch
like Ren, in warren, how to seize his prey.
But hold, we wander from our first intent,
the rise and progress of Diana's court.
The all directing Goddess, having viewed
the vast extent of hills, and dales, that run
from East, to West, and all a mossy turf,
the noted, great, and proper distant woods
and close recesses, here and there dispersed,
the badgers' earths, where foxes oft retreat,
when hard pursued, not trusting to their speed,
to each of these, some rustic name She gave,
which so continue to this present day;
by this She meant, to assist her little court,
when warmly glorying in their Goddess' praise;
how to report, and how describe, the chase
And next, with foxes brought from Northern climes,
and secretly turned out, by her command
She stocked these mossy hills, and bosky vales,
and then her thoughts, were where to choose her bank;
and such, who would her laws and rights maintain.
A Grosveneur, a name the Norman brought,
She thought was requisite to rule the whole;
since She, in decency could not appear.
The first firm maxim, she laid down was this,
that blood, in every vein should be the best;
to answer this, the first brave youth She chose,
had graceful mien, with waving locks adorned,
but empty head, tho' sprung from Royal loins;
vigorous he was, and Monmouth was his name;
with him came Tankerville, associate he,

in all his follies, and his infamy,
how could a Goddess be so much deceiv'd?

Diana, still unheeding all events
went on, in forming rules of government,
the best bred hounds of vermin kind, well known,
were all collected, into one choice pack;
and horses too, the best of blood were bought,
and all by her directions, they were chose
of middle size, with nostrils wide, and red,
the muzzle small, and lean the head, and jaw,
with open throat, no vives along the chawle,
their crests, and shoulders then, their withers sharp,
too far, they can't run backward to the chine,
nor can the fillets, be too broad and round,
an oval even croup, the tail set high,
large ribb'd, close flank'd, and cushioned well behind
his brisket deep, his sides both long, and full,
his joints well knit, his legs, both flat and short,
his feet, both hard and round, and rather small,
than large, for those no speed can ever show;
These very rules, she gave to choose her hounds.
All hitherto proceeded well; but yet,
She thought her pack requir'd some better skill,
Ropero, then She brought, and gave to him
the care and management, of all her ment:
He, deep in knowledge, by experience taught,
could talk upon her darling subject well,
pleas'd with the sage, she gave him ample power,
to cast, to cull, to breed, and do his best.

With pleasure great, the Goddess saw her court;
each day gave joy, each day increased their sport;
Bacchus and Ceres, did their board supply;
and Martha made their beds, and made their pie.

But now alas, confusion seiz'd the land,
And Mars, with malice calls his sons to arms:
First Monmouth's breast, he with ambition fir'd,
to head his army, soon away he flew,
and took, the then thought faithful Tankerville,
along with him, to share his fortunes all:

but Oh! how far unfit, was Monmouth's skill,
to lead on British troops, or seize the throne:
he went, he came, he fought, betray'd, was ta'en;
he lost his head; and Cupid lost a dart.
Guiltless Ropero too, was forc'd to fly,
in those bad days, when honesty, was crime,
enough, for Jeffrys to pronounce his doom:
to France, then went, the ablest huntsman here;
and made acquaintance, with Saint Victor there
'till William came, and settled peace at home.
Diana calls, Ropero soon returns;
his Queen as soon declares him Grosveneur.

Fame now had loudly sung, of Charleton sports,
from France, Saint Victor came to see his friend,
the great Tuscanian Duke, too, had been there;
William the third, the great, once saw a chase.

Hence jealousy, that gnawing fiend, began
to rouse the spleen, of a much prouder man,
the Second Duke of Britain, and his name
was Seymour; Somerset, his title was,
his Castle Petworth, distant three small leagues,
not far from which, a worthy knight there dwelt,
a sportsman good, as ever Sussex bred,
his castle hospitable, Burton call'd.

To him the Duke: Sir William who's this man
that daily, boldly dares, thus in my sight,
to scour along those azure hills we see?
nay, even up to Petworth walls he comes.

My Lord; Diana's hands they are; I know
Ropero, good old man, her Grosveneur.
Diana's Grosveneur: — that place, I'll have.
My Lord, a Temple She at Charlton has,
at Compton too, another still she has,
at Findon likewise, does a Temple stand.

With ire stamm'ring his slaves he loudly call'd;
I'll have hounds, I'll have horses, see't be done;
Sir Knight, Diana's huntsmen we will be,

what land pray has Ropero here, good Sir?
where do his manors lie? what right has he?

My lord. – I'm told his land, in Kent does lie,
his right I doubt the goddess will maintain.

The Duke – nor Gods, nor Goddesses, I heed,
but straight a Temple I will raise with speed,
Diana, then may like it if she please.
He gave the word; twas done, he call'd it Twines,
a pretty spot, and just upon the downs,
in stalls magnificent his coursers lay,
in spacious kennels, all his hounds did play,
three times a week, he sent his cooks o'er night,
and made a feast, the Goddess to appease;
for she, to see his pride was angry grown,
and bid her old Ropero keep his ground.

A civil war, of course was now began,
She knew her power, and stood by her old man;
in Andrew's form, herself was spy to tell,
ere dawn of day appeared, which way he went;
then after them, under the wind he drew,
and often took their fox, and swore 'twas his,
had found in such a wood, and ran two hours.

This discord lasted for some months or more,
till one day, when the knight, the Duke not out,
in friendly manner to Ropero spoke,
Brother, I think we spoil each others sport;
I think so too, but who is most to blame?
strong were the arguments on both sides held,
the two old champions both were loath to yield;
at last, preliminaries strong were drawn,
all war, and future discord, should desist;
but soon the haughty sovereign's pride rebelled,
he gave away his hounds, and left the field.

Now peace returned, Sir William joins the court,
All lucky days now bless their rural sport,
neglected stands the stately temple Twine,
a nest for vermin, or a sty for swine.

G

When now, another noble Duke appears,
graceful his air, and blooming were his years,
he long a faithful votary had been,
and paid due homage, to the huntress Queen;
but now, he begs admittance in her band,
fresh troops he brings, all under his command.

Ropero paus'd, but liked the kind of hound,
which told, he soon the Goddess willing found;
and now they cull each pack, the choicest keep,
they found no fox that ever did escape;
for now against poor Ren the odds were vast,
at every check two packs there was to cast;
John Gough, up wind, did all ways choose to go;
but, Harry Barratt, down he best did know.

Till now, in homely manner they had lived,
a small dark cell, and one poor light had served,
to tell the chase; and sing the Goddess' praise;
till Grafton's Duke, and Burlington came down,
to see their sport, so far beyond their own;
then Boyle, by instinct all divine began,
is this an edifice for such a band?
I'll have the honour to erect a room,
shall cost Diana's train, but such a sum;
they all agreed, and quickly paid it down,
and now, there stands a sacred Dome, confessed
the finest in the country, most admired.

And now the Sylvan Queen began to think,
recruits would soon be wanting, to her train,
young novices She brought inclin'd to sport,
and placed 'em all under Ropero's care;
to be initiate in her rural rights,
and learn of him, the practice of the field;
the downy Nassau first she brought, a youth,
well made, and fair Boltona's chiefest care,
and then tall West, of old patrician race,
whose warlike ancestors at Boxgrove lie,
this youth adept, to all he undertook,
soon took to hunting, and forsook his book;
the old man pleas'd, with so apt a scholar

call'd him his son; and wished for such another,
West in return, did all he could to please,
he walked, he talked, he dressed, his boots, his sleeves,
nay more his very shape, was grown like his.

But Lo! the fatal catastrophe draws near,
Ropero, quite worn out with years, tho' full
in health, yet all his strength and vigour gone;
at Findon, he and Herbert, sportsman true,
and Andrew, his most faithful friend, went out
to mountain Furres, fatal was the day!
a fox just found; get on he cries! and then,
that instant fell, and life that instant fled.
And thus Ropero died, at eighty-four
a quick and sudden death, and in the field;
could Julius Cesar ere have wished for more?
Bolton's great Duke, now him succeeds, in all
the whole command of hounds as Grosveneur,
the train increases, and the sport goes on,
pleasing were all the Delian virgin's rules,
and happy was great George's gentle reign
and now Diana's leave first asked, there came,
from different parts, sportsmen of different names,
from Hadrian's wall, two northern peers there were
Montrose – the Duke, and Forester the Lord;
with Honeywood the gay, and Kirk the grave,
a stripling too, who to the first was kin
sedate he was, and sly, and hunting lov'd.
As visitors, came full many a one
of Germans, French, and Irish one, to see
the Sussex sport, or taste a Charlton pie.
The Grafton's Duke, and farming Halifax,
and Walpole's Lord, and Delawarr, once West,
their different palaces and stables had,
the gentle soft and meagre Jennison,
from Humber's banks, on little Toby came.
Godolphin too, would once essay to see,
on foot, for fear; the side hill chase, the best
when winds set right, and foxes take that way,
and Churchill – Churchill's best rider in New Park,
for there is scope, to lay his courser out;
but such as he, the Goddess did disdain,

so gave him back to Venus, and the maids.
The Ciprian Queen was not content with him,
her thoughts, were fixed on Delia's choicest man,
whose breast, nor she nor Cupid yet had touched.
A nut brown wench, with lightning in the eyes,
white teeth her beauty, and a warbling voice,
outdid herself, in acting of Distress:
admired by all, but most by Bolton's Grace;
the Queen of Love, who watched him smiled with joy,
he's mine she cried, I have him he's my own;
long obdurate, he has my laws refused,
but he'll repair that crime by constant love.

Now, he to Charlton for awhile did come,
unwilling and asham'd to leave the sport;
till forc'd at last, by loves resistless power,
resigned his place, and hounds, and left the court.

Diana vexed, at being thus beguiled
by Venus, and that wicked imp her boy,
resolves to try how Hymen would agree
with early rising, and with long fatigue;
then strait on vig'rous Lennox She does pitch,
who oft from Goodwood near, did use to come,
to pay her homage, at her stately Dome;
he gladly takes the proffered place, but begs,
that Delawarr sub-Governor may be,
to keep her rights, and rule, when absent he,
at Aubignie, or George's Court, must be.
Consent She gives, and thus approves his choice;
he lov'd Ropero, and Ropero him,
in Rufus wastes, he bears despotic sway,
where Bolderwood high elevated stands,
there in the Spring the hounds shall always go,
there end the sport, and pleasing dreams retain,
while basking in the Summer sun they lie.

That care be his, to see them kept all clean,
to view their kennels oft, and see them feed,
to register their names, and how they're bred;
that incest, foul, may never once intrude
to spoil the race, and vitiate the blood,

be it likewise his studies care, to choose
the proper shape, well bon'd, and wind with nose,
let not thin beauty ever tempt his mind,
to make a nurse of female kind so shap'd
nor of the males, a stallion ere to choose,
because at head, he once did foremost run;
let just proportion be in both the rule,
what shapes in this are wrong, let that amend;
in this, idea strong, must be his guide,
and trust to nature what she will produce;
let crossings of the kind be most his care,
for hounds incestuous bred, will soon be curs,
nor think, a steady pack of hounds to breed,
because the whelps by steady hounds were got,
the sexes both, must not with age be worn,
a youthful hound of three years old, well tried
for wind and stoutness, and sagacious nose,
when North East wind, or frost exhaled leaves
the tainted turf, or fox got far before,
by cunning turn, the scent by youth o'errun,
when they do wildly stare, or rattling fly
to every thing they smell, or takes their eyes;
then he, if backward soon he casts to try,
shows innate judgement, in a hound so young.
To him, a wise old female put, who is
at most but six or seven years, well known
for finding first, or hitting faults, the same;
or to a wise and aged steady hound,
in foreign pack, or in my own remarked,
his pedigree, and most of all his nose;
to him conjoin a bitch of two years old,
whose blood, without a stain long clean has run,
altho' no wisdom yet she ere has shown,
her progeny will answer all his care,
both strength, and beauty, thus will they produce,
whereas old age, in both will still deceive his hopes,
beware another error, seen too oft
in many sportsmen, when their youth is past;
they breed for speed, when they no more can ride,
prepost'rous thing! a boy I could forgive.

All hounds while young too hard are apt to run,

they lead with ignorance, and burst the rest,
who breathless come, to mend the faults they make;
which done, away again they heedless fly,
despise the wiser heads of middle age,
till off their speed, or foiled, with sheep,
unwillingly, submit to them to guide
the future chase, in hopes of getting blood.

This then, with care avoid, tho' his great weight,
and even yours, should be a reason good;
to teach you both, what hounds you ought to breed.

But since Ropero, and his friend likewise,
in this one article did both mistake;
I can't too much enjoin this future care;
remember this, that scenting days are rare,
the reason why, e'en to my self unknown,
nature's dark works, as yet to us untold,
consider then what hounds, without good nose
can do, when cold East winds shut up all pores,
nay more, a bright sun shining day that's warm,
will cause the same effect, as rising storms;
then speedy noseless hounds will creep, or stare,
while right bred, vermin, kind will hunt
and stick at mark, and walk a fox to death.
Nor let him think, tis shapes alone gives speed,
in hounds, and horses, both his wind does that,
tis blood gives wind, proportion just, the rest;
then stoutness shines, when breathless jades stand still.
Consult the country first for which you'd breed,
for this, or that, must different hounds be bred,
my Sussex hills require short backs, and wind,
for no slight boneless baubles those can climb.

Early in Spring, let all the puppies come,
winter starvelings n'er are worth the rearing,
then four or five, he ought at most to keep
of every litter, they the prettiest marked,
the Spaniel colour, or the brown, reject
the black tanned dog, does never take the eye,
the all white hound, of snowball kind, don't please,
the black pied dog, with bright tanned edges round,

with buff, or yellow head, and white the ground,
be this their colour, they'll by marks be known.
Let country walks be got, when once they're wean'd
at butchers, tanners, farmers, and such like,
where not o'er fed, they'll keep their shape and grow
and some small knowledge learn, by prouling out.
Whereas in towns, they're often fools, or spoiled;
ten nurses forty whelps will raise, each year,
and ten times two, will scarce supply the pack.
In spring, again, collect the scattered youth,
in separate kennel let them all be clos'd,
two moons at least, and blood them all at first,
last madness, mortal bane to all my hounds,
should lurking lie, yet hid in their young veins.

And here good judgement mostly is required,
to choose for bony strength, for shape and size,
and all partiality be then forgot,
the slaves who tend the hounds, may take the rest,
the season past, the youth be then their care,
to make them bold, but still obedient too:
to know their names, to come when called and this
by daily walking out, in couples joined;
till Autumn does draw near, the game yet weak,
take out some few, with them, some steady hounds,
to find, and guide the yet unknowing fools;
till be instinct, by nature taught, they stoop
and know a vermin scent, for which they're bred,
avoid the hare. I cannot that approve,
'tis sloth in Summer, or want of game,
makes northern sportsmen argue wrong in that;
their reason's only this, to make hounds know,
when right, when wrong, and mind the huntsman's rate,
my hounds when made no rate at all should hear,
it frights the guiltless, and baulks the old,
conscious they seem, expect the coming lash,
at distance humbly creep, or look dismayed;
nor anxious more to find, they heedless walk
behind, and show distaste, nor will they beat
the thick grown coverts, whose inwoven shades
the listening fox conceal; but pass him by.
Whereas when hounds no other scent do know,

they'll wind him far, they'll dash unawed by fear,
with emulation fired, they'll drive him out;
with vermin scent inspired, they'll tear their skins,
or loose an eye, unfelt, whilst in pursuit
with eager haste, they force their thorny way.

November come, another draught must be,
he then must cast, the oldest worn out hounds,
a thing, ungrateful! yet it must be done,
Mars does the same, with old, tho' valiant men.
The young ones too, by this time tried, and known,
which enters not, which cannot run, or tires;
away with such, let all be good he keeps,
and threescore couple be at least the stock,
to furnish hounds for thrice a week to hunt;
and thirty couple at a time's enough.

Let Terriers small be bred, and taught to bay,
when foxes find an unstoped badger's earth,
to guide the delvers, where to sink the trench;
peculiar is their breed, to some unknown,
who choose a fighting biting cur, who lies
and is scarce heard, but often kills the fox;
with such a one, bid him a beagle join,
the smallest kind, my nymphs for hare do use,
that cross gives nose, and wisdom to come in,
when foxes earth, and hounds all baying stand.

This beagle blood, for this alone allow'd,
reject it in the pack in every shape,
the ignorant, who oft have bred too high,
do falsely think, the nose thus to regain,
the cross is wrong, it alters quite the breed,
makes foxhounds hang, and chatter, o'er the scent,
as vermin blood; makes beagles overrun,
the beagle, for the hare alone design'd
tho' foxhounds some so falsely term, when small;
if he marks well these hints, he cannot err.

Your slave, who guides the pack, I don't approve;
I have one in my thoughts, as yet engaged;

with this I prophesy, some dire mischance,
be not dejected, but on me rely.
Nor guides, nor hounds, nor ought, shall wanting be,
whole packs I'll send, and that shall be my care;
when Lennox thus, with Heart o'erjoyed replies,
Goddess of woods, tremendous in the chace,
of mountain foxes, and the savage race,
my constant study it shall daily be,
to mind your orders, and commands obey,
with awful reverence will your rights maintain,
with hunting songs still celebrate your praise.

Near Compton, where Ropero used to hunt,
is seen a castle fam'd for prospect fine,
o'er sea, and land, the view does far extend,
Upparke tis called, thus nam'd from site so high :
here Tankerville, the friend of Monmouth dwelt,
and now a noble Earl, of stature low,
and haughty mien, good humoured tho' : when pleased;
this castle owned, and the same title bore;
his youth with northern sportsmen he had spent,
his father dead, to Sussex straight he comes,
with large estate, and vig'rous youth endued,
and hounds he'd have, without the Goddess' leave;
this could not please, because 'twould interfere,
Diana soon foresaw, it would not last,
She knew the youth, so flattered him a while;
at last contrives, with Lennox he should join,
about two years, this fickle Earl did well;
when on a sudden, he abruptly breaks
and ties of friendship, and from Charleton goes;
takes half the hounds, which chanced to be the best;
while thus distressed, the Goddess vows revenge.
Another petty, thoughtless, squire appears,
and he foxhounds, and coursers too, would keep;
Diana soon demolished all his schemes,
She took away his pack, and steeds, and all.

But Oh! mishaps! no pleasure, without pain,
the fatal accident she had foretold,
at last befell her hounds, so much renown'd!
that vilest slave, the huntsman, Ware, his name;

alone, and drunk, went out, and let the pack
kill fourteen farmers' sheep, all in one day;
Oh! fatal day! and fatal so the next,
now melancholy scenes, each week produc'd,
some hounds were hanged, some cast, and still the best;
to France some went, where farmers ne'er complain;
the best thus lost, the rest of little worth,
nay Emperor, that fine tho' wicked dog,
was all besmeared with blood of harmless sheep;
and Luther too, killed lambs, the shepherd's care.
Enrag'd at this, the Sylvan Queen declares
She'll still support her train, new hounds supply,
her fav'rite Lennox, she one night surprised,
in Husko's shape, she came, and thus she spoke;
'Cheer up brave youth, for fortune smiles on thee,
'the finest boy, and noblest post, thou hast;
'the best old huntsman, with no bad hounds I bring,
'accept the present they from Spencer come,
'the youth obliges me, and gives them you.'

To Bolderwood then straight repair, and there
you'll find Tom Johnson's hounds, and Delawarr,
there try, and choose the best, and form again
a formidable pack, for Sussex Downs.

Twas done, the sport again once more reviv'd,
with transports new, the youth came posting down,
to Charlton, where new Sportsmen daily come,
to hunt, to shoot, to dine at Goodwood some,
Goodwood! the place where all exotics are,
from Cooks exotic, to exotic bears;
but there too, conjugal affection shines,
the finest Dutchess, and finest Duke,
hail happy matron, hail most happy wife;
still blessed, still loved, tho' many years are past.
what amorous planet reigned when this fond pair
were got, or born, or happily conjoin'd?
the longest honey moon that ever shin'd,
and then, their blooming progeny to see;
but Emelia's picture who can draw?
the prettiest, prattling poppet e'er was seen,
petite tripone, jolie mignone des cieuses,

Soiez benite, soiez en toute heureuse.
Here shine the nymphs, in Amazonian garb,
by Delia trusted to Richmond as care,
look how the keen Haralda foremost rides
attended by a youth on either side.

Fitzwilliam, Pembroke, now comes cant'ring on,
of graceful stature, this Hibernian maid,
her size and limbs for Hercules a match;
some other nymphs, at sundry times did come,
but these their beauty, or complexion fear'd,
so soon returned, for softer sports prepar'd.

A hundred speedy coursers now are seen,
by different names they each distinguished stand
in sep'rate stalls, attended by a boy,
and one sage groom, does all those boys command;
each sportsman has his stalls, and groom apart,
(who also tries his master to direct)
more regular than formerly was seen,
the whole, in every part does now appear;
with velvet caps, in azure vests they're clad,
with golden loops alike, they all are made,
and each for use, wears couples at his side.
A warm, but small apartment, each one has,
the Duke's alone appears magnificent,
conspicuous it stands, above the rest
and uniform, and nearest to the Dome.
The Alban Duke, the next best palace owns,
just in the centre of the village, where
in sacred spot, white pallizado'd round
appears a mast erect, of monstrous height,
on top of which flies waving with the wind,
the emblematic standard of the Queen
of woods, whose fav'rite colour's always green,
in which a golden running fox is seen,
and near in verdant field enclosed, thro' which
the Lavant winding runs, and lends his aid,
to clean three spacious kennels for the hounds,
who here all walk, to stretch their stiffened limbs,
and in this field, the governor resides;
from whence he sees the management of all.

And here a regular front, full South appears,
a double palace, which three friends did rear,
the strong Cavendo owns the part of one,
Fauquier his friend, in attic storey sleeps,
young furious Harcourt, did the other build,
and great was the expense and charge of both.
Adjoining this a large old fabric stands,
and three Northumber youths, in that do dwell,
then East of this, close by the Lavant side,
a certain Brigadier has built his hut,
here he, his slaves, and strong made coursers all,
with Pompey too, under one thatch do lie.
'Tis thus we're told, the Tartars fierce still dwell,
fond of their horses, of their dogs as fond;
some more there are, but not worth remark,
where some, as little worth do sometimes come.

INDEX

OF CHI
OF CHASE

Liger heath
Comb hill
Stubhill Common

Road from Portsmouth to London
Sheet bridg
Slade
HUNDRED
Maiden Oak
Rogate
Trotton
Ipeing
Steadha
Durford Priory
Terweek
Parsonage
Durford bridg
Habent bridg
Parsona
Chithurst
Petersfield
Wenham
Haben Cross
Heath house
Downpark
Dumford
Goldrings
Minstead
Upperton
Ellstead Marsh
W. Harting
DUMFORD
Ellstead
Dary house
CH
Ditcham
Bohemy
E. Harting
Parsonage
Fizsals
AMP
Harting place
S Harting
Harting Windmill
Trayford Place
Bepton
Cocking pa
Trayford
Lynch
Didling
Hurston
Uppark
Ladyholt
Little green
N Marden
Fillet
Elland
Monking
Cocking Warre
Winchester
Greenlands
Compton
Compton Wind.
HUNDRED
IRE
Upmarden
E Marden
Ben hill
Chilgrove
Compton Down
Westmarden
Warren Lodg
Northwood
Lodg
OF W BOURNE
W Dean
Burston
AND
Stainsted Park
Watergate
SINGLETON
Stoughton
Stainstead Park
Walderton Place
Preston
Lordington
Walderton Street
D
Cromhole
E
A
Pound house
Adsden
Binderto
Rooks Wt.
Stonermeer
Racton
Racton
P
y White Way
Two Stone gate
R
A
Midlavant
Aylsworth
HUNDRED
W Stoke
W. Bourne Common
OF
W. Stoke place
W Lavant
E Lavant
Woodmancote
Funtington
E. Ashling
Ray mee
Parsonage
W Ashling
Deanswod
W. Bourne
BOSHAM
OF
W Hampt
Inland
Saltbox
Brile
Hermitage bridg
Hambrook Common
Napp
BOX
Prinsted Nutborn
Broadbri
Ham
CHICHESTER
W Hampt
Chidham
Bosham
Prebend
Fishbourn Saltwater Mill
Fishbourne
AND